The UFO Investigator's Guide

The UFO Investigator's Guide

David Coomer

BLANDFORD

To Julie, Jake, Christian and Danielle.

It'll come right in the end... it always does.

First published in the United Kingdom in 1999 by Ward Lock

Text copyright © 1999 David Coomer

Design and layout copyright © Blandford, 1999

Distributed in the United States of America by Sterling Publishing Co., Inc. 387 Park Avenue South, New York, NY 10016–8810

A CIP catalogue record for this book is available from the British Library

ISBN 0–7137–2782–9

Designed by Gwyn Lewis

Illustrations by Julie Hadfield and Richard Lucas

Printed and bound in Great Britain by MPG Books Ltd, Bodmin, Cornwall

Blandford, Illustrated Division, The Orion Publishing Group, Wellington House, 125 Strand, London WC2R 0BB

Contents

Acknowledgements

I would like to thank my Dad for getting me out of bed at some god-awful hour in July 1969 to watch the moon landings on television and for firing my initial interest in all things 'spacey', and my Mum for not giving him grief when he did. Thanks also to Julie, for being patient while this book was taking shape, for sharing my enthusiasm, and for not complaining while I was typing and retyping for days on end to the exclusion of everything and everyone else – and for keeping me supplied with copious quantities of tea, coffee and food.

Thanks also to Cynthia Hind and Graham Birdsall for their help and encouragement; to Dr Colin Ridyard for allowing me to use his notes and reports freely – you're a star; and to my agent, Chelsey, and Stuart Booth at Blandford, both of whom held my hand and mopped my fevered brow when the need arose. And thanks to Sarah, bless her cotton socks, for not being too heavy-handed with the editorial secateurs. To Peter Harrison, for proofreading and positive input.

To all these I say a big 'thank you', but the biggest thank you of all goes to all those unsung heroes of ufology who actually did most of what constitutes these pages. All I did was draw the threads of their work together and compile them into what I hope is an understandable and practical volume of useful information, adding a few observations and bits of my own along the way. A lot of the groundwork was already done by others far more qualified than I. You all know who you are, and if I've somehow missed you out or not credited you by name, I ask you to please accept my apologies. Any omission is entirely unintentional.

Introduction: An Historical Perspective

It is generally accepted that the era of modern ufology started way back on 24 June 1947, and so that seems a reasonable place to begin. On that day, Kenneth Arnold, an American fire appliance salesman and experienced pilot, was flying his light aircraft to Washington State when he took a detour to help look for a C-46 military transport plane that had apparently crashed in the Cascade Mountains region. During his search, he noticed nine crescent-shaped objects flying in formation around the summit of Mount Rainier, coming from the direction of Mount Baker at speeds estimated at 2,700km (1,700 miles) per hour. He described their motion in flight as being 'like a saucer would [move] if you skipped it across water'. Bill Becquette of Associated Press, who was present when Arnold landed at Pendleton, Oregon, misinterpreted this, and reported that the objects were saucer shaped, and thus the term 'flying saucers' was coined. This was not the first time that such things had been sighted that year, but now they at least had an identity of sorts. The story made international headlines, and Arnold's place in the history books was assured.

As if this sighting wasn't enough, Arnold went on to experience a second mass sighting five days later on 29 June, again while he was flying, this time over La Grande Valley. However, this second sighting – of about 25 brass-coloured objects approaching to within 370m (400yd) of his aircraft – attracted less media attention. Within days, hundreds of flying saucer reports were being filed, not just from civilians but also from pilots and the military. No doubt many of these were knee-jerk reactions or hoaxes fuelled by post-war paranoia and angst, but they came in none the less.

What allegedly happened that same year is to this day one of ufology's most controversial and enduring mysteries. The magic word is 'Roswell', and there can be few, if any, researchers who have not heard of the infamous New Mexico town and the alien craft that were said to have crashed there. Many books have been written about the 'Roswell Incident', along with television documentaries and movie scripts, and readers who are interested should have no difficulty in locating them. As for the cover stories put out by the military – of weather balloons, and later top-secret radiation-detecting balloons, gone awry – it should be stated that very few, if any, ufologists today believe that such mundane causes are at the bottom of these events. On the contrary, most believe that government cover-ups are being instituted on a massive international scale – cover-ups, incidentally, for which there is absolutely no shortage of evidence.

CULTURAL TRACKING

So, if the kick-off was in 1947, what about the pre-match warm-up? Strange as it may seem, the football analogy is not wholly inappropriate: in much the same way as the game has progressed, with strips and management techniques maturing to fit the day, so it is with ufology. This is known as 'cultural tracking'.

To illustrate this point, 'waves' of other exotic craft over the years have included the 'ghost planes' of Sweden, which were only one step ahead of the then current technology. And yet, only a few short years later, monoplanes were commonplace in the skies of Europe as World War II raged beneath and around them. Then came Peenemünde and the V-2 rockets: German engineering at its best, and most frightening. Again over Sweden, 'ghost rockets' were another reported anomaly, but by this time rockets were well known. In 1946, there were approximately 2,000 reported sightings of this latest phenomenon, and it was widely believed at the time that they were being flown by the Allies, who, having captured them from the Germans, were attempting either to destroy or to analyse them for their own military purposes. Some were reported to have exploded in mid-air, others to have landed.

The problem was that neither the western nor the eastern powers would admit to flying the craft and, as is always the way with literal UFOs, these ghost rockets were exhibiting anomalous behaviour inappropriate to the level of technology generally acknowledged to be available at the time. When some of the fragments were examined by western scientists, they were found to be constructed from an organic material very similar to carbide. In 1967, a Greek investigative team announced that these were not in fact missiles, at which point they were ordered into silence by the army, the investigation was closed down, and the now familiar blanket of secrecy descended. However, it is worth remembering that were it not for some of those same German rocket scientists responsible for the V-2 programme at Peenemünde, and others, there would be no American or Russian space programmes to speak of today, at least not as we recognize them now.

Cast your mind back, if you can, to the mid-1960s. Around that time, a Swiss author by the name of Erich von Daniken was making his presence felt in the libraries and bookshops of Europe. He wrote (and continues to write) a series of best-selling books which postulated extraterrestrials as the possible progenitors of the human race, and provided a wealth of 'evidence' to substantiate his claims – the most profound of which supposedly proved that the Earth had been visited regularly by various alien species during our long and colourful history. Of course, von Daniken wasn't the first to postulate such theories, but he was probably the first to popularize them on a truly international scale.

It was, and usually still is, considered that the territories of the bona fide scientific Search for Extraterrestrial Intelligence (SETI) and the wild and unsubstantiated rantings of the ufologists are mutually exclusive, with historical precedents not even entering into the equation. It therefore has to be asked whether the decriers of von Daniken and his ilk were merely upset at having their own doctrines, belief systems and years of learning challenged by this Swiss upstart who was looking at things from a different angle, or whether they really were that off-beam. The net result of all this was that the 'ancient astronaut' theories lost much of their credibility, and consequently serious support from researchers.

As Colin Wilson has pointed out, far more convincing evidence has been presented by other writers. The likes of Immanuel Velikovsky, Zecharia Sitchin, Andrew Tomas, Alan Alford and Maurice Chatelain, to name but a few, have indeed provided us with such 'evidence', and have written some very creditable books on the subject of extraterrestrials as ancient gods. They have examined the best available historical, archaeological and cultural evidence and have convincingly postulated direct extraterrestrial intervention in the genetic make-up and/or subsequent evolution and development of mankind. Many of these books have been published quite recently and 'ancient astronaut' theories, it seems, are fashionable, and credible, once again.

Such writers have helped to generate, revive or otherwise facilitate these subsequently popular theories, suggesting to some that among other things these theories and beliefs fill a spiritual gap in the collective unconscious of the human race – a spiritual gap that some say was created by the apparent failure of the established Churches to tender to their adherents the pastoral welfare that is historically their due. It's certainly fair to say that many ufologists approach their subject with a religious fervour bordering on fanaticism, and it could be argued that this too can be counter-productive to the aims of serious ufology. None the less, these theories and beliefs no longer appear to be as without foundation as they were once held to be, because with the advances made in archaeological and genetic science, dating techniques and other recent discoveries, for many people the evidence is simply too overwhelming to ignore.

For many, the Church has never been able to explain satisfactorily 'where we came from' or 'why we are here', beyond the myths and legends associated with the schoolroom. The established Churches, in the main, have relied on their followers' faith in the written word of the appropriate deity, fear of divine retribution and dread of eternal damnation to keep them buoyant. Today, however, such concepts are generally held by free-thinking people to be out of date, leading to accusations that the Church is out of touch with the needs of its followers. The growth of science during the Middle Ages and the Renaissance saw theology having to compete with new ideas which could be scientifically proven, and this proof, by its very existence, became a potential nemesis of the established Christian faith, threatening to undermine its power base as the repository of all wisdom and lore. This in turn could be seen as one of the reasons for the large-scale suppression of scientific knowledge, along with others including simple greed and misanthropy. Mankind has inexcusably lost or destroyed much potentially wonderful and enlightening knowledge and mathematical data through the systematic suppression and decimation of cultures such as the Mayan, Aztec, Inca, Alexandrian and Sumerian.

More recently, those who were brave (or stupid) enough to suggest that ours might not be the only planet supporting life usually had very short careers. One such example is Giordano Bruno, who in 1600 was burned at the stake for daring to suggest, among other things, that the sun was not at the centre of the universe after all, but was in fact just one of millions of similar stars, thereby introducing the concept of infinity into the bargain. Going further back, Nicolaus Copernicus was the first to remove the Earth from the same universal centre, which was not only a profound move but also an extremely dangerous one – or rather, it would have been, had his thirty-year study of astronomy (which included his conclusions as to the status of the Earth) been published prior to the year of his death, in 1543. Galileo Galilei, a professor of mathematics and developer of the astronomical telescope, taught Copernicus' theories at the Church-run universities, providing plausibility for these heliocentric (sun-centred) theories so convincingly that his published works were banned by the Church authorities in Rome. He was then forced to recant his views by the not-so-tender ministrations of the Inquisition, and thereafter was required to spend the last ten years of his life under house arrest, until his death in 1642. Power corrupts...

However, let us get back to the point, which is this: many of the accepted doctrines and beliefs that people follow today are based on or contain much older writings and legends, some of which date back several thousand years. Many of these legends tell of gods from the skies and the wondrous feats that they were supposed to have accomplished. All the major religions and belief systems have certain common themes running through them, which include some of these legends. Unfortunately, it is only the Christian religion that seems to utilize these accounts for allegorical purposes: most other faiths consider such legends to be genuine accounts of events, meetings, prophecies, etc., recorded by the witnesses to these events at the time. Consequently, perhaps, some of these other cultures are not in the slightest bit surprised to find that the skies are once again full of gods in their fiery chariots.

If we move forward in time, could these same creatures be the ones represented in medieval woodcuts and engravings as angels and devils? Or in folklore as faeries, elves, leprechauns and goblins? Remember that although Christianity was the dominant religion of the period, there were still those pagans and nature-worshippers who may have associated the beings in their own close encounters with their personal pantheon of deities and their subordinates. Again, many of these creatures from folklore are associated with assorted magic, the abducting of babies for 'changelings', underground or aerial lairs, and aerial gymnastics, in much the same way that today we have reports of advanced technology, secret underground bases, UFOs, alien abductions, hybrid babies and motherships. Thus, the folklore legends become no less credible, and no less frightening to the people of the relevant periods, than do the accounts of those who believe in an extraterrestrial presence on Earth today – thereby perhaps providing further evidence for cultural tracking.

It is a strange fact that the various types of UFOs (in the sense of alleged extraterrestrial craft) that have been witnessed through the ages have not all been saucer shaped. Indeed, it has been noted that they appear always to be just one step ahead of 'current' terrestrial technological capability – at least, those reported since about the middle of the nineteenth century do (consider the mysterious airships that were witnessed by thousands of people during the latter part of that century, especially in the US, or the Scandinavian 'ghost planes' that were seen, particularly over Sweden, in 1933–4). Cultural tracking is seen by some as the final convincing evidence that UFOs are simply manifestations of cultural deficits in certain areas of the human condition; others have argued that the ubiquitous extraterrestrials are 'leading us by the nose', so to speak, in the desired technological direction, although quite what that direction – and the agenda behind it – might be remains open to interpretation. However, that these mysterious airships and ghost rockets were seen and reported is beyond doubt.

Either way, this trend of cultural tracking appears to be continuing. There are a number of parallels between these earlier incidents and current UFO sightings. I am thinking in particular of the 'black triangle' sightings of the late 1980s and early 1990s, which continue even as I write, and the way in which they appear once again to be just one step beyond our technological capabilities. A divisive issue, the black (or flying) triangle appears to give rise to two schools of thought: the first, that it is an alien craft piloted by either extraterrestrials or our own people, as part of an ongoing covert human–alien partnership; the second, that it is the new generation of Stealth aircraft – the fabled Aurora project, or similar – which is popularly rumoured to be the extremely hi-tech, state-of-the-art, cutting-edge-technology replacement for the earlier and comparatively pedestrian B-2 Stealth bomber.

Aircraft have to be test flown, not only for safety reasons but also to try out their overall validity and viability. This may indeed include fly-overs of civilian conurbations to assess noise, visibility, manoeuvrability and operational capabilities among civilian air traffic routes, etc. Considering that it is unlikely that any sort of craft would be brought into active service or prepared for sale to foreign governments without a thorough testing and modification to maximize performance and achieve optimum operability, it could be argued that such covert activity is likely to be standard operating procedure. Any such modifications may take years to perfect, quite possibly seven or eight. Rumours of a new Stealth aircraft were circulating for at least a couple of years before the B-2 Stealth bomber was unveiled to a largely uninformed public, and it seems unreasonable to think that any nation in possession of such hardware would make it public knowledge without some new generation up its sleeve, or, at the very least, off the drawing board and in the pipeline. Such a device is a trump card, and you never show your cards to the other players – not if you want to win. We all consider ourselves or our nations to be 'the good guys' and we all want to win, so we all want to have a trump card. So, could the prototype B-2, prior to its official unveiling, have been accountable for several UFO sightings?

The point is that we should not assume that simply because a craft appears to be beyond our current capabilities, it must be extraterrestrial. Too many researchers make the mistake of underestimating our own terrestrial science and technological capabilities, and the situation is made worse by the popular press. Their job is to sell papers, and if this means misreporting, misquoting or sensationalizing the issues, then so be it. This is in the nature of the business.

ANCIENT EXTRATERRESTRIALS?

And I looked, and behold, a great whirlwind came out of the north, a great cloud, and a fire infolding itself, and a brightness was about it, and out of the midst thereof as the colour of amber, out of the midst of the fire. Also out of the midst thereof came the likeness of four living creatures. And this was their appearance; they had the likeness of a man... Whither the spirit was to go, they went... It went up and down among the living creatures; and the fire was bright, and out of the fire went forth lightning. And the living creatures ran and returned as the appearance of a flash of lightning... As for their rings, they were so high that they were dreadful; and their rings were full of eyes round about them four.

As fantastic as it sounds, this oft-quoted passage of the Bible's Old Testament in which Ezekiel describes a desert UFO encounter (complete, in later chapters, with an abduction scenario and an account of what appears to be a merciless ethnic cleansing) has actually been given some serious scientific consideration. An engineer at the NASA (National Aeronautics and Space Administration) Marshall Space Flight Center, Josef Blumrich, who was chief of the Systems Layout Branch and had worked on both the Saturn rockets and Skylab, looked into Ezekiel's claims with the intention of proving them to be nothing more than allegorical. By applying his expertise in the relevant fields, however, he came up with the notion that it could indeed have been a space-ship capable of interstellar travel that the prophet saw. He wrote about his dis-coveries in a 1974 book entitled *The Spaceships of Ezekiel*, and then went on to invent a universal wheel based on his findings.

However, Ezekiel's account is not the only biblical encounter of its type that is believed by many to be extraterrestrial in origin. Consider the ascension of Jesus. What did he ascend into? And how? The bright cloud that led the people of Israel through the Red Sea, parting the waters and engulfing the Egyptians: was this possibly a UFO? And perhaps the best-known event of all: was the star that guided the three wise men to the birth of Jesus an extraterres-trial craft, given that 'stars' just do not behave in the way described? Several books have been written on the subject of Bible UFOs alone, but what about other texts, other 'Bibles'?

Well, wheels and discs are not a new phenomenon as far as written texts and legends are concerned. Prehistoric cylinders from Assyria show the figure of a man descending to earth inside a disc. Ancient rock inscriptions show the god Ahura Mazda inside a circular vehicle. Indian texts have many of their pantheon of deities coming to Earth via discs or wheels, often launching thun-derbolts or lightning – noisy and pyrotechnic parallels with Ezekiel's vision, perhaps? The winged disc of the god Vishnu was reported to be both a vehicle and a machine of war.

The Dogon tribes of Mali in Africa worship at a flat-topped pyramid where, it is said, the sky gods would land on their frequent visits to Earth many cen-turies ago. They call these gods the Nossos or Nommos, and they were said to be a semi-aquatic or amphibious race, fish-like in appearance. Via the oral tra-dition, the Dogon describe the landing of the ship in which the Nossos arrived as having the accompanying sound of four stone blocks being repeatedly struck with stones, and although author Robert Temple suggests that they are trying to convey the idea of a thunderous vibration or roaring, there are definite paral-lels here with present-day UFO sightings. The Dogon ship displaced a pile of dust and raised a whirlwind, and the violence of the impact roughened the ground as the vehicle skidded along it: a crash-landing perhaps? But compare this description of a landing with that given by Ezekiel in his account.

However, if we are to believe the Dogon, then this is only one instance of a Dogon spaceship, as there also appears to be a mothership orbiting at a very high altitude, which tradition relates as a 'new star'. This left the Earth along with the Nommos. Anyone who has seen the orbiting Russian Mir space station will remember that it looks like a very bright star, but any spaceship like the one the Dogon describe might be even more likely to appear so, as it would probably be required to remain in a geostationary orbit in order to maintain communication and transport links with the ground crew.

Compare the Dogon's semi-aquatic Nossos with an ancient Babylonian account of a similar race. The Babylonians were the successors to the Sumerian culture, which was founded around 4000 BC. No one really knows where the Sumerians came from – they simply appeared as a fully formed and evolved culture, but had a strange language that, according to Carl Sagan, cannot be allied to any known Indo-European, Semitic or other ancient language. The ancient texts relate that there appeared upon the border between Babylonia and the Persian Gulf a creature of reason. It was called the Oannes, and in appearance resembled a fish, with a man's head under that of a fish, and a man's feet under the fish's tail. He was articulate in both voice and language, and taught the people of the area the tenets of the arts, science and letters. He showed them how to build houses and to establish laws and temples, and conveyed the principles of geometry. He also taught them the basics of agriculture. In short, he gave them culture. All this took place during the day; at night, the Oannes went back to the sea, not returning to the land again until daylight. After he had gone, others like him came and continued the teachings.

Like the Dogon, the astronomer-priests of Babylon also claimed that their flat-topped pyramids were used as landing sites for the benefit of the sky gods (the Oannes), while similar structures have been found throughout Central America. Yea, even unto England: take a look at Silbury Hill in Wiltshire, not a million miles from Stonehenge and in a locality that is no stranger to crop circles, UFO sightings and other bizarre phenomena.

Moreover, a Babylonian poem from c.2700 BC entitled 'The Flight of Etana' appears to give a visibly believable account of ascent into space.

Again, a halfway decent telescope must be used to see the total number of stars contained within the Pleiades, an open star cluster in the constellation of Taurus, and yet in the Mediterranean basin there are cave inscriptions showing this constellation as having ten stars, and although there are more, no more than seven are visible to the naked eye.

Egyptian legends, too, are full of references to gods from the skies, to 'those who live among the stars', as well as to many forms of ancient wisdom reputed to be of extraterrestrial origin. Interestingly, one of the current controversies concerns the age of the Sphinx and its supporting temple complex. According to traditional Egyptology, the Sphinx was erected c.2500 BC, but according to authors Robert Bauval and Graham Hancock, weather and erosion patterns indicate that it was actually built at the end of the last ice age, closer to 10,500 years ago, during a time when Egypt was much wetter. Furthermore, they point out that for the astronomical and astrological alignment to make sense, the positions of the stars must be precessed back to 8000 BC (which can easily be done using the appropriate software and computer), to the age of Leo. Bauval and Hancock suggest that the Sphinx is a marker to Sirius, which is the star associated with Isis, a major deity in Egyptian culture, and, perhaps not coincidentally, the star from which the Dogon claim the Nossos hail. There is certainly no doubt that Sirius is very important in the calendars of the Egyptians. Furthermore, the god Anubis, usually represented as jackal- or dog-headed, is also associated with Sirius, the dog star. However, there is evidence to suggest that the Dogon are at least culturally descended from the ancient Egyptians and may thus have 'inherited' their knowledge.

The ancient Hindu texts dating back to at least 3000 BC contain many passages which refer to *vimanas* – wonderful flying machines that were capable of space travel. In one account in the *Bhagavata-Purana*, there is a recorded incident of an aerial attack by one of these vehicles, referred to as a 'flying iron city'; attributes associated with them include invisibility, and what would appear to be radar and radio communications. Vedic writings also include direct references to gods from other planetary systems.

Ancient Mayan records also maintain contacts with beings from the heavens, adding that they returned to the stars following their time on Earth. They initially arrived on a 'cloud-serpent', and taught the Mayans the requirements and arts of civilization. The Mayans knew long before modern man that the Earth was round, indicating perhaps an understanding of aerial surveys.

As if all this weren't enough, Jim Marrs tells of an archaeological find in 1938, when Chi Pu Tei discovered rows of regularly aligned graves in mountains near the Sino-Tibetan border. Several small, frail skeletons with large skulls were found beneath cave drawings of strange beings wearing helmets along with pictograms of the sun, moon and stars. In 1962, several stone plates that were found among the graves were translated by Professor Tsum Um Nui of the Academy of Prehistoric Research in Beijing. The translation told the tale of a group of beings who crash-landed on Earth about 12,000 years ago and, having failed to repair their craft or mingle successfully with the native tribespeople, were ultimately hunted down and killed due to their non-human appearance. *Plus ça change?*

Again in China, a 1959 joint Chinese–Soviet palaeontological expedition in the Gobi desert unearthed the perfectly preserved and very recognizable imprint of a shoe-sole that was estimated to be around a million years old. Ivan Sanderson, a former British Naval Intelligence officer, discovered a manufactured gold chain in a coal deposit in Pennsylvania, US, likewise estimated to be at least a million years old. Nevada, 1869, and miners unearthed a piece of feldspar (a mineral), inside which was a 5cm (2in) long metal screw. The stone itself is estimated to be older than mankind. In 1936, a fossil of a three-toed Miocene-period horse was discovered in the same geological stratum as a smooth, level pavement built of 12cm (5in) square mortared tiles. The components of the mortar did not come from anywhere near the region, and the estimated period for the origin of this pavement is a million years ago. Then, in Kentucky, workmen unearthed neatly laid stone slabs underneath the remains of a prehistoric mastodon.

A 2,000-year-old gold artefact was found in Colombia which appeared to be a delta-winged jet fighter. It was discovered four years before the Wright brothers even flew. In La Venta, Mexico, ancient parallels to modern parabolic optical reflectors were found in the form of ancient concave mirrors, and it is thought that these may have been used to generate heat by focusing the sun's rays. These and other finds are detailed in Alan Landsburg's book *In Search of Ancient Mysteries* (1974).

Could a nuclear war have taken place in the twenty-first century BC? There is evidence to suggest that it might have done. Consider the destruction of Sodom and Gomorrah. That Lot was given advance warning of the impending destruction of the twin cities and advised by 'angels' to quit town is a bit of a giveaway, as is the description of the actual destruction, as witnessed by Lot, from the safety of the city of Zo-ar:

> Then the Lord rained upon Sodom and upon Gomorrah brimstone and fire from the Lord out of Heaven. And he overthrew those cities, and all the plain, and all the inhabitants of the cities, and that which grew upon the ground...
> And he looked toward Sodom and Gomorrah, and toward all the land of the plain, and beheld, and, lo, the smoke of the country went up as the smoke of a furnace.

The area was not volcanically or tectonically active at the time.

Marrs states that Zecharia Sitchin relates archaeological finds that provide evidence to support the theory that communities at the southern end of the Dead Sea, reportedly the location for the twin cities of Sodom and Gomorrah, were suddenly abandoned at the time of the incident, and were not resettled until several centuries later. Furthermore, Marrs claims that water samples from the region showed unsafe levels of radiation, and that Russian scientists found further evidence for the nuclear blast idea from fused silicon and glassy sand in the region.

Or this, translated from the Indian masterpiece the *Mahabharata*, explored more fully in John Hogues' *The Millennium Book of Prophecy*:

> A single projectile, charged with all the power of the universe; an incandescent column of smoke and fire as bright as a thousand suns rose in all its

splendour from a shaft fatal as the rod of death... It was destructive to all living creatures... Hostile warriors fell to the earth like trees burnt down in a raging fire... Elephants... fell to earth uttering fierce cries... burnt by the energy of that weapon... blistering hills, rivers, and trees... All are being reduced to ashes... Corpses burnt beyond recognition... Their hair and nails fell out... After a few hours, all foodstuffs were infected.

All this prior to 6500 BC. Some imagination, huh?

These examples of course, are just that – thumbnail portraits of many of the researched and documented accounts and artefacts that may be learned about by trawling the literature. This, after all, is intended as an investigator's handbook, so I make no apologies for not discussing these examples in detail, but the idea should be clear.

From some of these accounts, it can be seen that there are many parallels with present-day UFO sightings and levels of technology – although to be fair, some of the instances put forward as evidence of early or prehistoric extraterrestrial contact, influence or sightings might possibly be explained by mundane causes such as natural phenomena and should provide a salutary lesson in not jumping to conclusions. Also, we should not discount the possibility that our terrestrial predecessors were not the intellectual dullards that we characterize them as being, and we should not be so arrogant as to think them incapable of greatness. History has a wonderful way of repeating itself, and the one thing that we learn from history is that we don't learn from history.

Twentieth-century archaeologists and geologists have found evidence to suggest that human brains and history go much further back than the 5,000 years 'cut-off' point proposed by many for ancient history. Humankind's historical span on the Earth can be measured in millions of years; equally, our ability to map the heavens and measure time is not new. Admittedly, our predecessors' tools were supposedly primitive by our standards, but there is enough testimony to show that they could do it, and do it accurately. Why shouldn't ancient peoples have been as curious, intelligent or educated as we like to think we are? Why should they not want to categorize and understand their world in the same way that we choose to do today? In 3,000, or 10,000, years' time, will archaeologists judge twentieth-century man to be any more advanced than we consider our ancient forebears? Will they know that we have been to the moon, or seen into some of the furthest reaches of space? Will they believe that we worshipped gods from the skies that arrived in spaceships, because of a few remaining fragments of the thousands of documented UFO reports? And why is it that so many of the advocates of the ancient astronaut theories do not believe in the existence of present-day UFOs and extraterrestrials, given that it is these very UFOs that are supposed to have brought the gods from the skies in the first place?

INVESTIGATING UFOS

So, there you have it. Ufology itself is not new, nor is the extraterrestrial hypothesis: it simply has a new identity. Unlike SETI, it is not an exact science (although exact science is a large part of it); but like SETI, it occasionally requires lateral thinking. It also requires an open mind, an ability to discriminate and a desire to question. It encompasses many other disciplines and, as I hope the above discussion demonstrates, historical precedent is but one aspect of a deeply divisive, emotive and highly controversial and political issue.

There are so many elements of UFO investigation to consider and angles from which to approach the subject that to be effective it almost becomes necessary to be an 'expert' in many different fields. Not only that, but it is your level of expertise that determines how you will be judged as a ufologist by your peers, and by the witnesses and others with whom you come into contact during your investigations – mere depth of knowledge about the Roswell Incident, watching a few videos and being a fan of *The X-Files* does not make you an expert ufologist overall. Remember, too, that for every expert there is an equal and opposite expert.

One of the main reasons for writing this book was to address some of the questions and observations raised not only by the sceptics, but also by those who have little or no knowledge of the UFO phenomenon: questions such as 'How come they always look like us?', or 'Why is the photographic evidence always blurred?', or even the old classic 'Why don't they just land on the White House lawn and be done with it?' These and others I hope to answer by explaining how the application of sound scientific principles and accepted physical and biological laws influences the way in which ET and his vehicles are manifested and are expected to behave. I have drawn on some of the principles and science of SETI to legitimize some of the claims of ufology. There is a great deal of witness testimony regarding extraterrestrials and UFOs that remains consistent across social, cultural and geographical divides, and some of this has also been included – not for sensationalism, but because it supplements or even confirms the existing and accepted scientific principles described. However, this is not purely a book of science: I hope that it is much more. Nor is it a book of 'who saw what, and when'. There's plenty of that material elsewhere.

If you are already a competent ufologist, then I hope that my contribution will at least supplement your existing knowledge base or act as a point of ready reference. If you are new to ufology, then I hope that you, in particular, will benefit from this book. I wrote it largely for you, because it struck me that anyone can call themselves a UFO investigator simply by joining a UFO group and paying their subs. I consider this a dangerous position to be in, as an investigator is likely to be interviewing witnesses to events outside their normal sphere of everyday activity – events that may have profound effects upon their social, professional and private lives, and that may significantly affect their emotional, psychological and spiritual welfare. Simply joining a club and paying a subscription, or setting yourself up as a UFO investigator, does not – to my mind at least – qualify you to undertake investigations into what could be a series of deeply disturbing occurrences at a very personal and individual level. Unfortunately, this is exactly what seems to happen in many instances. I am not implying that this handbook will make you an instant expert in every field – far from it – but I do hope that it will help you to become a more questioning, thorough, insightful and efficient ufologist. Read as much related material as you can, and then question everything you read and inwardly digest, including this book. Diversify into different areas, such as astronomy, SETI, biology, ecology, physics, geology, chemistry, history, archaeology and anthropology, and more. Ufology really is a holistic 'science', as I hope a look at the Bibliography will show.

Some of this handbook you may never have to use, but I'm a great believer in having something and not needing it, rather than needing something and not having it. Much of what follows should be useful in any country in which you are reading it (the UFO phenomenon is not confined to any particular geographical area), and I hope that it will prove instrumental in generating further serious research, investigation and evaluation of the UFO phenomenon wherever it is read. It really is time that ufologists stopped sitting in bars discussing the latest sightings, stabbing each other in the back and criticizing other ufologists for their viewpoints, and set about looking at the problem from a unified position.

There are many different mindsets within the UFO fraternity: there are the scientists, the new-agers, the channelers, the sceptics, the remote-viewers, the psychologists, the historians, the proponents of the ancient astronaut theories, and so on. There are even 'armchair ufologists' with a viewpoint, and they too may find this book useful. Any interest in the UFO subject, budding or otherwise, is better than none – it indicates a growing global awareness and acceptance of the UFO situation, and of the possible realities, implications and aspirations in store for the human race. Ufology, it seems, is at last 'coming out of the closet'.

The massive international government interest in UFOs is no longer questioned by ufologists, and the phenomenon is now taken more seriously at an official level than many people recognize. It is not difficult to see the huge public interest in the subject, too. Look at the popularity of television programmes such as *The X-Files*, *Dark Skies* and UFO-related documentaries and movies. There's no smoke without fire, as they say, and information and data continue to filter down to ufologists from military personnel, scientists and intelligence staff, often at great personal and professional risk to themselves – surely an indication of a growing awareness of public interest in UFOs within political and military circles, and one that maybe we should capitalize on by pressing for more freedom of information, more political action, immunity from prosecution for some official whistle-blowers and less overall secrecy. Oh well... God loves an optimist!

I hope you will enjoy reading this book as much as I have enjoyed compiling and writing it – but more than that, I hope you will find it useful, enlightening and (ufologically speaking) educational. We may never know all the answers, we may only ever be able to 'best-guess' at any alien agenda; we may be silenced, lied to, laughed at, or even respected and admired, but the truth really *is* out there, and one day, one of us just might find it...

1 Equipment

No professional or tradesperson can do their job effectively without at least a few basic tools, and the same goes for UFO investigators. Although the following list of suggested items is by no means exhaustive, it covers all the basics, most of which are inexpensive and readily available.

THE PANIC BAG

Several of the items listed are obvious requirements for the ufologist undertaking investigations and site visits, and these should be kept handy in a 'panic bag', either at an investigator's home, or at a central location accessible to the investigative and research team. With larger UFO groups, it may be as well to establish a call-out rota, especially during UFO 'flaps' (heightened periods of UFO activity), and have the person who is on duty in possession of the panic bag. This is a matter of expediency, especially in cases where there may be the opportunity to conduct site analysis and time anomaly tests (see Chapter 9), in which there is usually a sense of urgency, particularly if there is likely to be military involvement. Once the police or military have sealed off the area, you are unlikely to be able to gain access to carry out tests and analysis anyway, and the longer the delay between incident and tests, the less reliable and accurate the results are likely to be.

So, what equipment should the panic bag contain, and what kind of bag should it be? Ideally, the panic bag should not be too heavy or ungainly to carry, and should be compact enough to be stored out of harm's way when not in use. Other than that, the choice is limited only by the type of kit you are likely to be using. Where possible, the panic bag should contain most of the following:

Notepad and pens Note the plural on 'pens': there is nothing more embarrassing than beginning an investigation only to discover that your pen has turned up its toes. A waterproof notepad is a useful addition, available from camping and army supply shops. Equally, at least one pen should have waterproof and/or indelible ink: have you ever tried to take field notes in the rain?

Dictaphone/cassette recorder If your budget will stretch to one of these, they are worth their weight in gold. You can tape an entire interview and be sure of missing nothing, or record observations while in the field when taking written notes is impractical or difficult due to inclement weather. Also useful for dyslexics, or for when some poor person would otherwise have to type up your appalling handwriting! A 'must-have'.

Torch Do not forget spare bulb and batteries. A red lens filter allows you to read maps, follow trails, etc. without impairing your night vision, which once lost through exposure to bright light may take several minutes to recover fully. (Incidentally, a red filter is also useful for watching nocturnal wildlife, as a lot of these creatures cannot see red light.)

Camera Almost any type will do, although it has been suggested that using a Polaroid reduces the risk of allegations of hoaxing. In addition, you do not need to go to the expense of processing an entire roll of film for the sake of one or two pertinent photographs; however, this advantage is offset by the initial cost of Polaroid films. Conversely, negatives are preferred for computer enhancement techniques. Naturally, the better the camera, and the more adept the photographer, the more chance there is of a better picture – and arguably, the better chance of a good hoax. There's just no pleasing the sceptics.

It could be argued that two cameras are a better investment, particularly during skywatches, where a flash will be unnecessary as it will not illuminate aerial objects and may actually ruin the shot. Time-exposure photography, using a tripod if possible (see below), will often produce better results. This will eliminate camera-shake during long exposures, and is also useful for site investigation photography. Sadly, fast-moving objects only reveal themselves as a streak on time-lapsed photographs, so here at least a back-up or secondary photographic system is a boon.

Video camera Very nice if your budget can run to it – a luxury item, and one to be invested in if at all possible. Also very useful on skywatches: better results may be obtained while filming nocturnal lights by using manual focusing. Again, don't forget spare battery pack, adaptors, etc. May require a separate carrying case. If a member of your group is prepared to 'loan' or otherwise make available their beloved video camera to the group, then ideally everyone who is likely to be using it should be familiar with how to do so, even to the extent of being able to slot in a new tape or batteries in the dark. As this is an expensive piece of equipment, it might be wise to insure it independently of household items or other equipment.

Tripod Especially useful during skywatches or for site photography, to steady a photographic or video camera in order to reduce camera-shake and thus produce sharper images. The same tripod may also be used to steady other optical equipment such as binoculars, telescopes or night-vision equipment.

Binoculars/telescope For skywatches, especially night skywatches, binoculars are the preferred instrument. They are specified by such magical formulas as 7×50, or 8×40, and so on; the first figure in such a designation is the magnification, while the second is the diameter of the front lenses. I have heard it said that the best binoculars are the ones where both figures in the designation are divisible by five, such as 10×50, as 5mm is the optimum diameter of the human eye's pupil and such binoculars are easier on the eye, particularly over long periods of time. For a bright image and a decent field of view, the ratio between the two figures in the designation should be 1:5 – so 6×30, 10×50, 8×40, etc. With smaller ratios, such as an 8×20 designation, there is a narrower field of vision and a dimmer image. As usual, look to your budget and cut your cloth accordingly.

Night-vision scopes Prices of these have dropped recently, although quality has not suffered greatly. Extremely useful on skywatches, they can enhance night vision considerably, and are well worth the money if your budget can run to it. There are both monocular and binocular types, the latter being more expensive, but with the collapse of the Iron Curtain many military versions are now coming out of the former Soviet Union, and these can be obtained through specialist dealers or by looking through small-ad magazines and specialist publications.

Watch Apart from the obvious uses, it might be necessary to log the actual times of events, verify time anomalies or check variations in local magnetic fields. Personal wristwatches pack up at the most inconvenient moments, so having one in the bag will not go amiss.

Geiger counter/dosimeter By and large, these can be quite ungainly, heavy and difficult to read without training. However, there are some portable types available relatively cheaply which can be a useful addition to your kit, particularly during visits to alleged landing sites. Some of these emit sound signals or a digital readout, sometimes both. They should be used with the probe as near to the ground or other surface being examined as possible. Thermoluminescent dosimeters, although easily read, require a back-up service, which can result in delays in analysing data. If there has been exposure to any more than background radiation, of course, then the damage to the investigator's health may be already done.

Some other types, such as those used by civil defence authorities, can be worn on the wrist or carried in the top pocket, like a pen. The latter have a scale which is read by holding the 'pen' up to the light. They can be recharged, but will probably require a specialist service to do this.

Passive radar/UFO motion detectors Rather more exotic pieces of equipment, these are claimed to provide early warnings of craft within the local area, by detection of magnetic and static fields that are moving in real time at speeds of over 290kmph (180mph). Displays may be by LED (light-emitting diodes) or meter, sometimes both, with the more expensive models being more sensitive but giving more reliable readings away from high-energy power lines and radio transmitters. If you are wearing clothing that generates static electricity, this too may trigger the unit. Useful during skywatches, site investigations and UFO 'flaps', these detectors are relatively inexpensive and will occupy very little space in your kit bag. Often advertised in UFO-related magazines, they are available via mail order (see Useful Addresses).

Mobile telephone/CB handset Purely for communication. The former is likely to be the responsibility of the individual investigator, while the latter can be bought solely for group use. A CB handset will need someone to monitor the required waveband or chosen channel and an operator's licence, but this is a small price to pay for site-to-base communication. Make sure the set utilizes the CB wavelength of 27MHz and *not* the cheaper alternative of 49MHz. This is not a CB, and the range is severely limited. It is illegal to use CB radio in an official business capacity. Both these items may also provide early warning of an impending encounter due to the disruption of local electromagnetic fields as a UFO approaches.

Other hand-held communications systems are available, but these tend to be prohibitively expensive and in some instances require a specific licence in order to operate them. Such systems may be monitored by the licence-issuing authority, and misuse or abuse of the airwaves may result in the withdrawal of the licence and possibly criminal proceedings.

Scanner First, a word of warning: listening in to police broadcasts is allegedly illegal, in the UK at least. As I understand it, however, it's not the act of listening in that is illegal, but rather the acting upon any data or information that is received while doing so. If caught with a scanner during the course of an investigation in which there is police involvement, you may run the risk both of criminal charges and of having your beloved – and expensive – scanner confiscated. Nevertheless, these instruments do have their uses, despite being used nefariously by criminals and those with a desire to monitor private telephone calls, especially those made on mobiles. Your local dealer will be able to advise you with regard to the type of equipment you should opt for, based upon the type of frequency ranges you hope to access. While scanners are not cheap to buy new, there are many good secondhand ones on the market, so it's worth looking in small-ads magazines or the various specialist publications, many of which print useful articles and advice. You will need one that covers a frequency range of 30–1,300MHz, and if the set is fitted with AM and FM bands, so much the better. This is because civil aircraft use the FM frequencies, while military pilots use both AM and FM. The civilian airband is 108–142MHz and covers the aeronautical mobile band, most control tower and airline frequencies, beacons, and Search & Rescue. The military airband is 225–400MHz and covers fast jets, AWACS (Airborne Warning And Control System), Search & Rescue and many other military movements. Some interesting HF frequencies are:

- RAF Strike Command Integrated Communications System (Architect): 2.591; 4.540; 4.742; 5.714; 6.739; 8.190; 9.031; 11.205; 11.247; 13.257; 15.031; 18.018; 23.220.

- United States Global High Frequency System (Croughten, Ascension, Incirlik, etc.): 4.724; 6.712; 8.968; 8.992; 11.175; 13.200; 15.016; 17.976.

- Royal Canadian Air Force: 5.718; 6.683; 9.006; 11.233; 13.257; 15.031.

- Rescue: 3.023; 3.085; 5.680 (primary); 5.695; 8.364.

- Space Shuttle: 259.7: 296.8 (voice communications).

A log to record any interesting exchanges should ideally be kept with the scanner, with headings to record such data as:

- Date and time of the exchange
- Frequencies
- Mode (FM, UHF, AM, etc.)
- Any callsigns (identifying names, etc.) heard
- Location of listener/incident
- Any transcript of messages or exchanges. If you can record such exchanges on your dictaphone or cassette recorder, so much the better.

A good frequency handbook can be useful – see Bibliography for details.

ID card Useful to have with you if challenged by authorities or landowners, but don't expect it to carry much weight. However, you should always seek to secure permission to venture on to private land before undertaking site examinations. Furthermore, you should always have your card handy to present to witnesses prior to commencing an interview. It should carry a recent colour passport-type photograph, along with your name and any relevant qualifications, which should be printed, and you should sign it and have it countersigned by your director of investigations or research.

Tape measure/pegs and string This should be long enough to measure suspected or reported landing site perimeters and areas. Most people work in metric measurements these days, but if, like me, you prefer the 'old money', you may be lucky enough to find a tape that has both imperial and metric scales of measurement. String and pegs, or chalk lines, might also be useful for delineating any measured-out areas, but the kit you actually carry with you will depend upon the amount of room there is in your 'panic bag'.

Sundries These can be anything else you consider valuable to your investigations. Items can include:

- Pocket-knife (a scalpel, or at least a scalpel blade, is a useful addition)
- Soil-testing kits
- Resealable plastic bags, for sample-taking
- Sterile plastic gloves, for handling samples
- Tweezers
- Magnifying glass
- Good compass, for checking local variations in magnetic fields
- Local maps
- Telephone card
- Incident report forms (see page 180) – do *not* forget them, otherwise any credibility you did have will go straight out of the window
- Time anomaly test forms (see page 185) and watch kit
- Small petty-cash float, to cover contingencies such as taxi fares, extra petrol, telephone calls, etc.
- Don't forget a copy of this book!

A small, basic first-aid kit is also a good idea. If there is a qualified first-aider in your team, then this should ideally be their responsibility. Anything in the panic bag that is used or becomes out of date, lost or damaged should be duly noted and replaced. This is particularly true of first-aid equipment, batteries, pens and cash.

The equipment you choose should come with instructions. Use the various items wisely and they should serve you well. Look after them, and they'll look after you. And remember, it's better to have something and not need it, than to need something and not have it.

HOME EQUIPMENT

Equipment for use at home is dictated by the type of research you are likely to be involved in. Naturally, everything in the panic bag might be useful, although whether you duplicate these items or not is simply a matter of choice and finances. Indeed, some equipment might be interchangeable between the two.

A computer is a very desirable item, and it doesn't need to be 'all-singing, all-dancing' in order to fulfil a useful role. My own first computer has an old 386 processor, no math co-processor, a 20MB hard disk, and only 2 megabytes of memory. However, it has served me well, if sometimes a little slowly, for a number of years now and I would be loath to part with it. Sentimentality apart, it will run Microsoft Windows 3.1 and DOS 6.22, and software applications that run under these environments such as astronomy, satellite tracking, graphic manipulation (for photographic enhancement), desktop publishing and computer modelling packages that are useful for UFO research. What it won't do is allow me to access the Internet or fit a modem. However, if you are buying your computer new, there are many types of system available and your retailer should be able to advise you on what you need, according to your budget and specified requirements. A good word processor and desktop publishing package will do much to give your report forms, letters and so on a professional look. Apart from raising your credibility, it can also raise your profile. It's all 'headology', but it works. Naturally, the more advanced your machine, the greater the capability, particularly with regard to the Internet and communications with other groups.

Another piece of kit I find useful is a microscope. Apart from keeping the kids amused for hours looking at pond life, it is useful for analytical work, such as examining vegetation and soil or water samples from crop circles and alleged UFO landing sites, or tissue samples from alleged cattle mutilations. There are many field guides to aid you with identification of assorted microscopic biota, and if you do intend to use a microscope, then it's as well to know exactly what it is you're looking at. As a further piece of evidence for a reported landing, you could even try looking for stuff that doesn't belong in your selected sample, such as non-native fungal spores, unusual bacteria or organic matter, as these can be used to suggest that such debris has been 'transported in', perhaps on the landing gear of a UFO. Don't forget, though, that you will need to take several representative samples from the area in order to provide a frame of reference.

Other equipment will depend upon your financial resources and level of expertise. I don't suggest that you rush out and buy surveying equipment, mass spectrometry analysers, atomic absorption spectrophotometers and the like, unless (a) you know how to use them, and (b) they are going cheap. The latter is highly unlikely anyway, but any of the larger UFO organizations, such as MUFON (Mutual UFO Network), BUFORA (British UFO Research Association) and the other national or international groups, will be likely to have access to such equipment, and you should not be afraid to approach them with your samples (see Useful Addresses).

2 Witness Interviewing Techniques

The witness statement is probably the single most important element of a report, and will usually be the only 'evidence' available. It is therefore important that you get it right. Remember: what the witness has seen may not be a UFO at all, but also they may not realize it, and if you handle the initial report wrongly you could be personally responsible for generating a 'genuine UFO' report when in reality it is nothing of the sort.

INTERVIEWING RULES

The basic interviewing rules that apply to you as the investigator are simple and straightforward:

- Put aside your own personal beliefs for the duration of the interview. This lessens the likelihood of your own value judgements influencing the witness's statement.

- Remember that the witness may be mistaken about some or all of the elements of their report. No one's memory is infallible, and the mind has a way of adding details here and there, especially where a witness's perceptions may be prone to error because of the nature of the incident. There are hundreds of other things outside the normal sphere of everyday experience, and you could be about to confirm the identity of an easily misidentified phenomenon or occurrence.

- Be aware that the witness might be perpetrating a hoax, for whatever reason. If you approach them with any preconceived ideas as to the nature of the incident, you will ultimately colour the final analysis of the report.

- Establish beforehand whether or not there are other witnesses to the event(s), and whether they have met with 'your' witness to discuss it. If they have, there is again the possibility that some of the details are erroneous or secondhand, and possibly less valid as a result.

- If you are able to visit the site of the incident prior to interview, so much the better. If you can, visit at the same hour and under the same conditions as when the witness had their experience. This action may highlight environmental conditions pre-existent and conducive to the report, such as a known lighthouse shining through the trees, military activity in a known range, ground-to-air communications between an incommunicado light aircraft and an airfield, blimp tether-line lights, and so on.

○ Prior to interviewing the witness, and as soon as possible after receiving the initial report, establish contact with other agencies to determine if any mundane explanation could account for the report, such as civilian or military aircraft, weather balloons, etc. This is not always practical, but if you eliminate the most likely sources first you can narrow down your options, and this can help to alleviate the anxieties of the witness. List any such findings and offer them as suggested preliminary explanations prior to final analysis of the report. Remember, though, that not all witnesses want their experience to be explained away by mundane occurrences.

SETTING UP AN INTERVIEW

Before you approach a witness clutching an incident report form in your hand, you should determine whether or not they actually *want* to have their encounter investigated: they may not, although it seems reasonable to assume that if they contacted you in the first place, they will at least be willing to discuss what they claim to have seen. Other reports may be secondhand at best by the time they reach you, but you should not push too hard for an interview if the witness seems reluctant to talk or appears to be in denial of the events.

Initially at least, you should try to remain objectively detached – if you go in gushing enthusiastically, the witness is not likely to take you very seriously. Remember, the witness is not there for your benefit, you are there for theirs, and for the cause of serious ufology. It is important to remain sympathetic – the encounter is likely to be beyond the sphere of the witness's normal everyday experience and may have far-reaching implications for their belief systems, quite apart from the impact it may have on their social and professional lives.

Try to arrange a convenient time to visit the witness at their home, as they will be more relaxed there and their own familiar surroundings are more likely to be conducive to openness about the encounter. Ideally, such an interview should be conducted as soon after the event as possible, as memory fades with time, and embellishments, unconscious or otherwise, have a tendency to creep in once the witness has had time to reflect on the incident. A fairly comprehensive incident report form can be found on page 180, and while this is not the be-all and end-all of report forms, it will serve as a template should you choose to design your own.

If possible, arrange for two investigators to visit the witness, but don't push it. If the witness is reluctant to have you visit their home, then could you perhaps arrange for them to visit you? Failing that, offer to send them an incident report form, and include return postage – they'll be more inclined to help you out if you do. A covering letter put in with the form will go a long way to cementing a relationship with the witness, especially if it adds that personal touch: be friendly but respectful, and include a contact address or telephone number.

All covering letters, especially when written on a word processor, should be signed personally, as failure to do so may imply laziness or disinterest on the part of the investigator. The letter should also be tailored to the encounter and witness in question, and not just a 'standard' letter of approach, as this may be considered junk mail and will be filed accordingly. Depending on the nature of the encounter, you might wish to include details of other parties who may possibly be able to help with the investigation. You should, of course, affirm an air of confidentiality, and confidence in your own abilities as an investigator, without being pushy. Remember that first impressions count, so be professional – you represent both your organization and ufologists in general.

CONDUCTING AN INTERVIEW

Assuming that you make it past the front door, there you are, talking to a witness. How do you get them to explain what they have experienced if they don't particularly want to talk? And how do you know that they're not making it all up? The truth is that there will always be one or two who get past you, but there are ways to sort the wheat from the chaff, and that's what this section is all about. These techniques have been proven in the field of psychology and counselling for other reasons, but they are none the less valid for our purposes. They will not turn you into a counsellor, nor will they qualify you to practise psychiatry, and there are bound to be times when all the evidence points to a truth when other subtle body language signs say otherwise. These are tips and guides, *no more*.

Try to begin by offering an unstructured invitation to talk. Such invitations might be worded something like 'Please feel free to go ahead and begin', or 'Where do you think you would you like to start from?', or even 'Perhaps there is a particular aspect of your encounter that you would like to relate?' A structured invitation limits the witness's room for manoeuvre, and gives little opportunity for them actually to reflect on what it is they want to discuss. For example, 'Tell me about the size of the object' restricts the witness to a single topic and directs them down a particular avenue of investigation. Not that this is necessarily the wrong approach, but it might be inappropriate at that time – save it for when a particular aspect of the incident has been identified.

An 'open' question is far better than a 'closed' one. An example of the former might be 'How would you describe the object you saw?'; an example of the latter would be 'Was the object you saw disc shaped?' See the difference? A closed question may only get you a 'yes' or a 'no' response, which might not answer the question fully, whereas an 'open' question is likely to elicit a more generalized account of (in this instance) the object's size and dimensions, which in turn opens up a more generous dialogue that can then be traded upon to gain a fuller insight into the nature of the event. A closed question can generally be defined as one that will elicit only a one-word answer and is useful when trying to obtain a specific piece of information; it includes questions with the opening words is, did, does, when, where, who, what, etc. A closed question can be converted into an open question by rewording it, and, of course, vice versa.

Don't be put off by silence: pauses following questions are a common occurrence, particularly at the beginning of an interview, but once a rapport is established these are likely to diminish gradually. Silence may indicate that the witness is considering their response to your question, so it is important for you to be comfortable with it. Allow your witness to marshal their thoughts; remember that they may be nervous or embarrassed, and often the way that a witness begins will set the tone for the whole interview. One way in which silence is constructive is if you use it to focus on a particular moment or issue. By not responding to a given statement, you allow that statement to 'hang in the air', which in turn allows it to be heard and to have its impact felt even by the witness themselves.

It is important to pace the interview, to direct it to the best effect. This does not mean that you should 'script' the witness (in fact, you should take great pains not to, otherwise you'll have a report of your version of events rather than the witness's), but you should be aware of exactly what it is that you, as an investigator, wish to achieve in terms of the investigation. Nor does it mean that you should be dismissive of apparently unimportant information relating to the incident.

Although you are there to listen and record an account of an event, there are responses you can use to reaffirm your active listening role. One such technique is to restate a response to a question, but worded in such a way that it does not alter the statement's content or make you sound like a parrot. Similar to this is reflection, which mirrors the last statement made by the witness. Here, the wording may be altered slightly, if only to condense that statement into a verbalized observation. Neither of these techniques should be used more than once a minute.

It can often be useful to focus on the accent of a statement or response to a question. For example, if the witness says 'After my encounter, I felt absolutely exhausted', you might respond 'Exhausted?' This allows exploration of the cause of the exhaustion, which might highlight a new aspect of the encounter. A request for clarification can be under- or over-used. If over-used, it can distract the witness from a current train of thought. If, however, you are unable to follow the statements, clarification is better than allowing the witness to continue along an avenue that you do not understand. A request for clarification may be worded thus: 'Could you describe it another way for me please?', or 'What did you mean when you said...' As always, let common sense prevail.

BODY LANGUAGE

This is not the place for a lengthy discourse on body language, but suffice it to say that only about 7 per cent of communication between two people is transmitted verbally. A huge chunk of the remaining percentage is transmitted unconsciously by the use of body language, and if read correctly, this can give the investigator a great deal of insight into the personal feelings and attitudes of the witness towards their encounter. It can be useful in determining how much of what they relate is actual memory, and how much is embellishment or internally constructed – and remember that in some instances, the latter may also be unconscious.

It is even possible to modify a person's body language by a subtle shifting of your own. For example, if a person sits with their legs crossed and arms folded, and is avoiding eye contact, it may be that they are feeling insecure about the interview, perhaps preferring to shut you out. If you are aware of adopting a similar posture, the interview is very unlikely to get off the ground. Adopt a relaxed posture, perhaps crossing your legs at the ankles, rather than the knees, or lean forward slightly towards the witness. Show interest in what they are saying – after all, it's the reason you are there – but don't go overboard and invade their personal space, as that will have exactly the opposite to the desired effect.

Limit the number of barriers between you and the witness, such as clipboards or briefcases. A three-piece suit is actually a barrier, as indeed are sunglasses, a fastened waistcoat and even a beard or moustache, as it sometimes indicates psychologically to others that an individual may have something to hide. Remember, too, that there might be cultural differences of body language to be overcome, and it is easy to offend someone from a different culture merely by not being aware of what those protocols or differences in body language are. If you're not sure, try to take someone along to the interview who comes from the same culture or background – this is particularly important if there is also a language barrier.

Talking once more of barriers, come out from behind any desk or other obstruction that stands between you. If possible, sit at 90 degrees to the witness, as this offers them (and you!) a psychological 'escape route'. Do not have the principal light source behind you, or in the witness's eyes – this is an informal interview, not an interrogation. The women among you may indicate being open to the situation by exposing your wrists or palms: this may be a mating gesture designed to attract male interest, but if you're dealing with a reluctant male witness it has its uses – with caution. The subtle manipulation of your own body language can do much to establish trust, empathy and rapport between you – if you relax, they'll relax, and to be effective you must be in control of the interview.

Below is a list of generalizations that relate to eye movement and internal representations of events, which are taught as observational techniques in 'neuro-linguistic programming'. I include them here because although most people understand the basic precepts of body language, these techniques augment such knowledge and are not widely known. Readers wishing to learn more should try to study these techniques or 'transactional analysis', both of which are good interviewing/counselling tools.

Direction of eye movement	Functioning sensory system
Up to their left	Visual remembered
Up to their right	Visual constructed
Eyes focused straight ahead, pupils dilated	Internal visual images, perceived externally
Blinking, squinting, prolonged eye closure (especially when accompanied by rapid eye movements)	Visual
Horizontally to their left	Auditory recall (sounds/words)
Horizontal to their right	Auditory constructed
Down to their left	Auditory dialogue (internal)
Down to their right	Kinesthetics (body sensations)

All these eye movements are based on the supposition that you are able to see the witness's eyes clearly. However, if you can't, *don't* fudge the data. If there are two investigators, it may be of value to have one of you asking the questions, while the other notes down question numbers and any of the above responses to those questions. Analysis of the data can be done later. Of course, it is not always possible to determine beforehand what questions will be asked, so you may have to improvise. Devising and attaching some sort of alphanumeric code to the responses would be useful here.

Of course, if you have someone on your team who is a qualified and experienced counsellor, then so much the better. It's all very well being a keen and well-intentioned amateur, but it's no substitute for being a trained and experienced professional. Mess up this stage of an investigation and you're unlikely to get past the door again.

INCIDENT REPORT FORM

During the interview, show the witness your incident report form (see page 180), and explain exactly what you are doing and why you are asking the questions you are. Don't be afraid to admit to ignorance: a defensive witness will spot bluff a mile off and will be more impressed by your honesty, dedication and sincerity than if you pretend to know all the answers. You can still offer opinions, if prompted, but again remember that some witnesses may not want their encounters explained away by mundane or natural causes. Be sensitive to this. Do not impinge on their time any longer than is necessary, unless invited, and even then use your discretion – they still have a life to get on with.

Most of the form is self-explanatory, although some questions are designed to help discover early on whether a mundane cause could explain the sighting. You will need to refer to a map for questions relating to location and landmarks. You should not dissuade the witness from writing down their own version of events, either on the form or on a separate sheet. If the latter, ask them if they would be willing to let you have a copy. This should then be attached to the incident report form. Some of the questions on the form cannot be answered by the witness and are for the investigator's use only.

The section for medical data can be used to detail any biological effects of the encounter such as burns, puncture wounds, symptoms of other conditions, etc., although obviously you will need to ensure that you are not breaching any code of medical ethics. The section for on-site field analysis is for use during examination of the landing site, photographic evidence, etc. (see Chapter 9). Starcharts can be generated by the appropriate software on a PC and printed out for attaching to the incident report form; several inexpensive astronomy programs are readily available. Meteorological data may be obtained from the meteorological office appropriate to the location of the sighting, and will usually be sited in or around major conurbations – check your local telephone directory (in the UK, details can be found under the heading Weather Services; in the US, under US Department of Commerce).

If possible, any photographic evidence should be analysed thoroughly, initially by your own researchers using appropriate image-editing and enhancement software, but any suspect (or indeed, not so suspect) photographic evidence should be referred to appropriate outside agencies, such as professional laboratories, for verification. Remember: if there is any question of your professionalism or your codes of practice, ethics or whatever being compromised, then call in another party. If it is possible to obtain the film still in the camera without its having being wound on or rewound, so much the better, as this implies that the camera and film have not been tampered with. Record this as such. It also allows other photographs to be taken on the same film, under the same lighting and environmental conditions, to provide a frame of reference. For details of photographic analysis, see Chapter 9.

Details of how to conduct the MUFON time anomaly test are also given in Chapter 9, and template forms for use during such tests are provided on page 185. The necessary watch kits can be obtained from MUFON via courier postage so contact them for details (see Useful Addresses, although it is also possible to make up your own.

Towards the end of the incident report form is a section for the Vallée classification system (explained in Chapter 3), which neatly compartmentalizes all the data and should make it easier to use for statistical and analytical purposes.

AFTER THE INTERVIEW

Now that you have interviewed the witness and filled in the form as best you can, what next? It is all too easy to sit on a report for a while and dissect and discuss it in the bar over a few drinks when the occasion arises. Not only is this unprofessional, it is also lazy. If there are likely to be other groups or individuals with whom you might have useful dialogue, then notify them of events as soon as is practical and bring them in if appropriate. By all means dissect and discuss the report with the individuals or groups concerned, but be mindful of confidentiality and the witness's privacy.

Make any follow-up calls, such as those to determine whether there were any military aircraft or activities in the area of the sighting, or whether police or other helicopters were flying at the time, and check with the meteorological office regarding weather or science balloons.

So there you are: witnesses interviewed, forms filled in, investigations undertaken, data analysed, report filed, etc., but what else can be done with the information? Well, periodically you could re-evaluate your local position, do some number-crunching, and come up with statistics based on the contents of your reports. You could use the data you obtain to see if there is any pattern to reported sightings in your area, which in turn might offer you further avenues of investigation. In any event, don't be afraid to share your data with other groups and organizations, regardless of differences in mindset or particular opinions about the UFO phenomenon. Publicize your findings, not only in the relevant UFO literature but also in the local or even national press if you can get them interested. UFO magazines and group newsletters are all well and good, but 99 times out of 100 you'll be preaching to the converted anyway, and one of our aims should be to raise the profile of ufology and help lessen its 'giggle factor' by establishing it firmly as acceptable within the public psyche.

You may be one of those ufologists who wishes to share data with the Ministry of Defence (or your national equivalent), or indeed, the witness may have reported an incident to them. What happens then? If an incident is reported to the police, then sooner or later it will be directed to the MoD or equivalent (in the UK, probably via the Aeronautical Information Service, AIS), but if you have had the foresight to establish links with the local constabulary, then they might even notify the witness that you exist when they make the initial report. However, just because you're on a database of useful addresses, don't assume that any and all reports will automatically come to your group, either directly from the witness or indirectly via the police. They may, eventually, but this is most likely to be through the police press office.

In the UK, any Royal Air Force base will accept UFO reports, from you or the public, and these are then forwarded to RAF Rudloe Manor in Wiltshire, the home of the Flying Complaints Flight, which according to Tim Good is probably a lodger unit that deals specifically with UFO reports. From here, it seems that reports are sent directly to Secretariat (Air Staff) 2a at Whitehall in London, with some of the more 'interesting' ones being sent to the US Defense Intelligence Agency's London Liaison (DIALL). Good also adds that all US defence attachés are required to collect such reports, and that occasionally some of these reports are reciprocally forwarded to the MoD's Defence Intelligence Staff. It appears likely that a similar arrangement exists between the US National Security Agency (NSA, also standing for 'Never Say Anything' or 'No Such Agency') and the British Government Communications Headquarters (GCHQ) in Cheltenham, Gloucestershire. Well-known researcher Nick Redfern has unearthed evidence that reports received by Sec (AS) 2a are forwarded to RAF Airborne Early Warning squadrons and the RAF's Ground Environment Division as a matter of course.

If, on the other hand, the witness has reported the incident to a civil aviation authority, such as a local air traffic control centre, then the latter are required to notify AIS at the London air traffic control centre immediately, while a completed report form has to be sent to the MoD at Whitehall, so it all ends up in the same hands anyway.

For those new to the subject of ufology, and overseas colleagues, Timothy Good has written extensively on how UFOs are treated by the various international intelligence agencies in countries around the world, and his books are generally considered essential reading for budding ufologists.

3 UFO Classification Systems

A UFO is defined as a flying object or anomaly seen in our skies by an observer or observers who are unable to determine its nature. Fortunately, most UFO sightings can be explained as natural phenomena or misidentified aircraft, astronomical events, top-secret projects of a military nature, etc. (see Chapter 11). However, many UFOs defy the usual criteria for these explanations and this is where you, as an investigator, come in.

THE HYNEK UFO CLASSIFICATION SYSTEM

Dr J. Allen Hynek was formerly the head of the US Air Force's Project Blue Book – the US government's own attempt to study the UFO phenomenon, formerly Project Grudge, and prior to that Project Sign, the latter incepted by the USAF in 1948. While with Blue Book as a consultant, Dr Hynek devised the following classification system, which has long been the 'industry standard'. He initially divided UFO reports according to the distance from the observer – greater or less than 150m (500ft) – and then further subdivided these two sections into a total of six categories.

'Long-distance' sightings:

Nocturnal lights Light or lights seen at distance. There may be various fluctuations in intensity, changes of colour, and/or rapid acceleration or deceleration, and sudden turns or changes of direction. Often turn out to be no more than planets such as Venus or Jupiter, high-altitude aircraft or meteors.

Daylight (diurnal) discs Often seen at a distance, and varying considerably in shape and size – may be disc, cigar or cylinder shaped, egg or acorn shaped (the former usually seen on a horizontal axis, the latter on a vertical axis). They may be spheres, ovals, irregular shapes or (particularly lately) large black triangles. They may or may not exhibit similar patterns of behaviour to nocturnal lights. Often the result of misidentified weather balloons, blimps, aircraft, or even hoaxes.

Radar-visual Witnessed both as a radar reflection and as a visual sighting by an independent observer. Stand-alone radar sightings are often discounted due to the nature of false traces caused by natural phenomena such as flocks of birds, ground-scatter (a reflected signal from high ground), cloud banks and temperature inversions. Relatively rare, but important, as they may provide instrumental evidence to support the visual aspect of the sighting.

Closer-range sightings:

CE1 (close encounters of the first kind) Observations of phenomena with no interaction between UFO and witness or environment.

CE2 Visible physical effects on both organic and non-organic, animate or inanimate objects are witnessed. Such effects may include the cutting out of car engines or other radio and electrical interference (due to the electromagnetic pulse (EMP) effect on the electrical circuits; diesel engines are not usually affected), broken tree branches, scorched or flattened vegetation, imprints in the ground, scorched or newly exposed earth, and increased radiation levels or localized time anomalies.

CE3 The actual witnessing of occupants in or around the UFO. There is a bone of contention concerning these so-called 'contactee cases', as Hynek believed that such reports usually came from pseudo-religious fanatics, and cases such as those of George Adamski and the Aetherius Society are often quoted by sceptics to add weight to these arguments. To qualify fully for CE3 status, the occupants of the UFO should either be witnessed or have verbal or some other communication with the witness. There may be displays of hostility by or towards the extraterrestrial biological entity (EBE) or by remote devices.

CE4 Although this is not one of Hynek's classifications per se, it is included as a later addition to the above and implies actual abduction by extraterrestrials, in its literal sense of being abducted without the witness's consent and/or knowledge. Often these encounters begin with a CE2, and the abductee may have no knowledge of the abduction until such time as regressional therapy becomes necessary due to subsequent emotional or psychological disturbances. There is a wealth of material available about abduction scenarios, and investigators are urged to study this to gain a fuller understanding of the phenomenon, particularly as such claims appear to be on the increase.

THE VALLÉE ANOMALY CLASSIFICATION SYSTEM

This is a system used to categorize various types of UFO and supernatural experiences that was devised by Dr Jacques Vallée, the famous French ufologist. It is now more widely used than Hynek's classification system, as it is more specific for analytical purposes and narrows things down somewhat. The various sections are detailed below.

AN ratings are used to classify anomalous behaviour:

AN1 Anomalies which have no lasting physical effects, such as amorphous or flashing lights, unexplained explosions.

AN2 Anomalies which do have lasting physical effects, such as poltergeists, materialized objects, areas of flattened grass, scorched ground, broken or damaged trees, crop circles, etc.

AN3 Anomalies which have entities associated with them, such as bigfoot, ghosts, yetis, spirits, elves, goblins, or other such mythical or legendary entities.

AN4 Witness interaction with the AN3 entities, including near-death experiences, religious miracles and visions, out-of-body experiences (OOBEs).

AN5 Reports of anomalies in which there are injuries and deaths, including spontaneous human combustion, unexplained wounds, or even supernatural healing that may result from such an experience.

MA ratings are used to describe the behaviour of a UFO and are comparable with the Nocturnal Light, Daylight Disc and Radar-visual Hynek classifications:

MA1 A UFO has been observed which travels in a discontinuous trajectory – rapid acceleration/deceleration, vertical climbs or drops, manoeuvres or loops.

MA2 MA1 plus any physical effects caused by the UFO as per AN1 or AN2.

MA3 MA1 plus any entities observed on board, e.g. the airship cases of the late nineteenth century.

MA4 Manoeuvres that are accompanied by a sense of reality transformation for the witness.

MA5 Manoeuvres resulting in the permanent injury or death of the witness.

FB ratings are used to describe the fly-by of an anomalous craft or object:

FB1 A straightforward sighting of a UFO travelling in a straight line across the sky.

FB2 FB1 accompanied by other physical evidence.

FB3 A fly-by where crew, pilots or other entities are observed on board.

FB4 A fly-by where the witness has experienced a transformation of reality into the object or its occupants.

FB5 A fly-by in which the witness suffers permanent injuries or even death.

CE ratings are used to describe close encounters and are very similar to the Hynek close-encounter classifications:

CE1 UFO comes to within 150m (500ft) of the witness, but no after-effects are suffered by the witness or the surrounding area.

CE2 CE1 that leaves landing traces, or temporary injuries to the witness.

CE3 Entities have been observed on or within the UFO

CE4 The witness has undergone abduction.

CE5 CE4 which results in permanent psychological injuries to, or death of, the witness.

The SVP rating is an important rating of credibility. 'Marks' out of four are awarded for the three categories of reliability (first number), site visit (second number) and possible explanations (third number). For example, if a rating of 330 was awarded, it would imply that the witness was at first hand and reliable, the site was visited by a reliable investigator, but the sighting could be explained by natural or mundane causes, thus:

Source reliability rating

0 Unknown or unreliable source.

1 Report attributed to a source of unknown or unmeasured reliability.

2 Reliable source, secondhand.

3 Reliable source, firsthand.

4 Firsthand personal interview with the witness by a source of proven reliability.

Site visit rating

0 No site visit, or answer unknown.

1 Site visit by a person not familiar with the phenomena.

2 Site visit by a person or persons familiar with the phenomena.

3 Site visit by reliable investigator(s) with some experience.

4 Site visit by skilled analyst(s).

Possible explanations rating

0 Data consistent with one or more natural or mundane causes.

1 Natural explanation requires only slight modification of the data.

2 Natural explanation requires major alteration of one parameter.

3 Natural explanation requires major alteration of several parameters.

4 No natural explanation possible, given the evidence.

You will notice that on the template for the incident report form (see page 180), there are the appropriate headings for both the Hynek and Vallée classification systems. It is not absolutely necessary to utilize both, but neither does it do any harm. A flowchart is provided on page 184 to assist with the identification of various aerial phenomena. While it is by no means exhaustive, it does give an indication as to the nature of some anomalies. Naturally, it is intended only as a guide and an aid to identification, but it should provide you with a starting point from which to begin your investigation.

For example, if an apparently oval or disc-shaped object appears to be moving continuously and milling about, it can be seen from the flowchart that this is identified as a flock of birds. However, this is only a likelihood and not a firm conclusion. It is therefore imperative that the investigator is not dismissive of the report, but instead undertakes to check whether or not this 'likelihood' is indeed probable. In this instance, could you perhaps solicit advice from an ornithologist? Let's say you could, but that the ornithologist thinks that the only birds capable of flying as described over the site, which might be a particular habitat or migratory route, are seasonal visitors that are not appropriate to the date of the sighting – then you might have to consider other factors. So, could it perhaps have been a cloud of jettisoned aviation fuel, perhaps blown about by the wind? These are the kinds of questions you will need to consider, but remember that it might still turn out to have been a flock of birds after all. Conversely, during the course of the investigation you may find other witnesses, closer to the event, who can add their own details.

It is important also to consider your own views and belief systems. There is absolutely no reason why a die-hard sceptic should not make an excellent investigator: indeed, such a person will not have their judgement coloured by the desire for an investigation to produce a bona fide extraterrestrial craft. Try to strike a balance if you can. A healthy dose of scepticism is a very useful tool in its own right, and those displaying it should not be relegated simply to making the tea or answering the telephone.

4 The Abduction Experience

The Oxford Dictionary defines the term 'abduction' as the noun of 'abduct': '*verb*. To carry off (person) illegally by force or fraud'. Recently, there have been one or two surveys that have attempted to put the phenomenon of abduction by extraterrestrials into some sort of human perspective. The most notable of these is the Roper Poll, a survey of just under 6,000 Americans carried out by Budd Hopkins, David Jacobs PhD and Ron Westrum PhD. Another was carried out by the Intruders Foundation (see Useful Addresses).

From the outset, these surveys have come in for some criticism, largely because of the widely held belief that statistics can be manipulated to serve the purposes of those compiling them and can thus be made to prove anything. Having myself wrestled with such number-crunching in the past, I feel that statistics are usually misunderstood by most people, and consequently mistrusted. That said, statistics should not be dismissed out of hand. Much will depend on how the raw data was gathered initially, what the 'null hypothesis' was, whether this null hypothesis was accepted or rejected, and what kind of statistical analysis was applied to the data. A greater understanding of the mechanics of statistics and statistical analysis can lead to a greater or lesser acceptance of the findings.

According to the above surveys, somewhere between 2 and 4 per cent of the US population over the age of 18 believe they have undergone alien abduction experiences, the majority of which have been at the hands of the small, humanoid type of extraterrestrial with large, black 'wrap-around' eyes, known collectively as the 'greys' (see page 76). (These survey figures do not take into account those residing in institutions or dormitories.) A possible abduction scenario might arise as a result of a remembered close encounter, or it might be discovered following investigations of a medical nature into sleep disturbances, night terrors, anxiety attacks, or psychotic or neurotic episodes. All these can be symptomatic of possible abduction, as can fragmented memories, disturbing images during sleep, unexplained time losses, and so on. However, they should not be taken to imply abduction merely by their presence alone.

The witness, when aware of having being abducted, is often reluctant to discuss what actually went on, and this can be for a number of reasons. It is important when interviewing abductees that you adopt a sympathetic and understanding approach, while remaining detached and scientifically objective. It is very easy to fall into the trap of shaping the experience of the witness to fit in with your own belief systems, and this is beneficial neither to the witness nor to your investigation. You must only work with what is known to have been experienced, and with what your witness relates. Anyone who has undergone a profound personal experience may be prone to suggestion as to the origins of and reasons for it, and input from you might re-shape or re-identify their experience, which is beyond your remit. Just record and submit your report as it is given. You should not offer opinions or 'fill in the gaps', unless invited to do so and you are very well informed. Any such personal input should, of course, be duly recorded, although you can offer up comparisons with similar cases to provide a framework within which a witness's personal assessment of the scenario can be formulated.

A witness may feel more comfortable with their own belief as to the nature of the event and may consider it a safer option, considering that they still have to get on with the rest of their lives. Unless you are a qualified regressional therapist, you should not attempt to hypnotize or regress a subject, as you will only make the situation worse and may awaken latent psychotic or neurotic behaviour in the witness. People often equate regressional therapy with stage hypnotism, but the two disciplines are poles apart. Experience with one does not qualify you to undertake the other. Having no experience or training in either means you are simply not qualified – period. Believe me, you do not want to mess about inside people's heads.

In fact, regression as a therapeutic tool of revelation has come in for a lot of criticism and, I think, quite rightly so. It is not the be-all and end-all of ufological investigation that it is often promoted to be, and should certainly not be offered as final 'proof' of alien intervention in an individual's life. British researcher Kevin McClure points out that regression as a technique for the retrieval of memories is both unreliable and often dangerous, sometimes having a profound 'knock-on' effect. The psychiatric profession widely accepts the textbook statement that memories produced under regression contain many elements of untruth and confabulation, distortions, cued responses and fantasy. This is not to say that the abductions are not taking place, but it seems possible that a lot less are actually happening than we would like to believe, given the general mindset that pervades the UFO fraternity regarding abduction. It has been said that regression can elicit both true and false memories, but that the subject will have an enhanced belief in the accuracy of those memories once the session is over.

We must also remember that we are all constantly bombarded by media images of UFOs and extraterrestrials, whether via television, cinema, computer games or whatever, but this in no way addresses the problem of explaining how it is that people from very different cultures and backgrounds (many of whom are not in any contact with these media sources) report the same or similar details of experience in abduction accounts.

'SYMPTOMS' OF ABDUCTION

Many of the 'symptoms' associated with alien abduction are akin to those found in people suffering from post-traumatic stress disorder – which, to be fair, may be exactly what the abductee is suffering from (if abduction by aliens isn't traumatic, then I'd like to know what is!). Symptoms include moderate to severe depression, anxiety and panic attacks, and irrational fears or phobias. There are often reports of disturbing dream images, nightmares or disrupted sleep patterns. The witness may display obsessive-compulsive behaviour and be terrified of being left alone, particularly at night. They may subsequently avoid previous haunts and routes. Mood lability (swing) is not uncommon, with irrational displays of extreme emotion, from love to fury. Younger abductees may later suffer from psychosexual problems.

above Alien logo seen on the outside of a landed UFO in 1964, during the Lonnie Zamora encounter.

right Some of the symbols allegedly associated with UFOs and alien activity. Sadly, most have known counterparts in astrology, science, electronics and mathematics, and this diminishes them as possible alien script.

left Alien script? This lettering was allegedly seen over a doorway on board a UFO during the well-publicized Antonio Villa Boas abduction.

The memory of the events may be partially or completely repressed, and there may be effects on the emotional, spiritual and mental health of the witness. Under regression, or with memory recall, the subject may remember seeing bright lights or what they believe to be UFOs, either in or around the location from which they believe they were abducted. They may have undergone an extended period of missing time, during which they were unable consciously to recall their actions or whereabouts. Images that are recalled may include hospital-type operating theatres, in which they might find themselves lying cold, naked and afraid on operating tables; various 'alien beings'; sensations or feelings of immobility or inability to resist; bright lights and odd smells; transport to the interior of spaceships; undergoing surgical procedures, such as being 'implanted' (in which a small device is inserted into the head via the nasal cavity, or positioned subcutaneously elsewhere on the body); and impregnation, abortion of an existing foetus, or removal of skin, hair, ovarian or sperm samples. Other reported phenomena include telepathic communications with these alien beings; various cylinders or vials containing liquids and human or hybrid specimens; strange writings or glyphs; strange marks or stains on the witnesses' bodies or clothing; and scars or bruises with little or no associated pain, the latter particularly appearing around the arms, legs and male genitalia. David Jacobs also reports that some witnesses subsequently suffer problems with their eyesight such as blurred vision and swollen or stinging eyes, with relief coming after a few days, months or sometimes not at all.

Other physiological features associated with abductions are muscle and joint pain, ruptured eardrums, nosebleeds and holes in the nasal passages. Among women, there may be vaginal or umbilical discharges, usually brownish in colour, vaginal haemorrhaging or scar tissue, and, perhaps more disturbingly, a rupturing of the hymen in sexually inactive children and young adolescent females. Unexplainable pregnancies are another reported feature among some female abductees, wherein a woman may present all the outward symptoms of pregnancy – a pregnancy that indeed may be verified by her doctor. Very often, between the time of discovering the pregnancy and the end of the first trimester (the first three-month period of pregnancy) the foetus 'vanishes'. There is no miscarriage, discharge, haemorrhage or any other outward sign of foetal loss – she is simply not pregnant any more. For the benefit of the sceptics among you, these are not 'phantom pregnancies'. The latter are a known medical condition (not unique to humans) and cannot be biologically verified, whereas the above pregnancies can. In his book *Alien Encounters*, David Jacobs explores the abduction phenomenon in detail, and provides some good case histories and transcripts of regressional sessions.

One of the highly popular current theories concerning the reasons for abduction is that of genetic harvesting, and the removal of samples for the acquisition of DNA. It is interesting to note that many reports of multiple abductions of the same subject over a period of years occur at times and ages that are pertinent to the genetic development and changes taking place within the witness, namely at 7 years, then 14, 21 and other multiples of seven, to within a year or so either way. Abductions are most apparent at around these ages and in many instances seem to be an ongoing thing, even from generation to generation.

Following an abduction scenario, many witnesses find that their self-esteem and self-confidence take a nosedive; they may undergo an identity crisis and suffer anxiety, disorientation, hypervigilance and show marked sexually inhibitive behaviour. This last should not be considered a cue to enquire about details of a highly personal nature: indeed, you should never need to broach the subject at all, but let the witness reveal it in their own time. Don't push. Depending on culture and background, many moral and personal issues are considered taboo, and an initial rapport and trust may have to be established before full details will be given to you.

While the foregoing sounds rather horrific, there are scenarios in which the contact appears friendly and of decidedly peaceful intent. In these cases, the witness is not usually abducted but rather is invited to enter the vehicle while fully conscious, where a dialogue usually ensues to the effect that the aliens are here to help mankind, but that we must change our ways to avoid destroying the planet before it is too late. Such witnesses often become a kind of 'evangelical missionary' or ambassador for the ETs, and are usually associated with the 'new age' philosophy of ufology. Conversely, some abductees feel that the friendly or more positive contact stems from their initial attitudes and approach when dealing with the alleged abductors.

Now, just because a witness relates any or all of the above scenarios to you, it does not follow that they have been abducted by aliens. There may be an underlying psychotic or neurotic condition in evidence that can be responsible for many of the same symptoms, although the Roper Poll found very little to suggest psychoses in any of their representative sample. Other causes for a belief in having being abducted include near-death experiences, birth trauma and so on. There is also the risk of an outright hoax. There is plenty of material available for the unscrupulous to study in order to perpetrate such a hoax, or it may be that the abduction scenario is put forward in order to draw attention to other underlying causes, such as some forms of abuse, about which the subject might feel more uncomfortable and be unable to relate their experiences directly. A report of abduction by aliens might seem a more acceptable option, and perhaps offers an in-road to the psyche of the witness or subject for a therapist or counsellor.

However, as a result of the surveys, five key questions were identified that can be used to indicate a possible abduction, and a 'yes' answer to at least four of them indicates that further investigation is warranted. These questions are:

○ Have you seen any unusual lights or balls of light in a room without knowing what was causing them, or where they came from?

○ Have you ever awoken paralysed, with a sense of a strange presence or something else in the room?

○ Have you ever experienced a period of an hour or more in which you were apparently lost, with no idea of where you were, or why you were there?

○ Have you ever experienced sensations of flying through the air, without knowing why or how?

○ Do you have any unexplained scars or marks on your body and neither you nor anyone else can recall when, where, or how you obtained them?

○ (supplemental) Since your encounter, do you find yourself suffering from anxiety, phobias, depression, altered sleep patterns, or disturbing imagery and dreams?

In cases that require you to deal with multiple witnesses, the order in which these questions are asked or organized on the report form should be varied. This limits the 'fudge factor' and helps to increase the chances of discovering a deliberate hoax. The final question is supplemental and optional, but in any event, the other five should be mixed in with a few nonsensical or irrelevant 'control' questions to determine whether the witness is likely to answer 'yes' to any and all questions in order to satisfy the investigator or reinforce a hoax. The closer to the criteria a witness becomes, the more credible the account.

ALTERNATIVE EXPLANATIONS

At this point, we should take a look at the more rational explanations for the abduction scenario.

There could be many psychological reasons why a subject would wish to propose an abduction scenario, and the first of these is a deliberate wish to perpetrate a hoax. Sadly, this might turn out to be the case in some instances. Such fabrication of events, when publicized, can make (for example) a social inadequate the centre of attention for a while, thus providing an immediate pay-off, and indeed a hoax can be quite lucrative financially for the unscrupulous. However, the reality is that genuine abductees rarely, if ever, actively seek fame or fortune from their experiences. Indeed, the costs to them socially, professionally, physically and psychologically would seem to preclude mass publicity as an option. The more familiar you are with the abduction phenomenon, the less likely it is that you will be duped in this fashion.

Over the last few years, much has been made in the press and on television of ritual and sexual abuse scenarios, and many families and reputations have been irreparably damaged by allegations from individuals and social welfare organizations alike. The fact that many of the subjects involved subsequently turn out to have undergone nothing of the sort compounds the problem for those who have been through it, with the result that genuine victims of sexual abuse are less inclined to report their abusers directly because of the fear of not being believed, and of the social stigma attached to such experiences. One theory is that the memories of abuse have become repressed into the unconscious mind by the traumatized victim, only to resurface years later as alien abduction 'screen memories'. Memories of abuse may be triggered in much the same way as abduction memories, and the subject may bear the symptoms of post-traumatic stress disorder. However, it seems that so far no such screen memories have been discovered, implying that the subject has actually undergone abduction, particularly as it is likely that suppressed abuse memories are likely to surface under regressional therapy anyway, and be addressed accordingly.

Mass hysteria is another oft-proposed explanation for claims of alien abduction, and quite a credible one too, given the fashionable interest in UFOs and all things extraterrestrial – or at least, so it would seem. However, such contagious hysteria requires a fair amount of mutual reinforcement between abductees, especially on the finer details, and in most instances the alleged abductees don't know each other at all. Ally this to the fact that not all such fine details regarding the abductions are broadcast, but bear so many similarities and consistencies between accounts as to render them unlikely to be coincidental, and hysteria seems improbable. The abduction phenomenon is a global one, and transcends all the boundaries of class, culture, language and geography, indicating that, like death, the abductors are great democrats. Nor is alien abduction a new phenomenon, and cases maintain the same consistencies and similarities in early reports, given before the recent publicity, as they do now.

Pre-birth experiences bear certain similarities to abduction scenarios and should not be discounted. During the early stages of pregnancy, the human foetus looks remarkably like the 'grey', with a disproportionately large head, large eyes and so on. Bodily features such as ears, genitalia and facial features are said to be either very simple or greatly reduced in size in the greys when compared to their human counterparts, and these attributes (or lack of them!) can also be found in the human foetus until quite late in its development (it is not recognizable as a human until at least the tenth week). In addition, the arms on a human baby are longer than the legs, another characteristic associated with greys. In the womb, human skin colour ranges through greyish, white, brown or even reddish orange until the third trimester, at seven months. Wrinkled skin and hair do not generally appear until the seventh and eighth months respectively.

These and other similarities between the human foetus and abducting humanoids have been proposed as the model on which descriptions of the abductors have been based. It has been suggested by Professor Alvin Lawson that pre-birth experiences can provide a very rich store of imagery that may be retrieved from the unconscious during regressional therapy. Such images as dark tunnels and bright lights, both common in abduction recalls, are similar to experiences in the birth canal and the sudden bright lights of the delivery room. However, as Jacobs points out, this fails to address the issue of how people could see another foetus unless they were the product of a multiple birth, or how those born by Caesarean section are able to recount parallel abduction experiences to those born by natural vaginal birth. None the less, our birth and our death are probably the two greatest traumas that the human condition knows, and this pre-birth experience argument is a persuasive, and indeed divisive, one.

Near-death experiences (NDEs) also bear some similarities to the abduction experience, particularly with regard to the appearance of bright lights, otherworldly beings and so on. There are reports of feelings of being lifted up, travelling or being transported through walls, doorways or solid objects into strange rooms, gardens, etc., only to be returned by the same means, whereupon the subject awakens and often reports a subsequent shift in consciousness or spiritual values. However, one major difference between NDEs and abduction scenarios is that in the former the subject often remains fully aware of the experience and rarely reports any negative effects, to the extent that the fear of dying is removed completely. Furthermore, many such NDE reports come from those whom one might expect to experience the phenomenon: people undergoing surgery and those who are ill.

Psychogenic fugue states are similar to some schizophrenic conditions and multiple-personality syndromes. An individual undergoing such a fugue may travel to another location and assume another identity, occupation, family life, etc., with no recollection whatever of the former life they once led. There are implications here for the experience of missing time, of being literally 'missing' from the former home and locale, family connections and so on. Usually triggered by great psychological stress, the fugue manifests as a kind of denial of the stressful situation which triggered it, and the subject adopts a new persona and lives accordingly. As an argument for alien abduction, however, it doesn't really work, as the two situations have no similarities other than the loss of memory or recall.

Temporal lobe epilepsy or dysfunction has been championed of late by certain clinical psychologists and neurobiologists, on the assumption that electrically charged particles released during the Earth's tectonic activity stimulate the brain's temporal lobe, causing instability and triggering hallucinations. It has been shown during laboratory experiments that such hallucinations can be produced when the temporal lobe is stimulated by electrical impulse. Some epileptic conditions also cause this electrical overload, and I have seen at first hand how this can alter a subject's perceptions. They often report other presences around them, strange or unfamiliar surroundings, false memory syndrome, and (to the observer) other equally bizarre experiences and tales. To the sufferer, these experiences, and the consequent fear and disorientation they generate, are very real. By and large, this theory is not accepted by either the UFO or psychiatric communities, and to be frank, the evidence for the claims is just too sparse and unsubstantiated to be accepted, even by geophysicists and geomorphologists.

These are just some of the theories postulated in order to explain the abduction phenomenon, but there are many others such as hallucinations caused by substance abuse, the simple will to believe, the product of fantasy-prone personalities, and the direct result of science fiction-related media. However you look at it, the phenomenon is stress producing and frightening to its victims, and it apparently continues unabated. That the abduction phenomenon is very real there is no doubt, but whether it is the direct result of alien intervention in human affairs remains an unanswered, emotive and divisive issue.

THE RICHARD BUTLER ABDUCTION EXPERIENCE CLASSIFICATION

This classification system was compiled by American researcher and author Richard Butler.

AE-1: Lucid dream These are dream experiences that are generated totally by the subject's own subconscious during sleep. There is no tangible human–ET interaction other than a dream in which there is no logical progression or sequence of events.

AE-2: Techno/telepathic lucid dream These lucid dreams are experienced internally, but generated by outside sources. According to Butler, they are extraterrestrial in origin and are accomplished by a technological enhancement of a psychic intrusion into the subject's subconscious. There may be a total collapse of the existing dream, or at least a dissociation from it. At the point of collapse, the desired scenario or message is inserted, which Butler believes is designed to influence the subject's ideals, belief systems or behaviour. Those who awake immediately afterwards sometimes report a glowing circle or oval on the ceiling approximately 1m (3ft) in diameter, and occasionally a shaft of light or energy retreating into it. Others report that the original dream picks up exactly where it left off prior to the psychic insertion.

AE-3: Psi-/bio-energy field extraction This appears to be an experience of the subject's 'life energy' being taken from their own body, to be placed temporarily in another, extraterrestrial one, as if they are borrowing it. It is similar in many ways to out-of-body experiences, except that the separation of this 'life-energy field' is externally induced. Subjects usually report that a bluish-white beam has penetrated their body, followed by a tugging or attracting sensation as the life energy is extracted. They then report that their sensory perception of external stimuli is greatly enhanced. This type of abduction would appear to account for a fair percentage of missing time and memory failure reported by some subjects. Memories are not hard and fast but there does appear to be some vague or shadow memory, and it is understood to be reflected somehow in the subject's bio-energy field, or aura, again implying that the subject's behaviour or belief systems have somehow been influenced.

AE-4: Physical abduction This is the actual and complete physical abduction from the subject's environment into that of the ET. The abductee is usually subdued or paralysed prior to the abduction. This type of abduction appears to follow a well-defined *modus operandi*. The subject is usually transported to the aliens' environment by direct transfer, a beam of some sort, or to a larger vessel via a smaller one. Some reports indicate that the ETs are able to 'fold' space–time in such a way as to make direct transfer immediate, without the need for linear travel. Solid objects often appear to represent no barrier at all, allowing the abductor and abductee to pass unhindered through walls, doors, etc. Once aboard the UFO, witnesses invariably report a battery of physical and medical examinations, often including the removal of sperm or ovarian material for supposed genetic experimentation. Following this, the subjects are usually returned unharmed to their original location. This is not always the case, however, and there are reports of subjects being returned to the wrong room, house or even town, sometimes inappropriately dressed or in the wrong clothes. One of two things then happens: either a false memory is implanted into the subject to alter slightly their perception of the reality of the event, or the human subconscious takes over and represses the event with something more acceptable, but in either case the memories of the abduction are never completely erased.

AE-5: Past-life recall In extraterrestrial terms, these are the most interesting in view of their implications. Under regression, subjects are able to recall lives spent in other incarnations, on other planets and in other alien societies. These experiences, although not often reported, can include being on Mars, on the moon, under the sea or in an underground military installation, on board a spacecraft or in some alien environment, which may often be multi-mooned. What makes these experiences all the more interesting is that they are recalled from an extraterrestrial perspective, not a human one. Butler proposes two interesting possibilities here: that (a) during telepathic communication some alien memories are actually transferred, or (b) the subject is recalling actual past-life memories of their own. The latter would suggest that part of the abduction scenario is a massive and covert surveillance operation. It could also be the reason why the greys say that they have every right to do what they do: if abductees are actually vehicles for souls that have been transferred from an extraterrestrial environment, then it could be argued that technically the aliens are abducting not humans, but rather volunteer ETs. The regressionist and author Dolores Cannon has done some excellent work in this area, and whether or not you accept the concepts outlined, her findings are none the less interesting reading and should not be discounted out of hand.

ANTI-ABDUCTION TECHNIQUES

One of the most disturbing features of an abduction is that the subject never knows when the event will happen again, or indeed if ever. In the case of multiple abductions of the same subject, the sheer helplessness that they feel can be very debilitating – emotionally, psychologically and physically. It is for this reason that I have included here some claimed anti-abduction techniques. Most are from suggestions by David Jacobs, but it would seem that the writers or inventors at least believe that they work, and if nothing else, when passed on to abductees they may help to restore confidence and some sort of control over events, or at least the comforting feelings of such. The psychological benefits alone are worth the attempt of applying them.

A very simple early-warning system that I learned during my ghostbusting days was the application of nitrogen tri-iodide on to surfaces over which an intruder must pass. It can be made simply and cheaply by mixing iodine crystals and household ammonia. The resulting brown muck is applied sparingly on to floors and stairs while it is still wet. Once dry, the slightest impact or compaction will trigger it off with a sound like a room full of Christmas crackers or 'caps' fired in toy guns.

Jacobs claims to have had limited success in preventing abduction using an ordinary video camera. This would make it impossible for any potential abductor to carry out their activities without being recorded. Jacobs and an alleged abductee set up a video camera and VCR on top of a dresser, aimed at the subject's bed. She had been abducted on the previous night, but there was no abduction attempt for several days following the setting up of the equipment. However, on the next attempted abduction the video camera ran out of tape at around 6am, and the subject claims to have been abducted shortly afterwards. Several weeks later there was another abduction of the subject; this time, she had not been in her bed, but was sleeping instead on the sofa to get away from noisy, argumentative upstairs neighbours.

Of course, the subject could have been pulling the wool over Jacobs' eyes and had never actually been physically abducted, or even visited, which I am sure the sceptics will be quick to point out. However, to give her the benefit of the doubt, the same tactics were tried with another suspected abductee and it seemed that as long as a running video camera was pointed at the subject, no abduction took place. Sometimes, as with other subjects videoing their sleep patterns, the video or VCR would mysteriously be turned off or would otherwise malfunction – then the alleged abductions would take place. It would seem from this that such tactics do not prevent the abductions, but they allow a pause for breath, so to speak. In no instance did an abduction take place while a camera was aimed at the subjects. Plenty of fuel there for the sceptics, I admit, but none the less, all these alleged abductees were convinced that something very unpleasant was happening to them, which implies that there is still a case to answer and that the phenomenon is all too real to those who experience it. Jacobs points out a secondary and certainly very valid point, in that the video camera can come to be used as a crutch, leading abductees into a scenario whereby they feel that they cannot sleep without it.

I have also read of instances where the abductees were so incensed at what was about to happen to them that they simply refused to allow themselves to be abducted. By virtue of sheer bloody-mindedness, self-will and determination alone, they were able to deter their abductors mid-stream, so to speak. Just saying 'No', it appears, does sometimes carry some weight.

IMPLANTS

One other disturbing feature of the abduction scenario is the insertion of a small (2–5mm/1/16–1/4in) implant of some sort, usually into the nasal cavity of the subject but occasionally elsewhere on the body, such as under the skin on the arm, leg, neck or ankle. There are several suggested reasons for these implants, and all in some way relate to a hidden agenda on the part of the abductors: they include monitoring devices which enable the abductors to track and locate the subjects for further abductions, or to influence the subjects' behaviour, development and thought processes. Of course, the act of doing this implies a removal of the subjects' free will and autonomy, and whatever your ideological and theological philosophy, this really isn't on.

Nicholas Reiter is a professional research technologist for a solar-cell manufacturing firm who has been interested in the UFO phenomenon all his life. He does not belong to any large UFO group but has been involved in research into abductions for the past few years. The following is a brief and edited   summary of his work as outlined in 'Magnetic Implant Response' and 'Magnetism, UFO Abductions and the Anomalous' in Dr David Gotlib's *Bulletin of Anomalous Experience*.

These tests and experiments were performed by Reiter and his colleague 'AR' in the Dallas, Texas, area in the autumn of 1990 with confirmed abductees, using a technique that can easily be duplicated. The experimental objectives of the two researchers were to determine first, whether or not the process of alien abduction could be understood in terms of available technology; second, whether the abduction implant devices, recalled so often under hypnosis, could be objectively detected, studied and possibly neutralized by electrical, magnetic or some other means; and third, whether it would be possible to develop a method of defence against abduction.

Several assumptions were made for the experiments: that there exists an unknown intelligence which is currently carrying out an agenda of experimentation on unwilling human subjects; that this is being carried out with the assistance of some highly advanced technology; that this technology is currently unknown to the accepted laws of physics; and that the human race has the undeniable right to defend itself to the best of its ability against such an agenda.

The first set of experiments involved trying to find a method of obtaining a measurable response from abduction implant devices. AR noticed a 'weird' sensation in her first volunteer (Volunteer 1) when a large horseshoe magnet was held up in the region of her head where, under hypnosis, the subject had recalled aliens 'doing something to her'. Volunteer 1 found the sensation extraordinarily vivid and disturbing; it seemed to be both mental and physiological in nature. In closest approximation, it was similar to a 'panic' response – a mental feeling of terror or extreme apprehension, coupled with a recorded rise in pulse rate and perspiration.

Volunteer 1 said that the panic response seemed to duplicate the feeling that she had been subject to in the past, shortly before an abduction would occur. Over the course of the following weeks several different tests were conducted with this volunteer.

o A large electromagnet was substituted for the horseshoe magnet. This coil was energized with 110V AC and later with 6V DC, but in different tests. The responses for both were smaller in magnitude than for the horseshoe magnet, although the symptoms were similar.

- While the horseshoe magnet was in use, a piece of steel was placed between the poles to divert the magnetic flux away from any external regions of the magnet. This test was performed to determine if the actual flux lines were involved in the response or whether the response was based on other 'virtual' effects of the magnet.

- The response (from here on referred to as the magnetic implant response, MIR) seemed to appear first when the magnet was moved within 45cm (18in) of the volunteer's response region (suspected area of the implant). From this distance inwards, the intensity increased.

- The Tesla coil suppression effect (TCSE) was thus discovered.

Reiter and AR then started testing other volunteers in January 1991. Prior to this, their research was being performed with the assistance of Volunteer 1 only. On 8 January 1991, they tested another 'confirmed abductee' volunteer. No communication was allowed between Volunteers 1 and 2. The symptoms experienced by Volunteer 2 were identical to those of Volunteer 1.

Over the course of the next few months, two other abductee volunteers were tested. Volunteer 3 showed a positive reaction with consistent symptoms. Volunteer 4, however, felt no response or sensations.

Reiter and AR started researching the nature of the abductions experienced by all the volunteers. They found that Volunteers 1, 2 and 3 were 'classical' abductees, although their specific experiences and ordeals were different. Through either regression or waking memories, each recalled the phenomena most often experienced by those who have been repeatedly abducted – grey entities, quasi-medical procedures, possible insertion of implants, etc. Volunteer 4's abduction experiences were quite 'non-standard' and may have involved different phenomena altogether.

It was decided that the research should continue. In the second phase, Volunteer 1 was placed in a chair and tested for MIR. Results were positive. A 45cm (18in) tall Tesla spark-gap coil was set up in front of Volunteer 1. The coil was turned on and allowed to operate for several minutes, after which Volunteer 1 was then checked again for MIR and the results were negative. She was checked again 24 hours later and the results were still negative. The nullifying effect lasted for approximately six days; when it did eventually return, it was at a much diminished magnitude. From this observation, it was inferred that the MIR had not been eliminated, but had in some way been deadened or temporarily stunned. Volunteer 2 was similarly tested with the Tesla coil and the results were identical: the MIR ceased for a period of time.

Another interesting effect was noticed by Volunteer 1. She was given the Tesla coil to take home with her, and on several occasions, specifically on certain evenings, would get the feeling that unseen entities were nearby. She found that by switching on the Tesla coil, the sensation would vanish, as though the coil was disrupting or driving away the invisible force. This more or less concluded the studies performed by Reiter and his associate AR.

Reiter has continued his research, however. Lack of volunteers prompted him to start in a slightly different vein. He began testing subjects randomly: business associates, friends, family and people on the street were tested, with some surprising results. The subjects were told that some people have the ability to 'sense' magnetic fields for unknown reasons and that Reiter would like to determine if the volunteers/subjects could detect them as well.

The volunteer was placed in a comfortable chair. A galvanic skin response (GSR) monitor, similar to those used in 'lie detectors', was placed on the second and third fingers of the left hand. The volunteer was then shown the magnet (similar to the one used in the original experiments). They were asked to verbalize any feelings or sensations which they might experience during the test. The subject was then blindfolded and a few minutes were allowed for the GSR monitor to 'settle out'.

At this point, the magnet was moved slowly and randomly around the subject's head. Spacing was kept at 5cm (2in) from the subject's head at all times. Sensations, feelings and GSR monitor response were observed and recorded. When the test was complete, the volunteer was thanked and released. If permitted, the volunteer's age, sex, occupation and name were recorded.

Of the first 24 subjects tested, five showed a positive response to this procedure. One or more of the following characteristics were noted in each case:

o A feeling of apprehension or panic.

o A sensation of pressure or tightness.

o A feeling of disorientation.

o Dark, formless shapes moving against closed eyelids.

o Uncontrollable finger twitching.

None of the five random positive response cases were totally identical in symptoms. However, the following characteristics were common to all five cases:

o The feeling was weird or unpleasant.

o Extreme nervousness and anxiety was present.

o The effect was vivid and definite.

o The GSR monitor tone increased, indicating increased bodily perspiration.

o The response occurred at a single, definitive location on each subject's head.

The areas included were:

Case 2 Left temple (in front of and slightly above left ear).

Case 3 Above nose, somewhere between and behind eyes.

Case 6 Behind and below left ear.

Case 13 Left temple.

Case 21 Above and slightly behind left ear.

The above test results were obtained during 1991 and published that same year.

Reiter has also designed some electronic equipment as a 'security' or abduction prevention system. The description and plans for these devices have been processed into files which can be downloaded from HIGH SCIENCE BBS (713) 688-2030. One such unit, it is claimed, has been used successfully to thwart abductions and seems to work by disrupting local electromagnetic fields. Reiter has several schematics for other shields as well – for details of how to contact him, see Useful Addresses.

5 Intelligent Extraterrestrial Life

Although some of this section might seem a little 'highbrow' in a book of this nature, the issues described are important, because an understanding of them is useful in deciding what parts of a UFO report concerning the pilots or other features could be scientifically accurate, and thus more credible. It also contains witnesses' descriptions of many of the alleged aliens that have been reported to investigators. At least some, as we shall see, are biologically credible. One cannot really look at UFO phenomena without also looking at the intelligences said to be behind them – that really is putting the cart before the horse.

ET'S HOMEWORLD

When Italian-American physicist Enrico Fermi posed the question 'Where are they?' with regard to extraterrestrials in 1943, he was merely asking for the hard scientific proof that ETs actually existed. Basically, his hypothesis was that if there was an abundance of intelligent life within the universe, then the extraterrestrials should, by now, have colonized the Earth.

The argument runs thus: the Earth is known to be much younger than the universe itself, so that if intelligent alien life can have arisen elsewhere, it will have done. Like most populations, theirs will have grown to such a size that competition for resources such as food and territory has become paramount. Faced with this competition, such a species will have only two options: self-destruction through all-out war and a return to barbarism, or the removal of the species into space, ultimately in order to colonize other planets. Given the accepted age of the universe of around 15 billion years, the age of our solar system, and the sheer size of our galaxy alone, many such species should have visited our solar system at some time within its 4½-billion-year history. They should be here by now. Yet evidently, at least to the satisfaction of the scientific community, they're not. Fermi thus concluded that we are, indeed, alone in the universe.

Our galaxy on its own is immense, pinwheel shaped and contains somewhere around 100 billion stars. It also contains enough material such as dust and gas to create billions more. So, just where is everybody? Well, either we are alone in the cold vastness of the universe, or we're not. Either way, it's a sobering thought. If life has arisen on Earth, then why not elsewhere? Why not on other 'Earths'? That life on Earth evolved at all seems, at least on the face of it, a somewhat miraculous occurrence, and if (and I stress the word 'if'), we are alone in the universe, then some would argue that as conclusive evidence for the existence of God as the supreme being. However, does this not, by definition, also prove the existence of 'extraterrestrial' intelligence?

If extraterrestrial life has evolved around some far-flung distant star, and for our purposes we assume it to be intelligent life, then how exactly might it have arisen? To answer this question, we first need to look at how life on Earth might have begun. This is not because I believe that the rules for evolution are constant throughout the galaxy (although the current belief, in the absence of evidence to the contrary, is that they are), but because it gives us an existing framework within which to operate.

Apart from the aforementioned miracle, in his book *Are We Alone?* Paul Davies, professor of Natural Philosophy at the University of Adelaide, South Australia, puts forward two other arguments: (a) that the evolution of life on Earth was a highly improbable accident, or (b) that it was the direct and unavoidable result of natural chemical, biological and physical laws, operating under the necessary conditions as and when the opportunity arose. As a scientist, I must favour the latter. So, what are the conditions necessary for the evolution of life? Here 'life', for our purposes, means something organic that we could recognize as such (and that would recognize us!), as opposed to silicon-based or other exotic life-forms – which, according to known laws of physics, are none the less feasible.

We, as carbon-based life-forms, have certain planetary requirements, not least of which is the presence of oxygen and water. So how did we come by them? Why have we got them while, say, Venus hasn't? First, we have to accept the existence of the sun as a given factor, although a fully detailed discourse on stellar formation lies outside the scope of this book. Suffice it to say that our sun is of a type that is not uncommon, and stars with similar mass, luminosity, chemical composition and dimensions are abundant throughout the universe, to the tune of around 5,000 million.

It is this very mediocrity that appears to be vital for the emergence of life. A heavy star has a short life but a fierce one. A star even twice the size of our sun will be twice as hot, but will only last around 1,000 million years, while our own sun is expected to last somewhere in the region of 10,000 million years. Along with this, the former will be emitting intolerable amounts of radiation under which carbon-based life cannot evolve. Conversely, lighter stars, such as the red dwarfs, will last a good deal longer but will not give out anywhere near enough light for the photosynthesis of plants, the Earth's 'primary producers' of food and thus energy, which is consumed in turn by herbivores, and then carnivores, and so on up through the food chain.

For the sake of argument, it is supposed that the physical laws governing any planetary formation around such likely life-giving stars also remain as constants. Because of these laws, those planets nearest to any sun-like star consist mainly of heavier, less volatile substances, such as the metals and silicates, while the outer planets (in our system, Jupiter, Uranus, Neptune and Pluto) are known as gas giants, and are formed mainly from the lighter elements, such as hydrogen. On Earth, the hydrogen became water through oxidization. Now, the hotter a gas gets, the more excited its atoms become, the faster they move, and the more difficult it is for a planet's gravity to hold on to them. The sun's intense radiation will have driven these lighter elements from the atmospheres of the inner planets, such as Mercury and Venus, while gravity and distance from the sun will have been instrumental in ensuring that the larger, outer planets held on to them.

So, we now have a planetary system, and sadly, for many ufologists the argument ends there. There's a tendency to believe that, since such laws of planetary formation are a constant, then there must be countless millions of planetary systems harbouring intelligent life, as if all that's needed is a planet and a star. However, such conditions need to be narrowed down even further.

The concept of continuously habitable zones has arisen from various mathematical studies, and implies that for intelligent life to arise on any given planet certain criteria must be met. These scientifically accepted criteria are, first, that such a planet must have roughly the same mass as that of the Earth. Second, this planet must orbit its star in such a way and at such a distance that the planet becomes continuously habitable (that is, extremes of climate and other environmental factors remain within the defined parameters conducive to the evolution of life). In fact, this orbital range falls within a very narrow band: had the Earth been much closer to the sun, even by only a few per cent, then it would have become as Venus is now; much further out, and it would have been akin to the frozen wastelands of Mars. Third, it would appear that the planet's star would have to have a mass within 20 per cent either way of our own sun's mass. All these criteria will have a bearing on factors such as gravitational effects, solar radiation, planetary evolution, availability of the necessary 'building blocks' for life, planetary atmospheres, availability of metals and so on.

There is now a wealth of scientifically accepted data from various NASA missions and others to suggest that not only are the correct type of stars available in abundance, but also all the other necessary items such as water and the organic building blocks for life are out there as well. Perhaps there isn't quite as much life out there as science fiction writers first thought, but there is none the less likely to be some. Then suppose that alien life-forms are visiting us, or have at least been here – would we be able to recognize them?

ET'S LIKELY APPEARANCE

In order to try to evaluate how ET might appear physically, we need to look at the kind of planetary environmental conditions which exist that are conducive to the evolution of intelligence. We have already referred to habitable zones, possible atmospheres and so on, and we now need to examine how these might affect the morphology of an alien species. In essence, all this is the science of exobiology, a relatively new branch of science wherein the possibility of extraterrestrial life is looked at from an ecological perspective.

When it comes to working out how ET will actually look, there are two main opposing views. First, there is the view that extraterrestrial life will look very different to us because it will have taken possibly very different evolutionary paths to that taken by ourselves, through arising in a very un-Earth-like environment. This is the 'exotic' viewpoint, and its adherents look to the possibility of such things as Fred Hoyle's giant gas cloud, maybe thousands of miles across, or Carl Sagan's balloon-like 'floaters' surviving in the mid- to upper reaches of Jupiter's atmosphere. The issue that the exponents of exotic evolution fail to address is the question of how such life-forms attain intelligence (and it's only intelligent life-forms that are likely to be flying UFOs).

This leads us into the other viewpoint: that intelligent life will, by necessity of survival, evolve a humanoid form as a natural by-product of ecological strategies employed by a species capable of both intelligence and conceptualization. There appear to be well-established and generally accepted criteria for a creature's rise to intelligence. It is because of this that we may assume that intelligent life throughout the galaxy will be humanoid in shape, however vaguely. There may be three eyes, a grasping proboscis or tentacles, different mass and bulk, but otherwise the life-forms' appearance will not really differ greatly from our own and they will have many features that we could easily recognize. Might that not be why the reported close encounters with aliens are invariably with various humanoid species?

Shape and characteristics

So, just how might they appear to us? Here we must draw upon several branches of science, including anthropology, zoology, ecology, biology and exobiology. If we begin with the primordial soup of our distant ancestors, we can consider the very earliest life-forms. We have already established that life would appear to be restricted to Earth-like planets with similar atmospheric pressures and surface temperatures, and that those planets, because of the chemistry, geology and physics governing planetary formation, will have water available for the evolution of life based on carbon compounds. Water suggests the presence of oxygen, although to be fair to the 'exotic' protagonists, many suggestions have been made as to the likelihood of non-humanoid life, some based on silicon and others arising in oxygen-free environments, both of which are feasible.

In fact, according to the theory of Russian biochemist Oparin in 1938, the spontaneous generation of life is only likely to occur on a planet following a period of abiotic, radiation-induced synthesis of organic molecules under conditions similar to those existing in the Precambrian period of Earth's history, and the kind of conditions now existing on Mars and Jupiter. It has been suggested that differences in atmospheric pressures, gravities and temperatures would result in very diverse evolutionary trends, giving rise to such exotic species as intelligent birds, fish, plants and insects.

Personally (and I am far from alone in this), I think this is highly unlikely. Evidence for the necessity of a sun-like star stems from the fact that the DNA molecule breaks down under ultraviolet bombardment and is sensitive to high levels of radiation. The 'exotic' protagonists further utilize the vast diversity of terrestrial life-forms to illustrate the number of possibilities that an alien species could take. That's as may be, but the fact remains that it is the species with the humanoid shape that shows the greatest feats of intelligence and conceptualization, and consequently rises to dominance within its environment.

To get back to the primordial soup, the simplest of life was formed from organic compounds in the world's oceans, such as they were then. It was in these very oceans that the first stirrings of the rise to intelligence were felt. It is all to do with shape of the body – bilateral symmetry, to be exact. By adopting this symmetry along the length of the creature, there was a reduction in turbulence and water resistance, and thus an increase in streamlining. This feature was crucial in establishing a predatory way of life, even in the simplest of creatures, and all the most successful marine predators have this bilateral symmetry – sharks, some other fish, otters, orcas, squid, etc. American scientist Robert Bieri points out that all these predators have certain grasping and sensing organs close to the mouth – again, consider the squid. Digestion and excretion in the predatory animal are most convenient when arranged in a tube-like formation, with a mouth at the business end and an anus at the other. A third and crucial survival strategy was to position the brain nearer to the sensing and grasping organs in order to reduce the transmission time for the necessary neural impulses. The chances of survival are greatly reduced unless a creature is quick on the uptake and can get prey into its mouth before it gets away. Those sea predators that have a radial symmetry, such as jellyfish and sea-anemones, have adopted a more sedentary way of life, with a subsequent loss of sensitivity and degeneration of active nervous systems, and have thus settled into an ecological niche not conducive to intelligence. Radially symmetrical extraterrestrials as space travellers or interplanetary colonizers are unlikely to make an appearance unless seeded by a higher intelligence.

In our intelligent ET, the internal cardiovascular, digestive and pulmonary systems might be quite different to ours, although the above tubular arrangement still seems likely. Much will depend on the relationships between individual organisms within food chains, the processes of acquiring and reprocessing food, and the method of gas exchanges in order to breathe and thus utilize the food energy, break down complex amino acids, and so on. That said, respiration is not a foregone conclusion, if a more effective means of maximizing food energy has evolved. The largest insects on Earth are not usually more than 30cm (1ft) or so across because insects breathe through spiracles – small apertures along the body – which is a slower and less efficient means of oxygenating the system than that found in cardiovascular circulation. Lungs have a highly complex structure and a massive surface area. So if respiratory spiracles, or their extraterrestrial counterparts, are present, there might be a similar process to that used by wasps, where air is pumped into the cardiovascular system by regular, rhythmic abdominal contractions, probably via an autonomic nervous system. None the less, the similarities with insects are likely to be limited, as we shall see.

Suppose, for example, that our life-form inhabited a planet with high surface pressures and temperatures, such as might be found on a planet orbiting Virginis 70, then it would need to evolve some means of venting excess heat or of coping with sudden extremes in temperatures. Such a creature might develop a tough outer carapace in order to avoid desiccation, or large sails designed to radiate heat, such as those found on some dinosaurs. Continuing survival would depend on the evolution of intelligence and the ability to cope with such a variable environment. Remember: harsh, but survivable.

After a few million years of fine-tuning, the first creatures left the seas for the land, and it was here that the next stage in the evolution of intelligence took place: the development of the capacity for conceptualization, the ability to see and understand beforehand the likely outcome or results from a considered course of action. But what about the whales and dolphins – are they not intelligent? Well, yes, they may be, but Puccetti (who worked with Bieri) proposes that conceptualization only arises in conjunction with the utilization of speech, a social existence and the use of tools. While they may be intelligent, communicate and have a social existence, whales and dolphins are not known for their use of tools. In fact, the development and use of tools under water or in any other liquid environment is both difficult and unnecessary, for reasons such as resistance, density and viscosity of the medium. Marine predators have already evolved 'tools' in the shape of speed, grasping appendages such as tentacles and teeth, and, in some defensive instances, camouflage, ink and the like. They will have already filled an ecological niche and are thus unlikely to develop much further.

It was only with the invasion of land that the appendages used for swim-ming became redundant and could thus afford to lose their streamlining and evolve into something more applicable to the adopted lifestyle, such as digits or appendages for grasping and manipulation. It then became possible to manipulate the environment for practical purposes. With a few notable excep-tions, it is only land animals that have the ability to manipulate their environ-ment. It is also these exceptions that prove the rule. Gradually, as the need for survival of the species dictated, these appendages became more complex, particularly in those higher creatures with larger brains capable of conceptual-ization. Look at your arm and your hand. Close the fingers together, shorten the limb, and you still have a useful paddle for swimming.

Likewise, it is unlikely that birds or other flying creatures, predatory or otherwise, could develop conceptualization as we have defined it. In order to fly, avian creatures require a lightweight frame and hollow bones appropriate to the homeworld's atmosphere, and blood is manufactured in the bone marrow. This makes the bones heavier and more solid, which rules out any chance of a large, intelligent brain because of such a brain's requirement for large quantities of blood and the necessarily heavy cardiovascular system needed to transport and oxygenate it. The result would be an impossible power-to-weight ratio. A species can either fly, or be intelligent with conceptualizing ability, but not both.

From the foregoing, it can be seen that an intelligent, spacefaring civiliza-tion is unlikely to be aquatic or avian. It looks as though our extraterrestrials will have to be land-dwelling predators, probably evolved from oceanic roots. Why predatory? Well, if we look again at our own evolutionary examples, predators are at the top of every food chain. So how did man get there, con-sidering that we are descended from herbivorous apes? Why, exactly, did our ancestors leave the trees? The general consensus of opinion is that they came down because of climatic and subsequent vegetation changes, resulting in the loss of established food sources as new pioneer species arose to replace those more appropriate to the previous climatic conditions. Brains would now be at a premium and in order to survive man had to eat, so he was forced to change his diet. Prior to hunting, it is likely that he underwent a carrion-eating stage, but eventually realized the advantage of being a hunter-gatherer over being patient and waiting for something to die – he would be more likely to attract the opposite sex, you see, and thus improve his chances of throwing his lot into the gene-pool.

It was here that man took the critical evolutionary path that put him on the final road to intelligence. A social existence was already well established, and this social grouping was adapted to hunting as man became omnivorous and learned to run on the ground with two appendages, while using the grasping and manipulating limbs to develop and use weapons such as clubs fashioned from thigh bones, jaw bones and wood. Paul Anderson has suggested that this would have been a necessary development, because nature did not arm man with natural weapons and defensive measures (in fact, there are several design faults!), and he would have had to conceptualize on the use of these items. From here, it was a relatively simple step to further this development into tool use and then on to a basic technology.

Why would an animal bother to develop tools, weapons and technology if it was already established in a herbivorous niche, or if it was already a competent and successful predator? The simple answer is that it wouldn't, and man is no exception to the rule. But a species could do none of this unless it was able to conceptualize. Man was quick to realize that competition for food on the hoof was keen, not only between man and other predators, but also between man and other men, and thus the development of technology, tools and weapons became paramount if he was to be successful in (a) putting food on the table, and (b) the procreation stakes. Man is the supreme competitor (on this planet, anyway!), and has remained the only species with any sort of real technology, purely because of this competitive and predatory predilection for the hunt. There are social and economic implications inherent in this, war being a good example, as competition for more and better resources, territory, etc. drive him ever onward. War is man's only natural outlet for his innate predatory, aggressive and competitive nature, and as man is merely an animal following the laws of evolution, why should we expect ET to be any different?

Tool use, it appears, is the sole preserve of land-based creatures, as is the evolution of an opposable thumb. A fully adapted herbivore is not going to develop tool use because it already occupies an ecological niche and is established in the food chain, with its own defensive methods of escape and evasion. Nor is tool use going to develop in already competent predators – there is no need. Therefore it appears that tool use, the manufacture of weapons and technology go hand-in-glove with the rise of intelligence and conceptualization in land-dwelling predators.

It can be seen from this that all intelligent species across the galaxy will have their origins in predatory land-dwelling species, themselves evolved from marine predators if, as we assume, the laws of evolution are a constant throughout the galaxy. There are animals that use basic tools, such as chimpanzees fishing out termites with sticks, otters using stones to break open shells, the thrush using an anvil to crack snails, and so on, but these are often learned or conditioned responses, and such creatures are not presently expected to develop their technological skills further – at least, not without considerable genetic intervention by man.

Technology, however primitive, requires the ability to hold and manipulate tools with some degree of skill and dexterity, combined with the ability to move quickly – thus primitive man learned to run and throw a spear at the same time. The absence of this ability would lead a species to rely on more naturally evolved methods of hunting and its intelligence ceiling would be attained relatively quickly, so it would be unlikely to attempt to modify its environment, preferring to remain in the one in which it is comfortable. If such an extraterrestrial species exists, then, like the bird or fish, it is unlikely to be building starships.

How our intelligent ET gets around is a moot point. We have four limbs because of genetic inheritance, but it is certainly true that a 'leg at each corner' allows a greater turn of speed and freedom of movement than, say, six or eight (although arachnophobics may not agree!). That said, it is only insects that have more than four legs, and the largest land insect (I use the term loosely – I know it's an arachnid) alive today is the tarantula, largely because of the way that insects grow, by casting off the exoskeleton of hollow tubes which surround the muscles and internal organs. This renders the insect or spider prone to predation, and is thus not a good survival strategy. It also limits the size to which an insect predator will grow, as does its mode of respiration, mentioned earlier. More than six legs is arguably too difficult or complex for a large land predator: each leg must swing through a wide arc for swift movement, and while gravity and atmospheric composition will play a role in this, with more than four legs such movement becomes difficult. One leg is totally impractical (consider C.S. Lewis's Dufflepuds in *The Voyage of the Dawn Treader*), and odd numbers cast bilateral symmetry right out of the window. Man (and, it is assumed, an intelligent extraterrestrial) has the evolutionary advantage of at least one pair of limbs modified for tool use and manipulation, while the other pair(s) is adapted to running and movement, thus optimizing between the two skills – pretty handy for running and chucking spears at the same time. We are where we are today because the bipedal humanoid is the most efficient and successful shape and size so far evolved on Earth.

Size

So to size. The size of our intelligent ET will be governed by atmospheric pressures and forces of gravity that are exerted on his homeworld. A planet slightly larger than the Earth would cause our alien to be more squat, with a powerful physique and heavy bones, because of the subsequently higher forces of gravity. He might also have two pairs of locomotive limbs. If ET is too small, there is unlikely to be a sufficient number of bodily cells for the transmission of the neural impulses that complex thought processes require. Furthermore, regardless of his possibly limited intelligence, if too small he is likely to be prey for larger predators, rather than the primary predator himself. Such a small creature might have less time to devote to technological development through needing to concentrate on camouflage skills and speed of movement. In doing so, he occupies an ecological niche, that of prey. A smaller planet with lower gravity will result in more spindly, perhaps taller and more delicate-looking aliens, with slender limbs and a narrower trunk.

Here on Earth, we have height ranges between the extremes of the Masai warriors and the pygmy tribes. ET may have similar height variances and, as here, there will be limits. (Interestingly, most reported sightings of EBEs fall within the ranges 1.4–2.4m (4½–7½ft) tall – about the heights of the two races mentioned.) If ET is too big, he will not be able to support his own weight. Imagine a human ten times the average human size. He will be ten times as wide and ten times as thick (physically, that is!), and these factors combine to produce a total weight about 1,000 times greater than that of the average human, or about 80–90 tonnes. Unfortunately, the cross-section of his bones is also only ten times that of your average human's bones, meaning that each square inch of giant bone has to support 100 times more weight than the human bone – and as the human thigh bone breaks under ten times the weight of the average human, our giant will break his leg every time he takes a step – hardly a useful bonus for a predatory organism. If our ET was very much heavier than man, there would be problems with running for long distances while chasing his prey, and he would thus require a great deal of food, which has to be readily available.

If ET was too big, the neural network would also be proportionately bigger, implying a greater time for the chemical impulses to reach the locomotive limbs. He might therefore be unable to react in time to dangerous situations. Dinosaurs got around this by having extensive neural networks in their posterior regions. Such large animals can live quite happily in a dense gaseous or liquid environment, which would possibly aid buoyancy, but environments like these are not conducive to the development of tool use and conceptualizing intelligence.

Senses

So now we know that ET looks pretty much like us, shape-wise. But what about other factors, such as sensory perceptions? Because we expect him to be basically a predator like us, we can assume that the mouth, nose and eyes will be placed in similar positions, as will his brain. It is the physical make-up of these organs that may be different, determined by the alien's planetary environment and illumination from his local sun or suns.

A successful predator requires stereoscopic vision, with the visual organs placed high on the body and near to the brain. Here, we can use raptors (birds of prey) to illustrate the point. The kestrel has a 150-degree field of vision, with an arc of 50 degrees where the two fields of vision, one from each eye, overlap. Owls go one better and have both their eyes facing forwards, giving them stereoscopic vision across the entire field. The eye is the most efficient way of sensing distant objects, and to be effective it must be capable of receiving signals within the electromagnetic radiation wavelength. Our own visible spectrum is of a wavelength that remains unaffected by our atmospheric constituents. Much depends upon the electron activity within the environmental gases, as this determines which wavelengths are actually seen. Hence, our ET's eye may receive wavelengths anywhere between ultraviolet and infrared.

Now, depending on which end of the spectrum our alien 'sees' in and the available amount of these frequencies, the actual structure of his eye may be very different to ours. Compound eyes, such as those possessed by some more successful predatory insects, hold some interesting possibilities. The bee can see a colour known as 'bee-purple', which can best be described as a mixture of yellow and ultraviolet, indicating that insects can see a very different spectrum to ourselves. To be honest, it's not even a colour we can truly imagine. It is thought that there is another visual 'window' at the long radio wavelengths, beyond 3cm. However, the drawback with this option is that in order to be able to pick out the fine visual detail with the same level of resolution that we do, our alien would need an eyeball approximately 0.8km (½ mile) in diameter. A single eye seems unlikely, as it affords no real depth perception – essential for a successful predatory species – and early on in its evolutionary development it would have had very limited survival value.

The advantage of a third eye appears to be minimal, biologically speaking, and certainly not as great over two eyes, as two eyes are over one. There is evidence to suggest that certain animals of the Mesozoic era (comprising the Triassic, Jurassic and Cretaceous periods of 65 million to 230 million years ago) displayed three eyes, all of which were at the front of the head. The tuatara lizard of New Zealand still possesses a 'third eye', which is little more than a light/dark sensor at the back of the head – a useful defence against predators, and in this instance of great survival value. Certain anatomists believe that the pineal gland is the last vestige of a third eye in humans, sometimes represented in ancient cultures and religions as the source of psychic abilities, such as extra-sensory perception (ESP). It remains extra-sensory only inasmuch as it is a sense that some lack or which remains underdeveloped, regressed or repressed, and seems to have its mechanics largely in the roots of endocrine and biochemical processes. Such a currently misunderstood ability would have immense survival value, and so psychic ability on behalf of aliens cannot be discounted and may indeed even be likely. Research in humans seems to indicate that as psychic ability is developed, the instincts and emotions appear to devolve. Could this explain the reports of indifference often said to be displayed by psychic extraterrestrials allegedly responsible for human abductions?

Echo-location such as that used by bats and dolphins cannot be ruled out, and there is evidence that some humans can sense high-intensity radar, although quite how they do it remains to be explained. This alone indicates that other forms of data sensing are potentially available.

Binaural hearing would need to function in stereo, and also be positioned near to the brain in order to enable rapid location bearing. The structure of the ear will depend upon the velocity of sound, which in turn will depend upon things like the density, composition and temperature of the atmosphere through which sound waves travel. A lighter planetary atmosphere will result in a smaller ear or a lessened sense of hearing, as such an ear has less value as a detective organ. It would devolve in favour of more effective sensory methods: a compromise might be pressure receptors, similar to our sense of touch, but acting like an eardrum. In an aquatic or dense gaseous environment, the dominant sense might be like our sense of taste or smell, and have sensory receptors allowing direct chemical analysis of gas- or liquid-borne molecules, similar to those possessed by snakes. Clearly useful for the detection of prey or predators, this would be a valuable survival strategy. Again, these organs would need to be positioned near to the brain, and probably the mouth as well, if not actually in or associated with it.

Other features

The number of fingers has implications for assessment of the aliens' type of technology and mathematical base. Although there may be variations, any more than ten to each hand or foot might be difficult to co-ordinate, while less than three makes the manipulation of tools and basic technology rather difficult. The development of an opposable thumb has been a bone of contention between various factions for years, particularly with regard to its place in the grand scheme of things, but nevertheless it has proved to be of immense practical value. It is alleged that the Roswell 'aliens' had four digits to each span, each digit having sucker-like appendages on the tips; I do not recall any evidence of an opposable thumb. These kinds of arrangements cannot be discounted on biological grounds.

We only have to look at the diversity of skin tones and colours here on Earth to understand the equally diverse range that might arise in alien environments. Pigmentations are there for a reason, usually protective, but sometimes for sexual, psychosexual or social purposes. The actual structure of the skin or hide must also be considered: polar bears have white fur but black skin underneath it, to attract and utilize as much solar heat as possible. Skin is more than a protective covering for us – it is an organ in its own right, and there is no reason to suppose that ET's skin is very much different in purpose. Depending on his genetic ancestry, there may be traces of fur or even whiskers, throwbacks to the days when other senses played a major role in the survival of the progenitor species.

Lastly, it is unlikely that ET will give up on his basic body appearance, if only for sociological and psychological reasons. I do not wish to 'humanize' them, but it seems reasonable to assume that the aliens too will recognize the best qualities of their species and would wish to emulate or generate them in order to have the opportunity to mate, put food on the table, improve their promotion prospects, and so on. They will have a psychology, although we may not initially understand it and may even moralize on it, but at the end of the day they are as unique as we are. There may be an active collective unconscious, or 'hive mind', evolved as a protective survival strategy against other competitive predators, and this again could indicate innate psychic ability. Even if they are by now a race of cyborgs, it seems probable that the robotics will be modelled on the original organic body shape. Any artificial aids will be manufactured to be as close to the original lost body part as possible, assuming they have a culture that encourages prosthetics. We should not judge them harshly if they practise a policy of survival of the fittest, with the weak or damaged falling by the wayside – after all, that is in the nature of the evolution whereby they rose to dominance, and it may be only our own species that manifests this kind of psychosocial responsibility (and even then, opinions vary from culture to culture).

There could be a difficulty in our determining the aliens' sexes, especially if they are either asexual or bisexual, such as with the earthworm or the oyster, which has the capacity to change sex as a matter of course. ET might appear to us to be androgynous, or have more than two sexes, but even to this there must be a limit, as nature rarely wastes her time on useless developments. There may be an absence of a navel, which raises questions as to the method of reproduction. Mammary nipples are mammalian by definition, implying a two-sex species, and absence of a navel would also seem to imply absence of nipples. Such absences naturally indicate non-mammalian origin. Conversely, if one is present, so should the other be.

There would appear to be only two other options. The first is a species giving birth to live offspring as a result of asexual reproduction, in which case the offspring would need to be almost self-sufficient from birth, undergoing a relatively quick rise to maturity. We have a long and relatively helpless infancy because our development depends more on learning than on instinct, and this is only possible through having protective parents or adults around us. The second option is that our ET might have hatched from eggs, probably a small clutch, and here we should expect to find some sort of ovipositor and possibly a quick rise to maturity. There may even be a system whereby the offspring tap directly into the parent's equivalent of a bloodstream, through the development of an organ specific to the task. Photosynthesis by intelligent extraterrestrials is ruled out on the basis that they would be unable to meet their heavy dietary requirements by photosynthesis alone. The fecundity of a successful species depends on how far up the food chain it is, the ready availability of a food source, and the rate of predation by other organisms. Either of these two options would result in a completely different psychological make-up, different drives and different personal agendas to our own.

We should not be too surprised to see a visiting extraterrestrial or ufonaut wearing some sort of space suit, particularly during the early days of 'first contact' with humans. We have evolved a respiratory system whereby we can breathe our nitrogen-rich air – in fact, over the preceding millennia evolution has modified this system so that it can now work only within narrow parameters. We have well-defined aerobic requirements. Our air mixture is probably unique to our planet, although similar atmospheres are to be expected elsewhere, given the nature of planetary evolution – so, if ET is not wearing a space suit, just what does that tell us about the atmosphere of his homeworld?

Space suits are not greatly in vogue these days, it seems. Neither the Pleiadeans nor the greys (see page 76) appear to be in need of them, if the abduction or contact reports are to be believed. Interestingly, both races claim to have been on, in or around the Earth for several thousand years, and the absence of space suits could be seen by some as evidence of co-evolution with regard to our air. Second, any visiting alien would be forced to consider the concept of the instant pathogen – a possibly slow and potentially painful death may result from failing to maintain and operate within a self-contained environment suit. Imagine the effects of an alien microbe upon terrestrial ecology: no predators. We could be looking at a worldwide pandemic of a disease against which we might have no defence at all. The process also works in reverse. We (or our microbiology) could inadvertently wipe out any visiting extraterrestrials in a matter of hours, which is not good for interplanetary relations. Here again, where an absence of some protective outer garment is witnessed, it could imply a long-term and gradual acclimatization or an engineered tolerance to our terrestrial atmosphere and microbiology (see page 75).

ET'S CIVILIZATION

So now we may have a reasonable idea of what ET looks like, but what about the broader concepts – his culture or civilization? Suppose we suddenly find ourselves inundated with extraterrestrial visitors from assorted planets – how might we categorize them? Just because they all arrive at the same time, this doesn't mean that they are all at the same technological level.

Perhaps the first man to categorize extraterrestrial civilizations was the Russian astronomer N.S. Kardashev, who postulated three types of technologically developed ET race by considering how they might transmit information and their energy use. Simply called types 1, 2 and 3, they are a workable yardstick for our purposes.

Type 1 civilizations will be in roughly the same position as we now. They will be planetary societies, with a developed technology that includes an understanding of physical laws, space and nuclear technology, and electromagnetic communications. There will be a global network of communications, food and resources. There may be early attempts at interstellar communications and space flight, possibly settlements in space and interplanetary travel. They may be starting to run out of planetary resources, and their energy consumption will manifest most probably as electromagnetic emissions and radio waves, intentional or otherwise. I wonder what ETs will make of our civilization when, in years to come, they pick up our radio and television broadcasts, particularly our earlier ones. Will they judge us on these, only to discover that when they visit us possibly several thousand years later we bear no resemblance to the characters in 1950s sitcoms or the technological wizards presented in *Star Trek* – even if, indeed, we are still here? If they have any sense, they will probably stay well away.

Type 2 civilizations will have their society possibly occupying most of their solar system, or at least living in space habitats such as Dyson spheres – giant artificial biospheres placed around the parent star in order to capitalize on its radiant energy (like an artificial hollow planet with the star at the core). Our recent Skylab and Mir missions, plus the Biosphere 2 experiment, are the progenitors of such space habitats, and these spheres represent probably the apex of type 2 civilizations' technological achievements. They would be detectable through thermal infrared emissions leaching out into space at approximately 300° Kelvin.

Type 2s are also likely to be actively involved with SETI projects of their own, and may even be enjoying ongoing dialogue with other type 1 or 2 civilizations. They are expected to have a long-lived society of between ten and a hundred thousand years, long-term planning objectives, and to have initiated interstellar travel and colonization. Their energy consumption is likely to involve the utilization of all radiant energy from the parent star, and will use electromagnetic emissions such as gamma rays, X-rays or even gravity waves to pass data and information through the galaxy. They may send out robotic probes or self-replicating machines on scouting missions to locate extra-solar life, and then undertake a mass interstellar transfer or migration of the species once the Dyson sphere is completed (estimated to take between 500 and 1,000 years, even for an advanced type 2 civilization). Such a migration may become necessary once the sphere reaches its ecological carrying capacity, and will perhaps be undertaken via stellar arks or through the practice of panspermia (the diffusion of spores, molecular building blocks, or engineered, microscopically encoded viruses through space as 'life seeds', designed to initiate the genesis of life once they become established in a viable ecosphere). Once such a migration has begun, it would logically leapfrog through the galaxy in waves of colonization as the species continually grows and matures. It is conceivable that a type 3 civilization would emerge or be established as a result of this stellar migration.

Type 3 civilizations are ultimately expected to be able to utilize and control the entire energy output and resources of hundreds of thousands of stars, if not the entire galaxy. We can only guess at the methods of communication and matter transfer likely to be used, but it's fair to say that to us they would appear magical. They may have mastered faster-than-light travel and use beams of supra-light-speed particles such as neutrinos or tachyons to transmit data and information. They may even use telepathy for the purpose of long-distance communications, and might even be travelling through black holes. We should not be able to miss them, if we actively seek them, as they would be a galaxy-wide race and more than capable of major feats of astro-engineering that we should be able to detect even with our comparatively primitive instruments. Their anticipated social lifetime would mean little to us – they are more likely to be considered as immortals, with long-term planning agendas and perspectives we probably could not even guess at.

Kardashev's civilizations classification does have its detractors, however, and they too should be given a fair hearing. Edward Ashpole proposes that advanced civilizations may not be big on industry or construction, or may follow a more sedentary or philosophical way of life that does not require vast energy expenditure, or that their optimum environment may be easy to maintain. He further proposes, quite reasonably, that only a species with the mentality of colonizing ants is likely to construct space habitats and colonies that are detectable to observers, pointing out that ants and termites do not have intelligence in the way that we do, and that it is evolution that has programmed all their behaviour patterns over the preceding millennia. This raises an interesting question: how long does a star have to live in order for a species to evolve naturally into a type 2 or type 3 civilization? The longest-lived stars might also be the ones that are not capable of supporting or encouraging the development of intelligent extraterrestrial life.

Alien morphology is one thing; alien psychology is another. They will, after all, be alien to us, and so will we be to them. Next time you settle down to watch an episode of *Star Trek* and find yourself wondering how it is that 'they always look like us', remember that the creators are probably not too far wide of the mark in their representations of what intelligent aliens might actually look like (although we must allow some artistic licence for their all being able to speak English, let alone cope with the complexities of language and the way that air currents play over various vocal chords to form sounds in different structural arrangements). Let us hope that we are sufficiently alike to get on, and sufficiently different to enrich both our species – we might turn out not to be at the top of the food chain after all.

CLASSIFICATION OF EBEs

The following descriptions of alleged extraterrestrial biological entities (EBEs) are based on both witness testimony and a classification system devised by Richard Butler. They cannot yet be verified beyond comparatively, and are included here because there is a remarkable level of consistency in UFO and abduction reports concerning descriptions of extraterrestrials and their alleged agendas. It might be worth questioning whether the recent upsurge in CE4 cases is due largely to the massive media coverage that the subject receives, and indeed whether they are a symptom of a cultural deficit in certain areas of human activity. Along with the descriptions, I have taken the liberty of adding the alleged 'planetary origin' where available, in the hope that it may add weight (or otherwise) in cases where claims of such origin tally with previous reports and can be compared.

Human Appear to speak and walk like terrestrial humans, height 1.5–2.1m (5–7ft). They are often described as wearing one-piece suits or overalls (mostly blue) and are usually blond with fair skin and blue eyes, although one or two red- or dark-haired specimens have been reported. Generally passive in nature, claiming to have been instrumental in shaping the world's history and religions etc. Often promote a 'brotherhood' concept, and show concern for our environment and our wars. Sometimes referred to as blondes, Swedes or Nordics. Butler proposes two main subgroups: non-Earth-born humans and Earth-born humans.

Non-Earth-born humans arrive from three distinct colony zones and genetically are almost identical to *Homo sapiens*, although generally taller. Eyes are almond shaped, and sometimes emphasized with a natural black liner. As a guide to colony origin, hair colour should be noted: blonde (Pleiades); black (Sirius); and red (Orion). There is claimed to be some sort of coalition between these three races, who are reported to wear an insignia of three spheres in a triangular arrangement.

Earth-born humans associated with these extraterrestrials can also be divided into two distinct subgroups. Class 1 (ancient) claim to be the humans who were the house servants and companions of the mining, military and occupation forces. Consequently, this raises questions regarding either time-travel capabilities or enhanced longevity on the part of the claimants. It is said that when the ET occupying forces left the Earth long ago, they took with them all humans with whom they had been in close contact, as it was felt that leaving them behind would inevitably influence natural human development (shades of *Star Trek*'s 'Prime Directive'?). It is said that class 1 humans and their descendants co-operate fully with all Earth-oriented projects undertaken by these races.

Class 2 (modern) humans work on the same co-operative level as class 1 humans, but were taken from Earth more recently. During some alleged abduction projects, identical or fraternal twins are induced in a female abductee. Then, at some time during the first trimester (the first three months) of pregnancy, one foetus would be removed, to grow to maturity among the non-Earth-born humans. There are reports of some abductees meeting their twins during abductions, although instances are rare and contact between them is very limited and controlled.

Genetically modified Earth-born humans Similar to the above human subgroups, and likewise divided into two groups, these are not to be confused with the greys or their hybrids. Both groups were allegedly created by non-Earth-born humans by genetic manipulation.

Workers are the smallest physically, reaching a height of about 1.1m (3½ft). They have large eyes and heads, and a very pale complexion. They appear to have the mental age of a 5-year-old human, and were designed to undertake menial tasks. They have a very limited reasoning ability and are incapable of violence. Workers may be seen in the company of non-Earth-born humans as 'pets' or companions.

Technicians are basically the same as workers, although they are a little taller, with a tan or yellowish complexion. Higher deductive and reasoning abilities are reflected in the higher mental tasks they undertake.

Butler suggests that both the workers and the technicians are telepathically camouflaged in order to make them appear as greys to abductees. This is done in order to conceal the true nature of these genetically modified Earth-born humans, as non-Earth-borns feel that were the real nature of these GMEHs as a human slave force to be known to Earth's terrestrial population, then it might prove rather difficult to establish friendly relations with us later on. This raises questions about the aliens' actual agenda anyway, and implies that (a) they do intend to establish contact at some point, and (b) such contact might be of covertly hostile intent, despite the 'peaceful brotherhood' angle.

The ubiquitous 'grey' – the alien face most often reported during encounters with extraterrestrials.

Reticulans/greys These are currently the most commonly reported types of alien encountered, and are colloquially known as 'greys'. They are said to come from the Zeta Reticuli system, a binary star system approximately 34 light years distant. They are reported to be about 1–1.2m (3–4ft) tall (although slightly larger, more spindly specimens are not unknown, and are usually represented as commanders or superiors, as in Spielberg's film *Close Encounters of the Third Kind*). They usually have grey skin, sometimes likened to that of a dolphin, a slit-like nose and mouth, and large, black, almond-shaped eyes. Current data appears to indicate that the greys are a cetacean-based life-form. The skin colour has been said to be off-white, brown, green, or even a kind of orange – a diversity that is not unusual, given our own range of skin colours here on Earth. There are three digits to each hand. Witnesses occasionally report a strong smell of ammonia or hydrogen peroxide accompanying these rather unpleasant individuals. Communication is via telepathy. They may be wearing blue, grey or silver close-fitting one-piece suits.

In any event, there appear to be three types of grey. Type 1 are devoted to technology and are generally intolerant, dismissive, or openly hostile towards their captives, although whether this is a purely cultural trait rather than conscious hostility remains undetermined at this time. Type 2 appear to be more 'evolved' than their type 1 counterparts, have a different finger arrangement, and are generally more passive and cognizant of their abductees' needs, fears and anxieties. They appear to fulfil the role of technicians and medics during abductions. Interestingly, one of the insignia associated with this type of grey is the staff of Mercury, the same symbol as used by our own medical profession. Type 3 greys appear to be little more than slaves, almost robotic in demeanour. Their lips are thinner than those of the other two types. It has been suggested that these type 3s are in fact either biomechanical androids or clones, or of a lower social caste. Some military-trained remote viewers have postulated that these greys are from a different time frame to their contemporaries, and are attempting to evolve their spirituality and technology to be more like those of the type 2s.

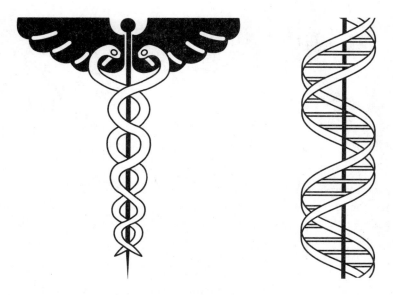

The staff of Mercury is reportedly identical to a symbol seen on the uniforms of the greys' 'medical technicians' during some abduction scenarios. This widely recognized logo of the terrestrial medical profession seems to be a ufological anachronism, until one considers that the entwined serpents may in fact symbolize the human DNA double helix (through which the vertical line is usually drawn purely for orientation purposes) – vital to any alleged alien agenda concerning genetic manipulation or harvesting. Note also the 'winged disc', long regarded as an ancient representation of the heavenly gods' flying machines.

Another startling feature of the greys, and one that appears to be a fairly recent development, is the ploy of appearing to abductees as either a pure human (there is at least one report of a grey having appeared as a 12-year-old human child) or a human-looking alien (compare with the telepathic camouflaging of workers and technicians, above). This point raises some very interesting questions regarding the agendas of both species, given that it has been said that the two are either at war with each other or have been, in which case this tactic could be of immense strategic and propaganda value from their point of view. Such claims are a new twist, and it remains to be seen whether these reports of illusory presentation are on the increase.

Grey/human hybrids It is said by some abductees that the greys are undertaking a hybridization programme in order to maximize on the potential and best mental and physical qualities of both species. Again, there is a question of agenda here. Hitler tried things in a similar vein, so questions must be asked as to why, exactly, they are attempting to manufacture a race that is superior to both us and them, and what they have in mind for the rest of us if they succeed.

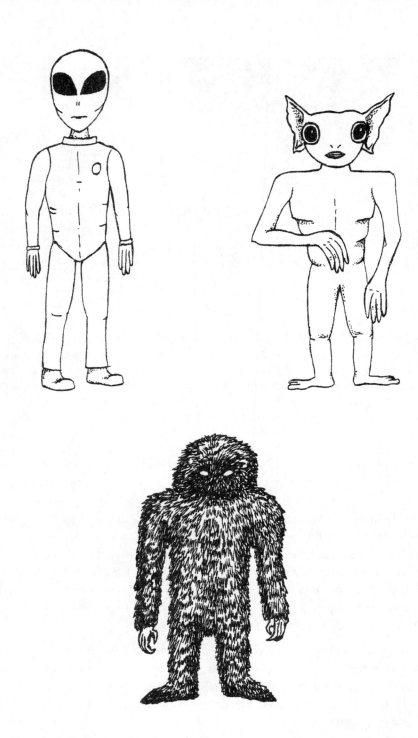

Representations of some of the reported alien types.

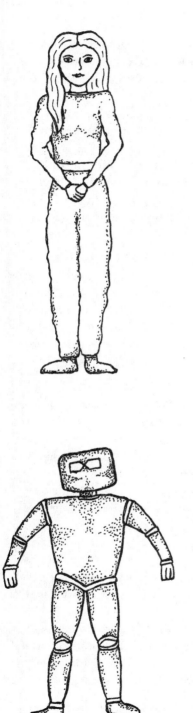

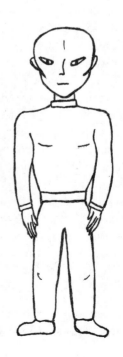

It has been speculated that the greys are hybridizing in order to overcome a genetic defect of their own, and are trying to survive as a viable race. Others suggest that they desire to understand our emotional make-up, as they seem to lack their own spontaneous emotional responses.

In appearance, these grey/human hybrids are like small children, with whitish-grey skin and blonde or very dark hair, which is usually worn in a ponytail. The head is larger and rounder than ours, and the features are very fine and attractive, if angular. They are telepathic, and adore human contact. They seem to be very tactile, and consider themselves to be more human than grey. They 'like' the greys and care about them, but find them terminally boring. The hybrids are said to have a great capacity for emotion, and are extremely proud of any attribute that is more human than grey.

Blues Looking very much like a subgroup of greys, but with a blue, almost translucent skin, these aliens are said to be more passive than the greys, and appear more concerned with what we are doing to our planet. Possibly a hybrid of or species closely related to the greys, they are friendlier, more communicative and more positive in their approach to terrestrial humans than are the greys. One theory holds that they are the most highly evolved of the greys -- the species or caste to which all others aspire.

Humanoid One type of humanoid that is often reported is the 'oriental', which is similar in appearance to a Chinese person, but slighter and more delicate-looking (compare with GMEH workers above). It was these orientals that were allegedly captured at Roswell, and as some were reported to be cadavers when found, this would appear to rule out their use of psychic camouflage, thus indicating a separate being altogether from the aforementioned workers.

The skin is yellowish and their heads are larger than ours, with only slightly different facial features. The upper arm is longer than the lower, and there are four digits to each hand. On each digit, there are four 'suction cups'. (Bearing these last two features in mind, it might be worth remembering that they are thus likely to count in base 4 mathematics. A verification would be useful, and might be achieved by clever questioning of witnesses under regression, with regard to the internal structure of ships, crew numbers, any geometric arrangements, etc. However, this is just theory at this stage.)

These orientals have also been associated with the black helicopter sightings of recent years, predominantly around alleged US/alien underground bases or other military facilities. They do not like humans getting too close to them, and will take off if spotted. Strongly linked with MIB (see page 83).

Animal These are the reported 'hairy dwarfs' often associated with the greys as manual labour, said sometimes to be the ones that undertake the actual physical abduction on behalf of the greys. They are about the same size as the greys, but more squat and solid-looking. Rough, capable, efficient and subservient, they are also physically strong.

Also in this category are the 'reptoids', and although reports of them are rare, they are said by some to be the race behind and dominating the greys. They are rumoured to be masters of genetic engineering, one report even claiming that the greys themselves are one of their genetic constructs. They are said to be thoroughly nasty and evil; their origin is unknown, but they are rumoured to be the oldest race in the galaxy, consequently seeing all others as being there for use as a resource. Personally, I doubt it.

The Nossos of Sirius B also fall into this category. They were said by the Dogon of west Africa (who worshipped and revered them, see page 13) to be a semi-aquatic or amphibious race, fish-like in appearance. The Dogon were instructed by these 'gods' to construct pits to be filled with water, and the Nossos would apparently divide their time between dry land and these water-pits. Interestingly, the Dogon found their benefactors to be rather ugly and with some unpleasant habits – not at all how one would imagine a deity to be presented by its worshipping culture.

The Babylonian Oannes were also said to be semi-aquatic and similar to the Nossos in many respects (see page 14). It is interesting to note that here we have two separate but similar species, both claiming to hail from the Sirius system. It is, of course, possible that one (if not both) has used the Sirius system at some time in its history as a mere staging post during the process of colonizing and exploring space, given that Earth's scientists do not believe Sirius capable of evolving and subsequently supporting life.

Over the years, there have been many cases or one-offs associated with certain animal-type EBEs. Lately, there has been much activity in Brazil and Puerto Rico from the infamous 'chupacabras', which are similar to greys but winged, with big red eyes and three digits with taloned claws. Believed by many to be a genetic construct of the greys, they are said to be vampiric in nature, totally draining goats, sheep, cattle and other domestic animals of blood via two small puncture marks. Some reports claim that there are three puncture wounds, through which internal organs have been removed. Given the comparative sizes of the removed organs and the offending puncture wounds, this procedure would seem to imply that these internal organs are liquefied prior to removal. This, in turn, would seem to preclude organ retrieval for transplant purposes as an option. Their *modus operandi* is distinctly predatory in nature, although at the time of writing there are no confirmed reports of attacks on humans. None the less, they have received massive international media coverage, and the Puerto Rican government takes the claims of witnesses very seriously indeed.

The sasquatch, bigfoot or yowie has sometimes been seen on or near UFOs, and while little is known about them, it has been suggested that they are the original species from which *Homo sapiens* was derived. They may also be associated with the yeti, of which Reinhold Messner, an Italian mountaineer, has some experience. He claims to have tracked 40cm (16in) wide footprints, and describes the yeti as being about 2.1m (6½ft) tall. Said to be shy, nocturnal and carnivorous, they appear actively to shun human contact (and who can blame them?). He also says that they communicate with each other by whistling. Dr Karl Shuker, a British yeti researcher and zoologist, has examined Messner's claims and added that yeti apparently fall into three groups: the original reddish-coloured creature, a taller black species, and a smaller subgroup of red yeti. He implies that it may simply be that the yeti is red while young, and changes to black as it grows and matures. Although there is plenty of evidence to support the claims of yeti witnesses, such as film footage and footprint casts, assorted skeletons and appendages, etc., there is no definitive evidence that they are the same creatures associated with UFOs, so the link is tenuous at best.

Robots The name should be self-explanatory, although they may vary in size and structure from a few square centimetres to humanoid shapes approximately 2.5m (8ft) tall. Shapes vary, from small boxes to spheres with antennas, and larger specimens have been reported. Some, of course, may be classified military or civilian projects. This latter explanation is, however, unlikely to account for the experiences of William Loosley, who on the morning of 5 October 1871 came across a mechanical device in woodland in Buckinghamshire which shone a purple beam of light at him, followed him, and appeared to be attempting to herd him towards a bigger metal box. The devices appeared to be collecting samples of some sort, and were leaving three narrow ruts in their wake as they moved. During Loosely's contact with them, they showed him holographic projections of himself, the planetary orbits of a solar system, a representation of atomic structures, and also gave him a mathematics lesson (all described by Alan Watts in *UFO Quest*). Above him, he saw a large, moon-like globe apparently signalling to the devices with lights. The previous night, Loosely had witnessed a strange light hover, bob about and then land in the nearby woods.

So, such machines or robots may be no more than remote devices, but they can evidently adopt a threatening posture none the less. They have attempted to abduct on occasion, as above, and have caused tangible physical injury. They may move in a stiff or jerky manner and may be techno-telepathic, but do not appear to be sentient or conscious as we understand it. Glowing eyes are sometimes reported in humanoid-robotic types. Machines or drones of some sort are reported more often than human-looking robots; however, the latter may sometimes be wearing padded suits and bubble-dome helmets when witnessed.

Exotics These are often quite bizarre in appearance. There may be human and non-human characteristics; they are generally bipedal, and may combine two or more characteristics from the other types. Chupacabras could arguably be entered into this category as well. Locomotion may resemble animal or human modes, or they may appear to 'float' along. Communication may be by telepathic or 'normal' means. There have been claims that some of these exotics are extradimensional or interdimensional in origin, and can thus assume various shapes. These latter types appear to be peaceful in nature – an approach which would be consistent with current evolutional theories.

Apparitional These appear to display many characteristics normally attributed to ghosts or other occult phenomena. There may be selective manifestation to individual witnesses, who may report shape-shifting, materialization/dematerialization, or telekinesis by these entities. There may be some overlap with the exotics. Apparitionals may be illusory or hallucinatory in origin, associated with other parapsychological phenomena, or indicative of some emotional or psychological disturbance, but they should not be disregarded and should be logged as EBEs if seen during an UFO encounter, for assessment and appraisal as appropriate.

MEN IN BLACK (MIB)

These are one of the most bizarre aspects of the UFO phenomenon, with many witnesses telling of visits from them following their reporting of UFO encounters. The witnesses state that these MIB usually attempt to dissuade them from discussing their encounters, often issuing threats directly or indirectly, while others state that UFOs do not even come into the conversation, with the reason for the visit never becoming apparent. They wear all black clothes, including turtle-neck sweaters, hats and sunglasses. They speak in a dull monotone voice, appear 'odd', and do not seem to be well versed in accepted social conventions, regardless of the culture from which the witness originates. The clothes are often described as shiny, not like silk, but as if cut from new material. Likewise, their shoes and wallets always appear new and not 'broken in'. There are reports of them arriving 'from nowhere', or crossing muddy fields following heavy rain with no sign of mud on their shoes or clothes. Females are not unknown.

Details of the MIBs' physical appearance vary, from dark complexions to very pale skin. Some are slightly oriental-looking, with a yellowish pallor. Otherwise, they all apparently look alike, with high cheekbones, pointed chins and thin lips. They are all said to be very sensitive to light, and although they will accept offers of food or drink, they will not consume any. Transport is usually in large, black, expensive cars; door insignias and registrations have never been successfully traced. The interiors of the cars have been seen to be illuminated by a purple or green glow. Some MIBs and their vehicles may be holographic representations. Generally, they visit in pairs, and sometimes leave hurriedly, claiming that their energy levels are almost exhausted.

Anti-MIB encounter techniques

Dealing with MIB encounters is fairly straightforward, if reliant on keeping a cool head and knowing your stuff. The counter-measures described below were laid out originally by former soldier Robert Parish, who based them on his US Army training.

Tactics utilized by both the recognized investigative agencies – Federal Bureau of Investigation (FBI), NSA, MoD, etc. – and the MIBs are often designed to frighten or intimidate people into keeping quiet about their UFO/ET encounters, particularly with regard to discussing the matter with UFO investigators. MIB encounters are only ever likely to arise following UFO encounters, and after they have been reported to the press or investigators. So what do you or your UFO witness do when, from nowhere, there they are on your doorstep?

The visitors announce that they are from this agency or that organization, flash an ID card at you and then put it away before you've had time to check it. You should then state that you wish to verify their credentials. You can do this by examining and comparing details on their official ID card, a credit card, and their driver's licence. Remember to compare signatures between these documents. You should advise them that unless they comply with your request to produce the documents, you will refuse to speak to them and report them to the police for trying to impersonate a government official, or whatever. If they are who they say they are, then they won't have a problem with this. If, however, they refuse, tell them that the conversation is now concluded. You should then ask them politely to leave, and warn them that if they refuse they can then explain who they are and what they want to the police. In any event, go back into your home and lock the door. Call the police and file a report anyway, whether or not you see them leave, as this makes things official and it will be acted upon.

If the visitors do produce the required identification, remember that it could still be stolen, borrowed, false or copied. Check the apparent age of the item against its printed date of issue – wear and tear are harder to fake. Are all the same names used on the items from the same individual? Check for use of a middle name or initial, ask what that initial stands for, and then see if you can verify it with the other ID. Likewise, check for the lack of it – if it doesn't show on one offered form of ID, ask why. Check for the individual's date of birth compared to their physical appearance, and don't be afraid to ask what it is and then verify this with the ID.

Ask for the individual's social security number, and advise them that this is purely for security reasons. Military personnel will easily remember their military serial number but have a problem with recalling their social security number. A social security number is apparently the best thing to use to run a computer trace on an individual to see if they are who they say they are and to check their date of birth, where they live, who they work for, validity of their driver's licence, etc. Write it down on the palm of your hand, or ask them to wait *outside* while you get a pen and paper. Most current police computers can identify anyone by running a social security number check. They can also 'run a make' on any vehicle (in the UK, via the Police National Computer, although you are unlikely to have access to it), so if you can, note down any vehicle registration numbers, along with descriptions of any insignia, make and model, etc.

Examine the state of the visitors' shoes. Most military and government employees wear only certain types of shoes and particular styles of clothes. Covert agencies, like the military, are likely to have a similar attitude to foot care as the policeman on the beat or the postman. Footwear must be appropriate to the type of work that they undertake: civilians will wear anything that is fashionable or that feels comfortable. Check that the shoes 'fit' with the clothes, for the right shoe on the right foot and matching socks. Is the mode of dress appropriate? Someone not familiar with Earth dress may have got it wrong. If you live in the country, check the footwear for the presence of mud or dirt – it may have been raining, or they may have had to cross a muddy field to get to your house.

If you still aren't sure, do not allow them to lead you into any sort of conversation – make them work for any information that you are prepared to divulge. Keep your answers simple: straight yes or no answers are best where possible; never lie, and do not elaborate on anything. Open questions require careful thought before answering. Never offer information, as once you start doing that they have hooked you, and it will be a great deal more difficult to break off the conversation.

Never, under any circumstances, invite them into your home! Conduct all business on the doorstep or in the porch, and where possible right in the open where others may see you, them, or all of you. Remember that they are not your friends and you really don't know who they are, and because of this you have no way of knowing what actions they may take once you have allowed them into your home and there is no one around to witness subsequent events.

If you smoke, offer the visitors a cigarette and light up one yourself. This gives you a psychological advantage on two counts: it might calm your nerves, and will possibly cause minor offence at the subliminal level. Non-smokers usually dislike being in close proximity to a smoker, especially if the smoke 'happens' to drift in their direction. If it does, note their reaction to it: do they move away from it, show discomfort, or are they indifferent to it? If they are smokers themselves, then they are likely to accept a cigarette from you as they will see it as an opportunity to establish a rapport, and consequently they are not likely to be bothered at all by the smoke. This might at least establish them as human. If they accept a cigarette, offer them your lighter. Try to offer and retrieve it in such a way that you are able to obtain a fingerprint. Once you have it back, store it in a re-sealable plastic bag until such time as you are able to identify the fingerprint. If they decline the offer of a cigarette, you could try offering them a drink, but don't forget to make them wait outside while you fetch it. Again, the object is to get a fingerprint sample from the glass or bottle. You should in any case take note of anything they do or do not eat or imbibe, and under what circumstances.

Finally, if they really do unsettle you and you get a strange feeling of uneasiness, then make any necessary excuses, get in your car, lock the doors and drive straight to the nearest police station, parking in the open in a highly visible position. They are unlikely to follow you. Go in and file a formal complaint.

No one can guarantee that these methods will work, if only because when you are faced with an intimidating stranger it is difficult to gauge exactly how you will react. It's all very well being wise after the event, but if you allow yourself to learn these guidelines beforehand, you may at least be in a better position to deal with the situation if and when it arises. Hopefully, it won't, but you never can tell.

6 Extraterrestrial and Space Laws

What follows should be of particular interest to American readers, as it concerns a wonderful piece of legislation which has already been passed by the US Congress. On 5 October 1982, it was announced to the world by Dr Brian T. Clifford of the Pentagon that any contact between American citizens and extra-terrestrials or their vehicles was now illegal, and had been since 1969. Pity that no one went to any great lengths to notify the American public beforehand.

THE EXTRATERRESTRIAL EXPOSURE LAW

Title 14, Section 1211 of the Code of Federal Regulations – the Extraterrestrial Exposure Law – effectively states that anyone who experiences extraterrestrial contact may be imprisoned and fined a maximum of $5,000. A designated NASA administrator now has the power to determine, with or without a hearing, that a person, persons or object has had extraterrestrial exposure and as a consequence may be subject to quarantine for an unspecified amount of time, under an armed guard – an order which cannot be broken even through the intervention of the courts. The number of individuals thus quarantined is unlimited, and what the law apparently says is that if a UFO were to land on the White House lawn tomorrow, any number of witnesses at the scene could be locked up indefinitely.

American readers probably realize by now that this is highly unconstitutional. This particular law was adopted prior to the Apollo moon shots, and it could reasonably be argued that it was designed purely to protect the inhabitants of Earth from possible extraterrestrial contaminants. The main concern of the conspiracy theorists is that the entire legislation is not worded clearly, is highly ambiguous and open to interpretation, implies that UFO contactees or witnesses have now become a criminal class, and that it was entered into the statute books without public debate, rendering it unsafe.

So, what does the Extraterrestrial Exposure Law actually say? Well, it establishes NASA's

... policy, responsibility and authority to guard the Earth against any harmful contamination or adverse changes in its environment resulting from personnel, spacecraft and other property returning to the Earth after landing on or coming within the atmospheric envelope of a celestial body...

and sets out security requirements, restrictions and safeguards that are deemed necessary in the interests of national security. The law applies to all NASA manned and unmanned space missions that land on or enter the atmospheric envelopes of other celestial bodies, including the moon, Mars, Venus, etc., which would render them 'extraterrestrially exposed'. This means the quarantine of

> ... any person, property, animal or *other form of life or matter whatever*, who or which has touched directly or come within the atmospheric envelope of any other celestial body; or touched directly or been in close proximity to (or been exposed indirectly to) any person, property, animal or other form of life or matter who or which has been extraterrestrially exposed...

To be held in quarantine under this law means the detention, examination and decontamination of any person, animal, or matter that the designated NASA administrator has deemed to have been extraterrestrially exposed. Well, there's no argument there, is there? Such an incumbent could be held against their will for up to a year, anywhere, under armed guard to ensure inviolability of security. Furthermore, if the person were to jump quarantine, or arrange for someone to break them out, both parties would face a $5,000 fine and/or a year in prison.

And that's about the gist of it. Given the various scenarios whereby witnesses have been injured through close encounters with extraterrestrials, maybe such a law is, in essence, not such a bad idea. In Chapter 5 I mentioned the concept of the instant pathogen, and many ufologists fail to appreciate fully what this means. Essentially, any extraterrestrial virus or microbe which makes its way safely into the Earth's biosphere is likely to undergo one of three fates. It will either (a) die quickly through an inability to adapt to a new environment or compete with native species, or (b) thrive and become an overly successful organism with no natural terrestrial predators or anti-pathogens (consider H.G. Wells' 'red weed' from Mars in *War of the Worlds*, and what eventually happened to the Martians themselves!), or (c) adapt to terrestrial ecology and find a niche in which it can conform to the constraints and restrictions placed upon it by its new environment. Even in the last case, this is still not a desirable option, as we have absolutely no way of knowing how it will behave as it evolves or the manner in which it will interact with terrestrial life-forms, which may have no natural defences against the interloper. As a consequence, there may be a total disruption of our own biosphere, which implies biological, ecological and economic damage. Any intelligent extraterrestrials may be carrying millions of little ET microbes about their person as they enter our biosphere. Theoretically, we could all be dead within a week from exposure to them.

There was one case where a young girl suffered approximately 60 per cent burns to her body from a low-flying UFO. She was taken to a USAF hospital, where no one was able to explain why it was that her clothes were not burned during the incident. In another case, a man received a sledgehammer-like blow that knocked him off his feet and rendered him unconscious, administered by what was thought to be the force field of a UFO estimated to be 30m (100ft) in diameter. Under these sorts of circumstances, maybe quarantine isn't such a bad plan, if only for the sake of ensuring intense and specialized medical attention. After all, such incidents could have implications for everyone on the planet in the event of mass landings, and it's a sure bet that if these steps had not been taken, we would lay the blame for our condition squarely at the feet of our respective governments for not having done something earlier to protect us. The only real problem with this law is that as it is, it is open to interpretation, and also to abuse.

THE OUTER SPACE ACT

The British government, in its infinite wisdom, has also passed a law pertaining to space and activities within it. Known as the Outer Space Act 1986, it expressly forbids, without a permit from a UK Secretary of State, the following activities:

- Launching, or procuring the launch of, a space object.
- Operating a space object.
- Any activity in outer space.

What are we to make of this? For the purposes of this law, outer space is defined as 'the moon and celestial bodies'. 'Any activity in outer space' as laid down in section 1(c) of the Act might imply that being abducted and transported into space is now an offence punishable under British law, depending on the desired interpretation at the time and upon who, exactly, is doing the interpreting. Likewise, could any extraterrestrials foolish enough to enter UK airspace find their vehicle impounded through not having the requisite permission from a Secretary of State?

The Act applies to all UK nationals, Scottish firms, British overseas citizens, and those under the protection of British law. Quite what the poor old Scots have done to deserve this singling out I have no idea – maybe it's just an English thing, although Scotland does have a fully fledged legal system of its own.

The Act promotes itself as a response to 'our international obligations', but is strangely quiet on the question of to whom these obligations have been made. One must therefore assume that they are to the United Nations (and we shall hear more of the UN later). By and large, the Act is concerned primarily with space activity regarding satellites and their orbital parameters, and lays down the conditions under which a licence might be granted. Offences against the Act are punishable by a fine 'not exceeding the statutory maximum', but again, it is not specified what that statutory maximum actually is.

There are currently five pieces of international legislation governing all space activity, and it is assumed that it is to at least some of these that the Outer Space Act 1986 owes its obligations. These are:

○ The Treaty on Principles Governing the Activities of States in the Exploration and Use of Outer Space, Including the Moon and Other Celestial Bodies 1967 (also known simply as the Outer Space Treaty).

○ The Agreement on the Rescue of Astronauts, the Return of Astronauts and the Return of Objects Launched Into Outer Space 1968.

○ The Convention on International Liability for Damage Caused by Space Objects 1972.

○ The Convention on Registration of Objects Launched into Outer Space 1975.

○ The United Nations Moon Treaty 1979, which, although it entered into force in July 1984, has still to be signed by the US and the countries of the former Soviet Union. Interesting...

An organization called the United Nations Committee on the Peaceful Uses of Outer Space was set up in 1953 by the UN General Assembly. It's their job to legislate and co-ordinate space law. There are two subcommittees, one to study and oversee the technical and scientific aspects of space activities, and the other to look at all the legal angles of those activities. The latter also has responsibility for deciding 'who speaks for Earth' in the event of our receiving a direct contact from an extraterrestrial species (presumably via the official SETI programmes), plus deciding upon the question of how we treat an alien visitor – especially if that visitor is perceived as being belligerent.

In 1989, a document entitled the *Declaration of Principles Concerning Activities Following the Detection of Extraterrestrial Intelligence* was approved by the Academy of Astronautics and other respectable and highly regarded astronomy organizations. Its basic statement is that should an intelligent alien signal be received, then other researchers should immediately be notified, and once the signal has been independently verified, then the whole world should be told. It also suggests that no return signal should be sent until international consultations have taken place. This is generally considered to mean that it will be the aforementioned UN subcommittee who will decide what is said, when it is said, who will say it, and how it will be said.

So, if officially extraterrestrials don't exist, why is such legislation in existence? Is the UN just hedging all bets? Or do the people in power really think that the likelihood of discovering extraterrestrial intelligence is a lot greater than the politicians are prepared to let on?

7 UFO Causes of Effects

In this chapter we will take a look at some of the methods by which it is possible or expected that UFOs are powered, and at some of the effects that witnesses to UFOs claim are produced. An understanding of the physics involved in UFO propulsion should help either to improve or to destroy the credibility of a report – it would be a shame to undermine a report's validity because of a simple misunderstanding or ignorance of some of the effects allegedly created by UFO propulsion systems.

UFO INTERFERENCE

There is much speculation on this topic, and I'm no engineer, but it seems to me that whatever the propulsion units employed by UFOs or alleged top-secret military craft, there does seem to be some tangible evidence of their passing within close range of automobiles. It is not unusual for a motorist to have their engine misfire, lose power or stop running altogether when in close proximity to a UFO flypast. When driving at night, headlights reportedly become dimmer or even die completely. Static is usually heard coming loudly over the radio, and it may stop playing altogether. The driver then usually stops at the side of the road and gets out to see what is causing the power loss, and sometimes it is only then that they may notice a large, glowing disc nearby, often hovering at low altitude over the car. This activity is often the preamble to abduction.

These effects are not limited to automobiles, but occur with all kinds of vehicles or pieces of machinery that are powered by internal combustion engines, with the exception of diesels. Incidents of engine or electrical interference or failure have been reported for aircraft, motorcycles, trucks, mobile telephones, radios, buses, power mowers, petrol-driven tractors and other farm machinery. Usually the engines will run normally once the UFO has departed.

There are cases where only one or two of the above effects have occurred, but then most people (excluding Volvo drivers and sensible motorcyclists) don't drive with their lights on during the day, and not everyone listens to the radio while travelling. In other scenarios, lights may dim, but there may be no discernible power loss to the engine.

From all this, it would appear that engines, lights and radios are about equal in their sensitivity to the proximity of UFOs. This is rather surprising, given the sensitivity of radios to ordinary electrical interference – driving close to power transmission lines which operate at 60 cycles per second usually causes static on the radio, without affecting the lights or engine. The implication is clear: the mechanism of the UFO interference is something other than low-frequency electromagnetic radiation.

Close examination of reports reveals a gradation effect, and it appears that the interference with the vehicle is directly related to the proximity to the UFO (or the strength of the emanations from it). One engine misses as the lights flicker, another sputters as the lights merely dim, a third runs normally as static is heard on the radio and the lights dim. A weak influence from a UFO at a great distance mildly disturbs the engine, radio and lights, whereas a stronger influence upon closer approach causes all three to fail completely. It has been shown that the intensity of the field radiated by UFOs is also variable; hence, the graduated response can occur while the distance to the UFO remains fixed.

Over the years, many components of car engines have been examined for signs of susceptibility to interference from UFOs, including the battery, alternator, spark plugs and ignition system. However, as power returned to the vehicle once it was away from the UFO, this would indicate that the power in the battery was not drained. Brian Lucas, an electrical engineer, proposed in a letter to the British *UFO Magazine* that the electrical circuits within a vehicle's wiring rely on the movement of electrons within the circuitry, along the wires, copper tracks and cables. When the voltage supply from the positive battery terminal travels to the ignition or lights, the existing circuit allows the electrons to transfer the battery current and thus provide power. Under very strong magnetic flux fields, this movement of electrons is slowed down, leading to power fluctuations. Increase this magnetic flux field, and sooner or later the movement of electrons will stop completely, producing a greater-than-normal resistance within the circuit, and the subsequent total loss of power is as though one had disconnected the battery and isolated the current.

Alan Watts, author of UFO books and lecturer in physics, set up an experiment using a DC power supply and a solenoid around an automobile coil, and ran the engine at full revs, gradually increasing the current. He was fully expecting to find that the resulting generated electromagnetism would affect the running of the engine. In fact, not much happened at all. He then changed the power supply to AC, and discovered that the engine slowed down considerably. From this experiment, Watts surmised that the UFOs were using alternating current as a power supply, and as it is known that magnetism is only created with the flow of electric currents, it was a simple step to calculate the amount of magnetism that was being generated by these UFOs in order for them to be able to affect a car. The result was somewhere in the region of one million teslas (a tesla being the unit of magnetic flux density in which the strength of a magnetic field is measured). Such a large magnetic field is only possible if one can eliminate electrical resistance, which we can – enter the superconductor.

When refrigerated to extremely low temperatures, certain metals and metallic compounds lose their electrical resistance in tandem with the decreasing temperature. This process continues until a critical temperature is reached – the superconducting point – which is usually within a few degrees of absolute zero (–273°C), whereupon the resistance falls to zero. Once this happens (and providing that the metal or compound remains below the superconducting point), any electric current induced by a magnetic field (say, in a coil) in a ring of the material or in a closed circuit continues to flow after the magnetic field has been removed.

Watts, among others, believes that UFOs may indeed be using superconductors in the structure of the skin of the craft, and it may be that this actually forms a part of the ships' propulsion and drive systems. Although we currently have no way of knowing, it seems reasonable to assume that our extraterrestrial friends have found a way of manufacturing superconductors that have no need of refrigeration. Terrestrial science is working towards these aims already – after all, the practical applications are manifold. For a full explanation of the experiment (and a complete discourse on the science behind UFOs), I suggest you read Watts' book *UFO Quest*.

OTHER FACTORS AND EFFECTS

So, immense electrical power, immense electromagnetic radiation. Captain Bruce Cathie, a former New Zealand Air Force pilot and author, postulated the existence of a worldwide magnetic power grid that he claimed was directly associated with UFO sightings around the globe. He estimated that the ufonauts could increase the efficiency of their craft while in the Earth's atmosphere by up to 15 per cent simply by drawing upon this naturally occurring system of geo-electromagnetic energy, known sometimes as 'ley lines'. It might, then, be worth examining a UFO's reported flight path to determine whether or not the craft was flying along known or suspected ley lines. Although ley lines can be found all over the world, they can sometimes be discovered easily by placing a ruler on a map and looking to find 'connecting lines' that link up any of the following features: churches (often built over much older, pagan sites of worship); prehistoric sites, such as stone circles and standing stones; holy wells; crossroads; tumuli or burial mounds; and prehistoric earthworks or settlements. Crossroads often mark the intersection of two or more ley lines, while holy wells often mark either end. To qualify as a ley line, such a line must have at least three of the listed sites along its length (but will often have many more), and there will possibly be tales of witchcraft, ghosts or other folk legends associated with these sites or particular areas along the line. It is understood that a ley line can be up to 10m (30ft) wide, and anything up to several hundred kilometres long.

Further evidence for the ufonauts' use of electricity as a power source comes from the type of sounds heard during encounters, usually described as buzzing or humming. This is because of the reaction of electrons (small subatomic particles) upon the air, as opposed to molecular bombardment – the latter cause shock waves to radiate out to the observer, who registers a deafening sound in their ears. Also, as there is usually no obvious emission of gases into the surrounding atmosphere with UFOs, their entire system appears to be self-contained, so that all reactions take place inside the ship and the only effect on the outside is the electromagnetic 'aura' that UFOs appear to generate (again, Watts gives further detail).

In some instances, these ships appear to be generating infrasound that appears to send waves of vibrations through the human body; this sound may or may not be heard as a very low-frequency humming. This in itself can be a health hazard, as there can be no way of knowing until it's too late whether these sounds are of sufficiently low frequency to disrupt the body at a molecular level. I don't believe that our ufonauts use this infrasound as a weapon – it seems more likely to be merely a by-product of the ship's propulsion system. However, this hum is not always low frequency. There are reports which indicate that the pitch increases with the Doppler effect as the ship approaches, sometimes reaching a voluble whining as the craft passes overhead.

Another sound often reported is uncannily consistent with sounds reported in ancient Mayan and Sumerian texts describing the arrival of the gods in their skyships (for want of a better word). This second, low-frequency sound is said to be like thousands of stones colliding with each other, or of gravel being tipped upon a concrete apron, while the ancient texts (which are several thousand years old) refer to it as being like a giant stone block being struck repeatedly by hundreds of stone hammers. Modern reports state that there is also something akin to electrical or static crackling within this sound.

One feature often reported by witnesses to UFOs is a strange black cone of energy, or vortex, seen underneath the hovering UFO as if it is resting on it. Francis Ridge, writing in the *UFO Intelligence Newsletter* in 1990, refers to it as the 'superdark cone'. It is also known as the Sorensen effect, after Niels T. Sorensen, who presented a paper on the phenomenon in 1975 at a conference in Los Angeles. The paper is entitled 'New Technology Related to UFOs and

Their Origins', and its central theory actually predicted a 90 degree cone and a 'null region' at the apex, which represents a region of apparent gravitational attraction. It seems that this area beneath the UFO may indeed be an energy vortex responsible for landing-trace circles. It may be invisible except when viewed under particular circumstances, such as under the ultraviolet flare of a lightning bolt or when viewed through polarized windscreens or the tinted windows of cars and trains.

This 'black cone' is not the only colour to be witnessed. The presence of a magnetic field as proposed by Watts would indicate that UFOs give off light as a by-product according to the strength of the magnetic field being generated. As the field is increased and the craft accelerates, there should be a colour shift (if the craft is stationary or landed, or from a 'standing start') from infrared, through red, orange, yellow, green, blue, violet, and up into bright white and then ultraviolet – at which point a witness may suffer the effects of 'sunburn' – while photon emission then carries on right up into gamma-radiation wavelengths. Obviously, what colours are seen will depend upon the speed of the acceleration and the human eye's ability to register them, and interestingly, oranges, golds and reds are often the last colours reported before the craft streaks off.

Another bizarre effect associated with UFOs is the apparent distortion of space and time that occurs not only inside the ship, but also at alleged landing sites. Contactees and abductees alike have mentioned that the UFO in which they find themselves appears to be larger on the inside than the outer dimensions would seem to allow (leading some perhaps to believe that they have been taken on board a mothership), and that the abduction takes place with a time distortion that is not consistent with currently accepted laws of physics. For example, some witnesses have claimed that their abduction lasted only minutes, while members of their family or other witnesses to the event may confirm that the subject has been 'missing' for several hours – or conversely, that they were abducted for several hours, and yet may only have been gone for a few minutes.

Most sceptics cannot accept that this does indeed appear to be the reality for the witnesses or abductees, and consequently label them as hoaxers, or as having fantasy-prone or psychologically disturbed personalities. So, is there a scientifically acceptable way of showing that the witnesses may be telling the truth? Well, yes, there is actually, and all those who say that faster-than-light travel is impossible are obviously not familiar with recent lines of mathematical thought. Enter Professor Maria Ruggero Santilli, a brilliant Brazilian-American physicist, and a new set of isorelativities and geometries that might just shed some light on such strange phenomena. But first, some background on the theories of Einstein, time travel, and faster-than-light travel.

RELATIVITIES

In 1905, Albert Einstein published his Special Theory of Relativity, in which he treated space and time on an equal footing, and illustrated that although accurate predictions could be made regarding the speed of objects at near light speed, faster-than-light travel was impossible because as an object approached light speed its mass became greater, requiring greater amounts of fuel to send it on its way – reaching infinite mass at light speed and requiring an infinite amount of fuel to propel it further. Thus, it was assumed that the speed of light in vacuum was the maximum possible, rendering interstellar travel impossible for all practical purposes. However, the Special Theory of Relativity also allowed the demonstration of 'time dilation', in which a moving clock will tick more slowly than one at rest, suggestively allowing for travel forwards in time. But this law did not allow for the gravitational effects of Newtonian laws.

As Einstein had established equality between time and space, in 1915 he constructed his General Theory of Relativity, which was consistent with both Newtonian law and the Special Theory of Relativity. This new theory attributed gravity to the bending, stretching and deformation of the flat space as implied in the Special Theory. The General Theory of Relativity allows for the distribution of matter in space, and predicts that space will become deformed according to the properties and pattern of distribution of that matter. It was formerly accepted that time and space were fixed and immutable, but these newer theories demolished that idea and implied that space was indeed flexible.

In 1994 at the University of Wales, researcher Miguel Alcubierre demonstrated that faster-than-light travel is possible because of the flexibility of space as allowed in Einsteinian laws. Alcubierre assumed the availability of what he called 'exotic matter' in large quantities, surrounding a spacecraft in such a manner as to cause gravity behind the craft to expand rapidly, and gravity at the front of the craft to contract equally rapidly. In effect, the ship does not travel in a linear mode, because the ship itself is not moving at all; rather, it is the space surrounding the ship that moves and the ship is carried along incidentally, as the rapid expansion and contraction of the surrounding 'envelope' of space shifts at a rapid rate towards its objective position. Imagine a bubble as it rises through a body of water: anything inside the bubble travels with it. This envelope of space effectively drags any ship contained within it in the same manner, but at near infinite speeds, simply because space and time themselves are distorted. The greater the expansion and contraction of the envelope, the greater the apparent speeds that can be achieved. Huge distances could consequently be covered almost instantaneously. This is your actual 'warp drive'.

Things have now been taken one stage further by Allen E. Everett of Tufts

University in Massachusetts. He examined the likely effects of such a ship moving under its own power while contained within the proposed envelope. He discovered that if the ship moved fast enough, then its speed as seen by an observer would appear to exceed infinity itself. In other words, instead of taking 'no time' to travel between two points, it would take a negative time, effectively disappearing up its own event horizon and travelling backwards in time. Pretty neat, huh?

But what of this 'exotic matter'? It is generally held among the cosmological fraternity that the cosmos became filled with such stuff following the Big Bang. It is this exotic matter which is held to be partly responsible for the rapid expansion of the universe, but it appears to be in much shorter supply these days. In practical terms, such a ship is still beyond our capabilities because we would require a mass of exotic matter approaching the mass of Jupiter, and then there are the technical considerations of how to contain it effectively. Back to the drawing board – for us Earthlings at least...

The behaviour of anomalous craft under visual or radar observation is not usually compatible with the theories of Einstein. However, most ufologists are unaware that Einstein's theories have well-defined limits of validity, and that beyond these limits they are merely inapplicable, rather than actually violated. Professor Santilli's relativities apply for conditions beyond those of Einstein and are based on new geometries and mathematics, whose basic units of space and time are arbitrary quantities 'U', which can be either negative (in which case they describe anti-matter) or positive (in which case they describe matter), as opposed to Einstein's basic unit for space and time, which is +1. UFOs appear capable of controlling space/time units, and it is here that Santilli's theories provide a geometric representation of the anomalous propulsion, flight patterns and behaviour, such as rapid acceleration/deceleration; sharp and apparently inertia-free turns; interior dimensions of ships greater than outside (as per Dr Who's Tardis, which, for those into trivia, stands for Time and Relative Dimensions in Space – a case of life imitating art?); lengthy periods of abduction without missing time; apparent 'jumps' in temporal space, etc.

Ultimately, UFOs are expected to be space/time machines, on the premise that no alteration of space is possible without also altering time, and vice versa. Santilli's relativities predict that time in the interior of such vehicles, and consequently in the immediate vicinity, will flow in a different way to our own. Therefore, there is expected to be a residual time difference in the soil at landing sites compared to test zones at different distances from the centre of such a landing site. This time anomaly is expected not to remain as a constant, but to revert to 'normal' time with exposure to the natural passage of our time.

If this all sounds too bizarre, remember that not only is faster-than-light travel theoretically possible, but that speeds of up to 76 times the speed of light have been attained by subatomic particles in linear accelerators, such as the 4km (2½-mile) long monster at Stanford University. MUFON have produced an excellent document about this theory and its applications to UFO investigation, which can be obtained from them directly (see Useful Addresses).

What witnesses generally report as a visual upshot of all this wonderful science includes both solid and tangible vehicles, lights, 'fuzzy' images or cloud-like structures, radar reflections (with or without visual confirmation), or sightings by one witness that are not seen by others in close proximity or whose testimony is in conflict with that of other witnesses. So, why should this be? Again, it may all be to do with the way that the ships are powered and subsequently behave. It has been proposed that the ionization or electromagnetic effects surrounding some of these ships might actually bend light rays around them. In some instances, this will apparently 'displace' the ship from its actual position so that it appears to be several metres away from it, or it can make it look as though there is more than one vehicle by reflecting images on to the inside of the charged 'envelope' surrounding the ship, which itself may be seen depending upon the observers' position and line of sight in relation to the ship.

Way back in 1964, the National Investigations Committee on Aerial Phenomena (NICAP) produced an excellent document called *The UFO Evidence* which examined many of the elements, traces, effects and other issues surrounding UFOs and is now hailed as a classic of UFO literature. Edited by Richard H. Hall, this work is now available again and although the data it contains is quite old (predominantly covering the period 1947–1963), it is none the less one of the most important, valuable and convincing UFO-related texts still available. Get a copy if you can.

WITNESS TESTIMONY

The following are extracts from statements made by witnesses themselves regarding the science behind the UFOs, and the amount of co-consistency is remarkable.

> Three ball-shaped landing gear were half lowered below the flange that covered them. On top was a round glowing ball like a heavy lens. Top of craft was dome shaped, with a ring of gears or heavy coil glowing at the base of the dome. Round portholes in the side wall but not above the position of the ball gear. The lower outside portion or flange was shiny but not one piece, built in layers in a reverse step fashion. Underneath the craft, there were two rings under the flange and a third around the centre disk. The inner and outer rings appeared to revolve clockwise and the middle one counter-clockwise in direction, when looking up from

underneath. Inside, a slight hum came from the floor and a coil built at the top of the circular wall. The coil glowed red but emitted no heat, and emitted various colours before, like a flashing prism. Many of the colour changes and glowing coronas are from different energy intensities radiating into the atmosphere similar to ionization.

A pillar about two feet thick extended downward from the top of the dome through the centre of the floor. This is a reversible magnetic pole to draw on nature's forces to provide power for flight. It also serves as a powerful telescope – one end to the sky and one end to the ground and [images] are projected on to the big lenses on the floor and ceiling.

Control panels and benches are placed along the outer wall. An instrument is connected to the central column and functions similarly to a periscope. Four cables appear to run through the floor lens or below it [and] join the central column forming a cross. Three cables carry power to the balls underneath which are hollow, and can be lowered for emergency landings, and are used as electrostatic condensers. The fourth cable goes from the column to two periscopic instruments, one next to the pilot's seat and the other behind him.

All the machinery is located underneath the floor and under the outer flange. Small workshop and storage areas are located here, along with the ship's environmental system. A porthole opened in the wall somewhat like an iris of a camera to a size of about 18 inches; the porthole is nearly undetectable when closed.

The ship has been described as glowing, an effect which is created when particles come into contact with the resonant field. Pulsations within this field cause a shimmering effect which makes the craft appear alive and breathing. This also can cause the light to bend completely around the craft and to become invisible. Also as field strength is varied ionization may shift through all colours of the spectrum to a part of the spectrum not visible.

The intense resonating field also serves as a shield to deflect debris from the ship, and at the same time serves as a atmospheric buffer reducing friction and atmospheric shock waves. The external field of the ship can cause the local air to condense and form a cloud around the hovering ship.

Photos taken around the craft may be distorted due to the electromagnetic flux around the craft. Tape recorders would not work aboard the craft; all that would be heard is a hiss on the tape. Approximately one-third of the circular interior room was devoted to instrument panels and in front of the panels was a frame containing some sort of viewing screen.

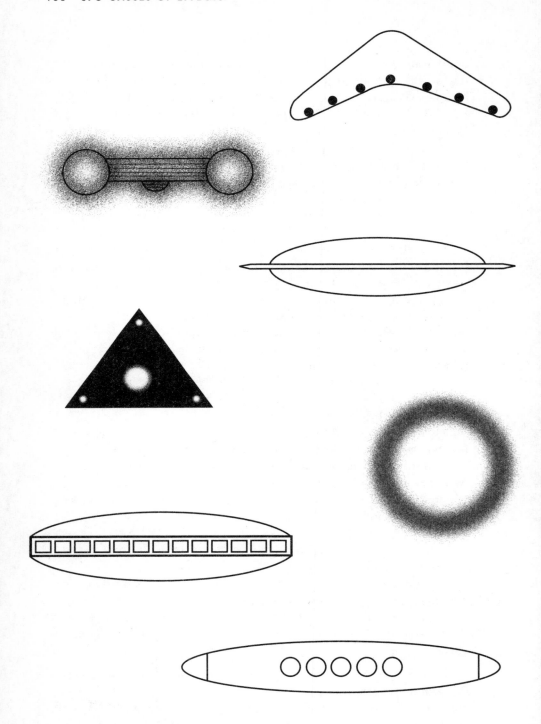

Representations of some of the reported UFO types.

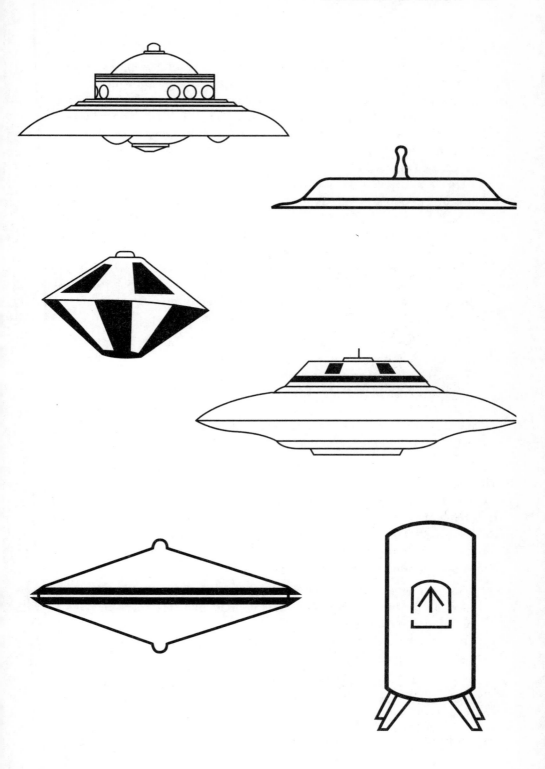

The dome had small round windows from which a similar light shone as if the interior was illuminated from all directions. The light which surrounded the disc suddenly changed colour from white to violet then to a deep orange. There was a flash, the disk becoming a ball of light. I could hear a slight humming sound. Then all at once it sped away and over the trees. A mist was left behind which gradually dissolved.

A light appeared which grew brighter and brighter. The outline of a large cigar-shaped object resting on the ground could be clearly seen. It was over 100 metres long and at its thickest reached to the height of the trees behind it. A long row of portholes emitted coloured lights that lit up the area where it was resting. From one end of the ship, one after another, four discs that shone so brightly as to appear as globes of white light. After a time the discs returned and a humming sound could be heard from the huge craft. The light around it grew stronger, changing from pearl white to orange gold along its length. Then it lifted skyward and streaked off like lightning and disappeared from sight.

It was a solid metallic thing with a dome, portholes and three bumps underneath. In the centre the underneath was darker and shaped like a cone. At first three portholes were visible but then it turned and I saw some more. There was what looked like a hatch on top of the dome and it seemed translucent. It glinted in the sunlight and looked as if made of metal. The upper dome and spherical landing gear were clearly seen. I heard a low humming sound as it came within a few hundred yards of me.

The above statement is supposed to have been made by Cedric Allingham, who has never been satisfactorily traced, although it is claimed that British UFO researcher Jenny Randles, on a tip-off from other researchers, discovered him to be none other than arch-sceptic and astronomer Patrick Moore. Apparently, Moore has never either acknowledged or denied the accusation. Just goes to show that you can't accept everything at face value!

There are three large-turn electromagnetic coils. Close examination reveals a doubling or displacement at periodic intervals, suggesting a pulsating slowly turning wave form. There are highly charged electrostatic condensers which double as landing gear. The condensers pulse in sequence and a rotating field is produced.

The craft was surrounded in a fiery rotating mass of some kind, you could see the craft in the centre of it. It then lifted up, dipped down and then went straight up into the sky.

There, apparently hovering a few inches above the ground, was a large shining disc. The diameter was about 60 feet, and it was about 25 to 30 feet high. Five windows or portholes were visible and it glowed all over with a dull fluorescent light. A sort of halo seemed to surround the craft. It appeared to hover 18 to 20 inches off the ground. We began to hear a slight humming sound like a generator running. A low droning pulsating hum.

The dim glow surrounding the craft took on an orange cast, then a bright red colour. It glowed like a huge ball of red fire. It rose up and changed to a brilliant bluish white and sailed off to the horizon.

The blue-white light turned to a dull green and made no sound. It slowly started to descend. We could make out what appeared to be three large round like ball [sic] objects equally spaced in thirds near the outer rim of the ship from which the fluorescent glowing light appeared to emanate. The ship appeared to bounce up and down and we could hear the pulsating hum increase and decrease as it bounced. The dull fluorescent glow around the rim brightened to a brilliant white then it disappeared from its location.

The field surrounding the ship acts on every atom and molecule in the ship force and acceleration is vectored in the same direction at the same time. All gravitational and acceleration effects from inertia are neutralized or non-existent.

As they got within 500–1,000ft, a very close lightning bolt lit up the area, exposing a 'superdark cone' that wasn't solid and extended below the craft. The cone was fuzzy on the edges and apexed below tree level.

The craft itself looked old, and the surface had the appearance of 'pickled metal'. This craft was operating in a severe thunderstorm and wasn't affected by the high winds.

It was a solid metal thing, with a dome and portholes, and three bumps or landing domes underneath. In the centre the underneath was darker and pointed like a cone. At first, three portholes were visible, but then it turned slightly and we saw four.

The last statement is taken from a case reported by Francis Ridge in 1990.

From these witness testimonies, it can be seen that there is, by and large, co-consistency in how these craft are constructed and how they appear to behave. Many of the claims are also consistent with the isorelativities and scientific theories outlined earlier in the chapter. No doubt some of these statements will generate intense debate and disagreement, and in a perverse kind of way I don't consider that a bad thing, so long as such argument doesn't degenerate into character assassination or a free-for-all slanging match.

8 UFO Wave Theories

A UFO 'flap' is a fairly intense period of UFO activity in a locally defined area. A 'wave', on the other hand, is defined as a national or greater equivalent – a flap's big brother, if you like. In a wave, UFO activity is seen over a much larger geographical area, and over an extended period of time. Flaps and waves may be associated with what are termed 'window areas', which are usually agreed to be well-defined areas of intense and repeated UFO activity, often with associated and sometimes disturbing paranormal phenomena.

A flap may develop into a wave, but it is sometimes hard to determine whether this is because there really is an increase and expansion of activity, or because it is 'helped along' by media interest. In the latter instance, it is common for the 'signal' to become lost among the 'static', as hoaxers and well-intentioned witnesses misidentify mundane or natural phenomena in the spirit of the 'I-saw-it-too!' syndrome.

Window areas are often thought to be some kind of interdimensional portal through which UFOs enter and leave our part of the space–time continuum. There is certainly some theoretical mathematical evidence to suggest that this is at least partly the case (see Chapter 7), although to many researchers and sceptics alike, this is simply too far 'out there' to be valid.

EARLIER THEORIES

Several theories have been put forward to rationalize UFO waves, the '61-month-wave theory' being one example. It was initially conceived by French researcher Aimé Michelle, who detected a general easterly drift of UFO activity, and was further developed by Dr David Saunders and researchers at the University of Colorado.

In 1971, the latter undertook a study of 50,000 sightings and first examined their reports for 1947, a year in which there were many sightings. They noticed the predictability in the UFO waves of 1947, 1952, 1957, 1962 and 1967. Dr Saunders determined that what distinguished these UFO waves from other, possibly publicity-generated UFO waves was the shape of their distributions: these were waves of UFO reports in which the frequency of daily reports began building slowly, increased to reach a high level, and then diminished rapidly. These waves occurred with a periodicity of 61 months

(5 years), with an accuracy in prediction of peaking to within a few days.

Another characteristic of the 61-month-wave theory was the progressively easterly tracking of the area of activity. The first noted wave crested in July 1947 in the mountain and Pacific states of the US. The 1952 wave reached its peak in late August, mainly in the American midwest and central American states, where there were over 20 times the usual number of reports. Subsequent waves appeared to move approximately 30 degrees east longitudinally, the 1957 wave peaking over South America with around 60 sightings a week, well over ten times the national annual average. The 1962 wave took place around the mid-Atlantic in September of that year, and the 1967 wave peaked in England. Dr Saunders made his first prediction that a major UFO wave would take place around 30 degrees East and peak in December 1972. There followed a UFO wave in South Africa towards the end of November of that year, in a country which had previously seen very few UFO reports. If the predictions were to be proved correct, there would have to be another peaking over Russia in the December of 1977 – there was, along with heightened activity in the UK and Chile.

However, most ufologists lost interest in the theory when the predicted waves for 1977/8 and 1983 failed to materialize – as far as we can tell. These waves should have occurred around Russia, Kazakhstan, Afghanistan and Iran in the first case, and in Russia, China and around the Himalayas in the second. However, with the collapse of the Soviet Union there is a wealth of data now emerging regarding UFO sightings that would seem to concur with Dr Saunders' theory.

Another theory that showed promise for a while was known as 'orthoteny', wherein all UFO sightings fall into 'straight line' routes. When sightings were initially plotted it was found that there was indeed correlation, but according to Gregory Van Dyke it was discovered that the same or similar results were found when random elements were plotted in the same manner, in place of the UFO sightings. The theory later fell apart under close mathematical scrutiny.

Jacques and Janine Vallée undertook studies for the period 1947–1962, and looked to see whether or not there was any correlation with Earth–Mars conjunctions. There was, at least for a period of six years (1950–1956), but they also found that there were sighting peaks around every 13 months within this period. It was then discovered that there is an Earth–Jupiter conjunction every 13.1 months. It remains to be shown whether or not these and other such planetary conjunctions can be in any way conducive to the upward swing in the frequency of UFO sightings.

The head of the rocket division of the Space Studies Centre in Toulouse, France, M. Claude Poher, has undertaken a study of his own. Over a four-year period he examined and analysed 1,000 sightings and arrived at the following conclusions:

- The phenomenon is global.
- Observations are related to population density and meteorological conditions such as cloudiness.
- Seventy per cent of cases were reports from multiple witnesses, and more were from adults than from children. Likewise, 70 per cent of these UFOs were seen at distances under 1km (2/3 mile); 80 per cent of reports were of round objects, which varied between 10m (30ft) and 30m (100ft) in diameter, and 20 per cent were of elongated or cigar-like objects.
- By day, the objects were of a metallic colour, while at night they appeared to be red or orange.
- There was not generally any sound associated with the objects, unless the witnesses were within 150m (500ft) of them.
- Ten per cent of the objects were stationary, 20 per cent moved away slowly, 50 per cent departed rapidly, and the remaining 20 per cent traversed the skies at tremendously high speeds.
- Fifty per cent of the reports were of irregular trajectories, and 20 per cent of the objects had apparently landed.
- Reports remained coherent despite the nationality, culture or sophistication of the witnesses, who were from a diverse range of professions, including several scientific observers.

CURRENT THEORIES

These figures were published in 1976, so what has happened since? Has the number of actual alleged visitations increased, or is it simply that through an increased awareness via the media, film and television, more people are coming forward with sightings of their own? Given the popularity of such programmes as *The X-Files*, *Star Trek*, *Dark Skies* and so on, and the sheer volume of UFO and extraterrestrial-related literature and movies, it does seem likely that UFOs have become more socially acceptable, and this appears to be reflected in the increasing number of reported sightings, but it is equally likely that there is also a greater incidence of hoax reports. The sad fact remains that there are many individuals keen to jump on the bandwagon of money-spinning ufology, or to have their 15 minutes of fame. However, it should also be remembered that many witnesses fail to report their own sightings for one reason or another, such as fear of social or professional ridicule. You can't blame them really – ufology is a very emotive issue. In any case, it would seem that on average these 'missing numbers' appear to balance the books.

Peter Brookesmith rightly points out that UFO flaps or waves can be amplified by a contagious public enthusiasm bordering on hysteria. None the less, there is now enough data available for enterprising ufologists to examine and perhaps come up with some new theories (here, NICAP's *The UFO Evidence* would be invaluable), or to re-examine and update existing theories and distribution maps that compare the number of UFO sightings with the by-products of natural phenomena such as tectonic activity and earthquakes. Canadian scientists Gyslaine Lafranière and Michael Persinger did this to great effect, and published their findings in *Space–Time Transients and Unusual Events* in 1997. The Swedish researcher R. Forshufud compared twenty years of UFO reports with known and measurable sunspot activity and found a distinct correlation between the peaks of both sets of data, with UFO activity peaking only very slightly before sunspot activity.

It is also interesting to note that cultural traits may have a bearing upon not only the number of reported sightings, but also the distribution of those reports. For example, Brookesmith points out that India produces almost no UFO reports at all, despite being one of the most densely populated and urbanized countries in the world. Australia and New Zealand, on the other hand, have only a tiny fraction of India's population, with a correspondingly low population density and distribution, but do, however, have a notable history of UFO sightings going right back to the turn of the century. In England, urban areas provide a heavier concentration of reports than rural areas, while in France, Jacques Vallée noted that the reverse was true.

Whichever way you look at it, the fact remains that over 95 per cent of reported UFO sightings are of mundane or natural occurrences being witnessed sometimes under unusual circumstances. Perhaps it is this area of knowledge that we should be promoting at UFO conventions, and not just the usual run of UFO sightings – after all, are we not then preaching only to the converted? Perhaps we should also remember that psychological studies have shown that, on average, only 65 per cent of an account will be remembered accurately, the remainder being 'filled in' as the subject feels is appropriate. So, if we have a 65 per cent accuracy with regard to a 95 per cent likelihood of a misidentification of a UFO in the first place, it's not too difficult to see where many of the discrepancies and errors in accounts arise.

Many other 'wave theories' have been formulated, but sadly, none seems to have withstood the test of time. Although they appear to answer or address the situation at the time, they quickly lose their appeal once they have been found not to work consistently over extended periods. None the less, reports continue to be logged, assessed and compared, and many attempts have been made to explain the distributions of these reports. Has anybody considered, though, that there might be no rhyme or reason to it at all – that UFO appearances might indeed be random, entirely at the whim of the pilot or commanding officer on board? Is it perhaps possible that we are guilty of 'humanizing' any extraterrestrial visitors – of automatically assuming that they will have a humanly coherent chain of command and will behave predictably or systematically? Furthermore, until all the 'white noise' of misidentifications and hoaxes has been effectively filtered out of incoming reports, we are unlikely to discover an infallible system anyway.

Perhaps even more importantly, any mathematically predictable pattern of UFO activity may need a little lateral thinking applied to it. Supposing, for example, that some extraterrestrial surveyor has given the order for the Earth to be mapped and assayed according to their own 'alien' system. If they only have eight digits – four to each 'hand' – then they are likely to have evolved that system from base 8 mathematics and *not* base 10, as we ourselves use. Therefore, perhaps we should attempt to undertake studies in base 6, base 8 *and* base 10 mathematics. It would be a shame to miss out on an opportunity or major discovery because of intellectual snobbery, rigidity or oversight.

9 In the Field

This chapter is probably the one that you will refer to most often. Although it is titled In the Field, this should be taken to mean the generic field of UFO study – it is not a treatise on what to do when you are standing in a field surrounded by cattle, sheep, the military or whatever, although there is some of that, too. I should also reiterate here that none of the techniques outlined in this handbook will turn you instantly into an expert, but for those with no training at all in the various areas they should provide a useful starting point.

The section on photographic evidence should be particularly useful, as photographs are likely to be the second most available source of evidence, after witness testimony (see Chapter 2). It is therefore essential that you are not taken in too easily by clever fakes and deliberate hoaxes – as with witnesses, there will always be one or two that get past you, but don't let this discourage you. Many of us have been embarrassed in this way: it happens, but hopefully, with the publication of this book it will happen a lot less.

CALCULATION OF HEIGHT, SPEED AND COURSE OF ANOMALOUS CRAFT

Based on the experimental results of Professor H. Rutledge of Missouri State University, this system has proved to be valid for calculating the height, speed and course of aerial objects, but requires a minimum of two sightings from independent witnesses whose linear distance from each other can be calculated. Furthermore, to be accurate it requires each witness to record the bearing and altitude of the object at 15-second intervals.

While it is recognized that it is unrealistic to expect 'right-place-right-time' UFO witnesses to record such details, this system may be applied during organized skywatches where two observation posts are established and in radio or telephone contact with each other, and where both posts are in a position to verify the sightings of the other. At the first instance of a sighting, the witness should verify it with the second observation post, and then both should record the altitude and bearing of the object at 15-second intervals. Such tracking can be undertaken using either a compass and a map aligned with the surrounding land, or with a map and protractor. Various estimated positions can then be calculated by trigonometry. This system is by no means perfect, particularly (as already stated) with reference to witness encounters, but it may prove useful in one or two such instances.

Imagine a giant triangle placed flat on the ground. The point on the ground underneath the UFO represents the apex of the triangle, while your two observation posts A and B form the other two points (see diagram for estimating UFO position). The distance C between observation posts A and B should already be known. Then, if the horizontal angles between both A and B and the UFO are measured, and imaginary lines drawn in the direction of the UFO's position, then logically, as the distance between the two observation posts is known, the distances between the posts and the UFO can be measured by noting the point at which the imaginary lines intersect.

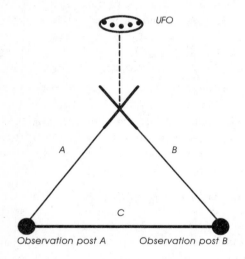

Estimating the position of a UFO.

Once the horizontal distances are known, the vertical angles between the observation posts and the UFO can be measured, similar imaginary lines drawn (D and E) and the height (F) calculated (see diagram for estimating UFO height). The speed of the object can be worked out using the formula *distance divided by time*. Accurate measurements at the time of observation of the object will mean greater accuracy in plotting of details of its course, height and speed of the object (see also Chapter 11, for aircraft flight paths and cruising heights).

As a further aid, it is possible to guesstimate the height of an object from its proximity to the cloudbase, especially if the object keeps disappearing into and reappearing from the clouds. Different types of clouds have different ceiling heights, as follows:

Stratus Often described as hill fog, stratus clouds are very low and form a uniform blanket-type layer. Often produce rain. Cloudbase has a maximum ceiling of about 1,000m (4,000ft), reaching a thickness of up to about 2,000m (6,000ft).

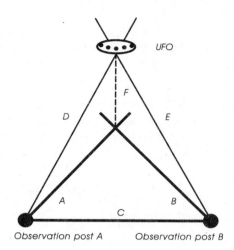

UFO

F

D   E

A   B
         C

Observation post A   Observation post B   Estimating the height of a UFO.

Cumulonimbus These are those dark and brooding thunderclouds which form the tall columns known as 'thunderheads' or 'anvil' clouds. Usually very dark at the base. The top of these anvils is usually smooth, and may reach 6,000m (20,000ft), while the base will be at around 300–1,000m (1,000–4,000ft).

Nimbostratus These clouds also have a fairly low ceiling and form low, dense, gloomy blankets of cloud, indicative of lengthy periods of rain or snow arriving within a few hours. Form a thick blanket from about 300m (1,000ft) at the base up to a little over 2,000m (6,000ft) topside.

Altocumulus At heights of between 3,000m (10,000ft) (base) and around 6,000m (20,000ft) (top), altocumulus are greyish white, thick and heavy clouds, often rounded, with well-defined shadows in them. They are frequently seen following storms. Also known as 'lenticular' or 'crenellate' clouds.

Cumulus These are the 'fluffy' white clouds that we all know and love. They very often have flat bottoms to them, which indicate the rising thermal currents favoured by gliders, paragliders and birds. When seen at sea, they usually indicate that land is beneath them. The maximum ceiling is about 800m (2,500ft).

Stratocumulus These are often presented covering the entire sky as a low, rolling, lumpy mass, with a maximum ceiling of around 300m (1,000ft).

Altostratus Little more than a grey watery veil, altostratus clouds may ultimately thicken to form rain. Height range is between 2,600m (8,500ft) (base) and 5,850m (19,500ft).

Cirrocumulus Often referred to as a 'mackerel sky', cirrocumulus clouds present as small rounded lumps, which might look like sand ripples. Usually appearing and then dissipating following a storm, they have a height range of 6,000–9,000m (20,000–30,000ft).

Cirrus Often referred to as 'mare's tails', cirrus clouds are actually formed from ice crystals high in the atmosphere and have a height range of 9,000–12,000m (30,000–40,000ft) plus.

Cirrostratus Very similar in appearance to cirrus clouds, these may appear as little more than white veins in the sky. Also made from ice particles, these clouds may form halos around the sun or moon and they have a height range of 5,500–7,500m (18,000–25,000ft).

When assessing meteorological reports, clouds are usually classified thus:
Low cloud = below 3,000m (10,000ft)
Medium cloud = between 3,000m (10,000ft) and 6,000m (20,000ft)
High cloud = above 6,000m (20,000ft)

SOIL TESTING ON-SITE

Soil testing on a reported landing site may help to determine effects of contact on the soil's biota, or microbiological life, and chemical composition. It is also worth examining any vegetation within the confines of the site for such things as burns, chemical change, or any cellular disruption or alteration, but you will of course also need to take control samples from outside the area for comparison.

There are many cheap and cheerful soil-testing kits that include battery-operated probes. However, these are limited in their applications and you will need several different probes for different tests: testers are available for pH, nitrogen, potassium, water content and so on, and most garden centres stock them. If you can, test for as many different criteria as you are able, and don't forget to run a range of tests outside the encounter area as well, otherwise you'll have no frame of reference.

Samples should be taken from at least the top 15cm (6in) of soil, with a minimum of six samples being tested from within the suspected landing site. An auger or core-sampler is an ideal tool to use for this. Remember that the underlying substrate will affect the type of soil you encounter, and differing substrates should be taken into account where they overlap within the test area. Samples should be collected at random from the site along a Z or W line (see diagram), and should total about 250g (8oz) dry weight. Store the samples in re-sealable plastic bags to maintain freshness, and label with the date, site and sample number, particularly where the samples are being removed to a laboratory for analysis. In these instances, time is of the essence, particularly as the sample may undergo subtle chemical or biological changes through confounding factors such as sudden changes in temperature or respiratory deprivation.

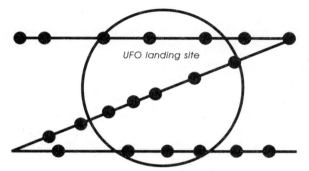

UFO landing site

Soil testing on alleged UFO landing sites. Soil is extracted from the points randomly marked along the line. Although a Z line is shown here, a W line is equally acceptable.

Where possible, pH testing should be carried out on-site, and an accurate way of doing this is to dissolve the soil sample in an equal volume of distilled water or, if the soil has a high clay content, in barium sulphate solution. The solution can then be tested with a probe or pH indicator paper. Remember that pH values may be anywhere from 1, which is strongly acid, to 14, which is strongly alkaline (for the scientifically minded, pH values are the negative logarithm of the hydrogen ion concentration).

When taking samples of any kind, it is important to be familiar with the protocols regarding their collection, protection, transit and documentation. The more thorough the protocols, the better the practice and the more valid the results. As already emphasized, one sample is not enough, so take several to give a better representation of the site, and don't forget to take some control samples from outside the site so that you have a comparison. If samples are being sent away for analysis, then make sure you get a receipt from the carrier or courier, detailing exactly what is being carried and from where it came. Keep written records of any samples that are taken, a logbook if you like, and if you keep computer records *make a back-up copy or two* and store in a safe place away from the other record systems.

It is worth drawing a sketch map of the site, with the sample points marked on it and numbered. Pay particular attention to areas of apparent compaction – for example, where it appears that landing gear has made depressions in the ground. Apart from the soil samples themselves, take a look at the actual soil texture in and around the site, to see if there is any marked variation in the types of soil, and make a note of that too. Textures range from sand, through loam and silt, to clay, and mixtures of the same: sandy-loam, clay-loam, silty-clay, etc. If you are examining an old site, remember that many wild plants can act as indicators of the prevailing soil conditions, and there are excellent field guides available to help you with this.

If you have access to a microscope, it is worth taking soil samples to study at leisure, but preferably as soon as possible after collection. Under the microscope, identify and check the condition of the soil biota – amoeba, nematode worms, bacteria and so on – looking for signs of life and general health, and comparing with other samples where appropriate. Likewise, vegetation samples may yield some startling results, although it helps if you know a little about cell structure and biology, to help you better understand what you're looking at. Please remember that under the provisions of the Wildlife and Countryside Act 1981, in the UK it is actually illegal to remove soil or dig up wild plants, and even picking flowers could land you in court under the Theft Act, so make sure that you obtain the landowner's permission before removing any samples from the site.

If you can employ the services of a competent pedologist (soil scientist) or geomorphologist, so much the better. They will have access to all the necessary materials and equipment, not to mention specialized knowledge, and although possibly expensive, will be able to carry out tests for hydrogen ion activity and colorimetric or spectrophotometric analysis, including atomic absorption spectrophotometry. The principles of these tests are based on the absorption of electromagnetic radiation by chemical substances and their measurement, so they will be able to tell you which substances are present and which aren't. You may even uncover an unknown substance that warrants further investigation. In summary, soil and vegetation analysis can be quite exacting, and may require specialist help to assess and evaluate fully all your survey results.

PHOTOGRAPHIC AND VIDEO ANALYSIS

Any one of us can take a photograph, and some of us can take a photograph of what we think is a UFO. These days, it is relatively easy to 'manufacture' a UFO photograph using well-known photographic techniques or computer software, as happened not too long ago with an Italian picture that was widely published and destined to become internationally infamous as the 'proof' of a government cover-up. The picture showed an alleged UFO just inside a military aircraft hangar. It was subsequently shown to be a hoax, a picture made using the Adobe Photoshop computer program – good advertising for the software, but bad publicity for ufology.

If you find something in a much-trumpeted photograph which tells you that what it shows is obviously not an alien craft, it is important that you do not rubbish the photographer as a result. People's beliefs and perceptions are funny things, and the hapless photographer may really believe that they have captured a UFO on film, so it can sometimes be embarrassing for them to have it pointed out that it is nothing of the sort. Be tactful and diplomatic, but honest. If results are inconclusive, then say so. Ask if they would mind having the photographs sent away for professional analysis. If they have nothing to hide, this shouldn't be a problem, but that said, you should make a few copies from the original first, as it is not unknown for really good UFO photographs mysteriously to 'go walkabout'.

It is a simple enough mistake to misidentify mundane objects as UFOs, and it is equally easy to misinterpret unexpected images that appear on a photograph. I have received well over 200 photographs from one source alone, who states that the UFOs he claims are in the photographs were not always visible to the naked eye at the time that the photographs were taken, and only showed up following development of the film. This mysterious appearance of unexpected images on film is a common enough occurrence, and indeed many such credible photographs have been offered as evidence of extraterrestrial visitations, but unfortunately most of these UFO photographs contain nothing more unusual than the results of developing, film or camera faults.

Because of this, we now need to take a look at some of the problems associated with photographic evidence. Not that what follows will turn you into an instant expert – however, it should give you some starting points from which to begin an analysis of 'photographic evidence'. Perhaps I am simply jaded, but I find that going in with a negative attitude (no pun intended!) towards the photograph puts me in a better position to be critical and, hopefully, more objective. This is not a treatise on photography and photographic techniques, and so what follows is merely a list of instances which might indicate that further investigation is required – or not, as the case may be. Beyond access to a reasonable computer and decent image editing/enhancement software, no special equipment is needed, although a magnifying glass might be handy.

Perhaps the first thing to do with any suspect photograph is to examine it as a whole, and compare it with details on the incident report form and with witness testimony. For example, what kind of photograph is it? Is there a sequence of pictures on the roll, or are the pictures separated by other mundane pictures? A series of pictures will provide far more information, while an interrupted sequence (which can be found by noting the manufacturer's frame numbers) suggests a set-up of the photographs and therefore a hoax – particularly where the witness is unwilling or unable to provide the pictures that interrupt the sequence of UFO pictures. Was a filter used, and if so, what type? Was there any grease on the lense? Is the film from a Polaroid camera, a 35mm SLR (single lens reflex), a 110 cartridge camera, or are they digital photographs? What kind of lens was used? What kind of film? What developing process was used, and who undertook it? These determinations are important, as they may influence the way in which you, or an expert, examine other elements of the photograph, and may be useful information to have if it becomes necessary to pass the photograph 'up the line'. If possible, visit the site at the same time of day that the photograph was allegedly taken. Look at the shadows: are they consistent with the photograph with regard to length, angle, the sun's position and so on? Measure and check the distances to known site landmarks in the photograph with those reported by the witness.

Record as much information as you can about the photograph, including the date it was taken, the location, make and model of camera, film type and speed, shutter speed and any other technical details. Even things like the age of the film (contrary to popular belief, they do not have infinite lifetimes), how and where it had been stored, for how long and under what conditions, will all have a bearing upon the results of the final analysis. You can usually obtain such details from the witness or photographer – and if you are really lucky, you might be able to obtain the undeveloped film while it is still in the camera. If possible, ensure that the film has been neither wound on nor rewound, and that all settings have remained unchanged since the photograph(s) was (were) taken.

The advantage of this is twofold. First, you should be able to return to the scene to take another photograph from the same position, at the same time of day, in the same direction, under the same conditions, and of the same subject (minus the anomaly, or unless the anomaly *was* the subject), in order to provide another photograph for comparison of detail such as lighting, shadows, environmental effects, distance from the photographer's position to landmarks in the picture, and so on. Plus, of course, you will be able to verify the pictorial sequence for yourself. Details of the photograph can be verified by checking the sky background with known or recorded weather conditions at the time – contact the meteorological office. Second, if the film is still in the camera it implies that neither the film nor the camera has been tampered with since the photograph was taken. This can make life very much easier, especially if the subsequent photographs show similar anomalies when printed, which in effect renders the photograph possibly suspect because of probable film or camera fault.

If you are dealing with a Polaroid film, the film-still-in-camera scenario is not really an option. It also means that there is no negative available for examination, and for computer enhancement – this can still be done, but the results are not likely to be as conclusive as with a negative. However, it should still be possible to return to the site and re-shoot the photograph as above. It could also be argued that there is less chance of a hoax with a Polaroid camera, at least inasmuch as tampering with the negative is concerned, although it is still possible to 'set up' a photograph. Again, it is possible to verify the order in which the pictures were taken, by comparing the maker's sequential numbering of the prints with witness testimony.

The next thing to do is to examine the photograph under a magnifying glass. Is the grain (the quality of the print, if you like) consistent across the entire photograph, or could the object or anomaly have been superimposed in some way? Could there be a mundane, rational or natural explanation for the anomaly? Could the photograph be not the original, but an enlargement? Could it be a photograph of a photograph, with something else added? Does it 'look' right? If not, then you have reason to be suspicious. For example, is the background in focus but the object not? Could this be due to motion blur? This could imply that the object is moving, or it could be because it is closer to the lens than stated – this has implications for the size of the object, so compare it with witness testimony. A smaller, closer object can produce on the photograph an object that appears to be larger and much further away. The sharpness of focus may provide a few clues, especially where there are reference points in the picture such as trees or buildings, whose heights or distances from the observer are known or can be measured.

Conversely, is the object in focus, but the background out of focus? This might imply that the photographer 'tracked' the object with the camera as it moved, but it could equally imply that there should be evidence of camera-shake or motion blur across the entire photo, and motion blur should be consistent with the object being tracked. Again, compare with witness testimony.

Remember, too, that some autofocus cameras will have their focus sensitivity in the centre of the frame, in a small area. Thus, if the focus is fixed upon a background point (i.e. infinity, in which case the object will be nowhere near the centre of the photograph), then the near and middle distance will be out of focus. If such a camera is being used and the anomaly is in the centre of the frame, then it should be in focus. If not, question it. Under dim or dark conditions, autofocus functions often don't work, thus requiring flash and manual focusing in order to take photographs. A hoax picture that fuelled speculation and debate for ten years was taken by schoolboy Alex Birch, by painting UFOs on a window pane and then photographing the scene through it.

What about lighting and shadows: are they consistent with the anomaly's position in the photograph, with regard to natural sunlight or any artificial light sources that may have been used? For example, compare lengths and directions of shadows in the foreground, middle distance and background with each other and any shadow cast by the anomaly: are they consistent with the object being where the witness says it was in relation to the light source? Is the object casting a shadow, and is that shadow where it should be? And talking of lighting, remember that in the northern hemisphere, north-facing buildings and objects never receive full sunlight, except around midsummer, when sunlight falls on these buildings or objects very briefly, just after dawn and just before dusk. In the southern hemisphere the situation is, of course, reversed, but the midsummer rule still applies. This is a small point, perhaps, but none the less valid for photoanalytical purposes.

The closer the light source is to the objects in the picture, the greater the diversity of the angles of those objects' shadows in relation to each other. If it is possible to measure both the height of an object and the length of its shadow, then the position of the sun can be calculated using an ephemeris or nautical almanac. The sun moves one degree in four minutes, ten degrees in 40 minutes. As a rough guide, a hand held at arm's length with the fingers spread will measure out 22 degrees between the tip of the thumb and the tip of the extended little finger. If the thumb is tucked into the palm, then the remaining four fingers will measure out approximately 15 degrees, and if you then make a fist, the width of one knuckle is about two degrees. From this, and the measurement of shadow lengths and directions, it can be seen that if a witness claims that a sequence of photographs was taken a few seconds apart, but the sun has apparently moved through a few degrees between the first and last shots, you know they are lying.

Next, look at the 'UFO' image itself. What kind of image is it? Is it a 'ghost'? A blob of colour? A blur? A trail? A cloud? Or is it something more tangible – an obviously structured object? These latter are obviously more use for publicity purposes, while the former usually indicate camera or development faults. Below are listed just a few of the problems that may be encountered with photography and photographs that might be misinterpreted as UFOs. An expert would probably identify hundreds more, but at least you should get some idea of what to look for and how such problems might be rectified. Once you have an understanding of the basics, it should be easier for you to decide whether or not a photograph is worth the extra time, money and resources that will need to be spent on further examination and analysis.

Fogging May be misconstrued as a UFO or anomalous entity, or the result of such an object's proximity. Fogging sometimes appears on films as a result of light entering the body of the camera, usually through the back where the film is loaded. The result is often bars, lines, crescents or rings of fog on a print and negative, which frequently manifest as an orange or yellow discoloration around the edge or base of the photograph. A loose or faulty catch is often the cause. Fogging may also occur through exposure to X-ray machines, such as those found at airports, and the greater the exposure, the greater the likelihood of fogging. Loading a film in sunlight often results in bright orange fogging streaks occurring parallel to the edges on those frames closest to the opening in the film's cassette. Check the camera by loading a short length of unexposed film, and slowly turn it around in your hands near to a bright lamp so that all parts of the camera have been exposed to the light. When processed, bars of fogging will occur on the film at the point where the light is entering the camera. Fogging may also occur where there has been some light overspill from an enlarger (particularly in black-and-white pictures).

Lens flare This usually occurs when there is a relatively bright light source (which may be just out of the frame), and also where the lens is quite old, scratched or greasy, or where the camera is a cheap one. What usually happens is that the light becomes spread in shape and size, and the result is called flare. If the light source is out of the picture, lens flare may manifest as bars, rays or lines of light radiating out from the point of origin of the light source. If the light source is in the picture, it may be seen as a star-like shape due to flare. Such flare may be misidentified as a UFO. Check the effect in the picture against the size and shape of the lens diaphragm and the exposure time, as these are the two elements used by photographers to control lens flare. The larger the aperture used, the more circular the light spread is likely to be. More modern and expensive cameras usually have anti-flare coatings applied to all lenses, thus reducing the incidence of lens flare. Flare is more likely when there is dirt, grease or a scratch on the lens.

Iris flare This manifests as a series of ghost-like images of the shape (usually hexagonal) of the aperture on the film, which are likely to be spread out in a line across the print. The more complex the lens, and the more elements it con-tains, the more aperture ghosts are likely to be formed. Droplets of water in the air close to the lens produce the effect of a number of lights, each one resulting in one or more such ghosts. These ghosts may be pink, blue, red, orange, etc., as they take on the reflection colour of any surface lens coating. Iris flare hap-pens when there is a particularly bright light source imaged just off-centre or even just outside the frame. It is unlikely to occur in direct vision (but see lens flare, above) or twin reflex cameras, in cameras fitted with the appropriate lens hood, or in situations where a light source is well outside the frame by a rea-sonable distance. Flare can also occur indoors and from any light source, including studio lights and windows.

Double exposure This may happen as a result of failure to advance the film between shots, although it is unlikely to happen on most modern cameras due to their design. In some larger-format cameras it is possible to double-expose by accident, but generally speaking if only one or two frames on an entire roll are double-exposed, it suggests that there is a fault in the camera. If all frames on the roll are double-exposed, it is likely that the roll has been run through the camera twice. Other apparent double exposures can occur where a photo-graph has been shot through a reflective surface, such as a car or train window.

Damaged film Sometimes the result of film storage, damp may cause strange marks, discoloration and odd patches of colour to arise because of condensa-tion causing water droplets to form on the surface of the film within the cas-sette. This in turn causes the emulsion to swell, and it is not unknown for fungus to grow on the film under these conditions. Unwrapping cold film under warm and humid conditions may cause this to happen, and the film may have been put into the camera before a sufficient period of time had elapsed to allow the film to warm up to the surrounding temperature. The only real problem with photographs taken in hot climates (that are not subject to other mishaps or mishandling) is a colour shift in the film itself once it is developed, especially if the film has been stored for any length of time prior to developing. Water marks may arise either through excessive condensation on the film, or from immersion in water that is not immediately wiped dry. These generally manifest as pink or reddish blotches or marks on the prints.

Dark crescents or marks These may be the result of poor loading of the film into the camera. What sometimes happens is that the film gets slightly bent or creased while being loaded into the film spiral. The resulting pressure damages the emulsion on the film, and the damage manifests when developed as dark crescents or lines.

Development faults There are a number:

- Streaky white marks on black-and-white negatives may be caused when the film touches on itself as it is loaded on to the spool for the development tank. The developing solution cannot then reach the touching parts of the film and the result is light or creamy white marks on the negative. These will then, of course, be transferred to the prints unless noticed. Creasing the film while loading it on to the spool also causes white marks or crescents (see above).

- A bright blue or white streak is usually caused by chemical contamination or insufficient agitation of the fluids during development. The latter usually occurs as pale bands in highlighted areas of the frame such as patches of sky, and next to the sprocket holes (along the edge of the film, that allow it to be wound on or rewound).

- A slightly blurred black line appearing on one or more prints that wasn't visible through the viewfinder or on the lens may be a hair or other debris inside the camera body. Check the camera and eliminate as necessary.

- White spots or flecks on a print are usually the result of dust on the negatives. They are obviously more profound on prints that have been enlarged.

- Fingerprints on negatives can have some pretty bizarre effects once printed, and are the result of poor handling of negatives.

- Coloured lines running parallel to the frames' long edge across prints and negatives are usually the result of dust or grit in the camera, which scratch the emulsions as the film is wound on.

○ Other developing faults include 'static marks', which appear as jagged black lines caused by electrical discharge when dry film is rubbed. Small, sharp-edged black specks may be caused by chemical dust or undissolved particles in the developer. When dry, films occasionally become accidentally splashed with chemicals, resulting in small droplet-shaped marks, sometimes with darker edges. Uneven drying causes similar damage. Small and distinct round spots which appear clear or light in density are caused by air bubbles clinging to the surface of the film during development.

Basic computer enhancement of photographic evidence

Anyone with a personal computer and the appropriate image-editing software can have a bash at enhancing photographic images, and the techniques which are employed can all highlight suspect elements in photographs, such as threads suspending an object reported as a UFO. Several excellent packages are available including Photoshop, Graphics Workshop, Paint Shop Pro and ProImage Plus, all of which allow basic manipulation of photographic images.

You will, of course, need to scan the photographs into your computer first, or have them digitized to disk. Once in the computer, they should be converted to monotone (black and white) – this makes manipulating the image both quicker and easier. Particularly useful techniques with which you should make yourself familiar before you actually need to use them include edge enhancement, embossing and image sharpening. Remember, though, that as the picture is enlarged it becomes coarser, as the original scanned image's pixels (picture cells) are also enlarged.

More complex photoanalysis is best left to the experts – photographic labs should be listed in your local telephone directory. Some of the larger UFO organizations such as MUFON and BUFORA have their own experts 'on tap'. Contact them for details of how to submit photographic or video evidence.

Video analysis

With video analysis, the technicalities really are best left to the experts, but there are a few pointers that you might find useful for an initial examination of video evidence.

The expression 'the camera never lies' is itself a lie. However, most video misidentifications are of either (a) an aeroplane's navigation or landing lights, or (b) the planet Venus, with the occasional Jupiter or Sirius thrown in for good measure. On video, aircraft light colours are usually lost, and thus are seen on tape as moving white lights. Remember also that without a fixed and stationary point of reference, moving lights in a video may be nothing more than camera movement. Without at least two such fixed and stationary reference points, apparent changes in size, brightness or motion away from or towards the camera may be no more than changes in zoom focusing, auto or otherwise. Autofocus mechanisms need something to focus on, and they will thus hunt for a subject on which to fix. This 'hunting' may result in blobs of light becoming bright points of light, and vice versa.

Jeff Sainio (MUFON's photoanalyst) also points out that birds or insects flitting about may not always be seen during the original filming, with the result that when the tape is later examined they may appear to be flying behind tree branches or through clouds – thus giving a false impression of size and distance from the camcorder. This is because they may be 'smeared out' from motion as they pass in front of objects or materials of a similar brightness and colour, and their small size prevents an accurate colour display.

When sending videotape away for analysis, apply the same conditions as for photographs and record as much information about the film and its provenance as possible. Again, make any necessary checks against witness testimony, weather conditions, etc. as are needed to verify the film's authenticity and validity. Although photographic and video evidence can be ambiguous, it can often corroborate or contradict witness statements.

UFO LANDING-SITE TIME ANOMALY TEST

This field investigation, originally designed and set out by MUFON, is based upon some new isorelativity theories developed by Professor Santilli and others (see Chapter 7). It is because of these isorelativities that it is expected that some of the anomalous behaviour exhibited by UFOs will include time-distortion fields, both on board the ship itself and as a residual effect at alleged UFO landing sites. Such time anomalies are not expected to appear at every site, but may indeed be apparent at many.

The test presented here is modified only very slightly from MUFON's original for reasons of immediate practicality, time limitation and accessibility. MUFON would be grateful for feedback concerning any anomalies associated with UFOs that you may discover during the course of your investigations (see Useful Addresses). They may also provide you with the required watch kits, but unless you can get them fairly quickly they may only be of limited value, due to the lessening effects of the distorted fields with increasing time. All the necessary data sheets are provided on pages 185–188.

Pre-test preparations

For the test itself, you will need five identical wristwatches (MUFON may supply them on request), synchronized, and weatherproofed by removing the straps and placing them in re-sealable plastic envelopes. If possible, once the watches have been synchronized (and they should be fairly reliable timepieces if you wish to limit the scientific variable), remove the winding mechanism to render them tamperproof. Number the watches 1–5; watch 5 will act as the off-site 'control' and must remain undisturbed in the custody of the field investigator, in a safe location; apart from the time when measurements are being taken, it should be kept well away from the landing site.

To synchronize the watches, take the control watch and as soon as the second hand reaches '00', look at watch 1 and record the exact time in hours, minutes and seconds on the Watch Inspection Data Sheet (see page 185). Repeat the procedure for each remaining watch (2–4), entering the data as appropriate. If there are any differences at this point, record them in the 'difference' field on the form. If there is no difference, enter '00'. This test should be repeated if the watches are not to be placed on-site within 48 hours of the initial test. In fact, if circumstances permit, it's not a bad idea to do this anyway, if only to determine any operational differences between the watches before the time anomaly test commences. Before placing the watches *in situ*, check the site and the watches for any magnetic fields, and record any apparent anomalous needle deviations.

Landing site test procedure

Survey the site for suitable watch locations and mark them, ready for later. Watch 1 should be located in the middle of the landing site, watch 2 halfway along the radius of the circle, watch 3 on the perimeter of the landing site, and watch 4 about the site's width again away from the perimeter. All the watches should be positioned in a straight line from watch 1 in the centre to watch 4 well outside the alleged landing site (see diagram). Watch 5 is the control, and is kept separately away from the landing site. Make a map of the site, noting its dimensions, and indicate the direction of magnetic north and true north, allowing for the magnetic deviation (if known). The map should be to scale, and should give the scale of reference (e.g. 1cm = 1m).

Test the site for local magnetic deviations, using a compass or other magnetic field detector. Flight maps used by pilots of light aircraft show local

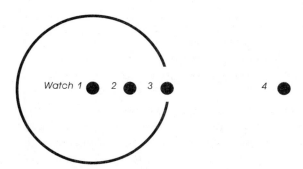

Time anomaly test at alleged UFO landing sites. The watches are positioned along the radial line at the points shown. Watch 4 should be placed at least one landing site's width away, and watch 5, the control watch, should be kept away altogether, preferably at the investigator's home.

magnetic deviations, but remember that the area might have a large deviation, due possibly to underground ore reserves or whatever, but any such map should indicate if this is the case. The whole area should be checked, not just that within the defined landing site. MUFON suggest that this be accomplished by marking magnetic north well outside the landing site, and then describing a spiral outwards from the centre of the landing site of at least two 360-degree turns, marking any strong deviations in the magnetic field as you walk. Continue this spiral out to some point beyond one and a half diameters.

More specifically, also check the chosen watch locations and record any magnetic fields on the magnetism data sheet, then check the watches themselves for magnetic fields and record accordingly.

If another time synchronization test is to be undertaken, do it now, before the watches are buried at the predetermined locations. Enter the results in the '1st visit' field on the field data sheet. All data results should be entered in 24-hour format. Now, leaving the control watch well away from the landing site, take the remaining four watches and bury them 5–8cm (2–3in) into the soil at the selected locations using a trowel, spoon or similar tool. You should wear gloves at this stage, and be careful to avoid breathing in any dust or soil that you disturb during the procedure. If you have a face mask, wear it. Mark the locations of the watches on your site map.

The first time checks can be made one hour after the initial burying of the watches, and you will now need to take watch 5 into the site to take readings. If, following the first test, time anomalies are found, conduct the tests at one-hour intervals thereafter for as long as is possible or practical, or for as long as there continue to be changes. It may be necessary to use additional data sheets. The reason for these multiple tests is to determine a possible decay rate for a time-distortion field, and to track the intensity of the field affecting the watches. Obviously, the more readings that are taken, the more useful the final data, but for them to be statistically viable you will need a minimum of 30 readings. Of course, it may be that you are not able to take more than one or two readings a day, but don't let this put you off – any data gained is not wasted data, even though the purists may disagree. Even if you cannot take another reading for seven days, record those readings, and if no discrepancies are noted, enter them as your final data. I recommend that you do not run the test for more than ten days; MUFON suggest seven days as being adequate. In any event, throughout the test remember to take watch 5 to the site watches, and not the other way around.

Each time you perform a time synchronization test, you should also repeat the magnetic field variance test, entering the data on the magnetism data sheet as appropriate. Check the watches with the compass as well, and record any changes accordingly.

ORGANIZING A SKYWATCH

A skywatch is an organized event during which the participants actively look for anomalous aerial phenomena – that's UFOs. They can last from an hour or two right up to a weekend or even longer. The number of participants will depend entirely upon the willingness of people to attend, sometimes not coming on duty until the early hours of the morning, although my own experience has been that skywatches are ideal opportunities for like-minded individuals to get together to share a common interest, a beer or two, and the odd joke. The social aspect of skywatches is valuable for cementing relations between different groups or individuals who may have travelled many miles to attend. Very often, the appearance of a UFO is purely incidental, a bonus if you like, but the national skywatches organized by Britain's Quest International and *UFO Magazine* have produced several interesting incidents, plus some useful contacts and enduring friendships.

Of course, you do not have to be a member of any particular group or clique to enjoy a skywatch, and there is absolutely nothing to stop you undertaking one on your own, although it is generally wiser from a health and safety point of view to have at least one other person accompanying you, as accidents can and do happen.

So, how do you go about organizing a skywatch? First, decide where you are going to hold it. The best places are generally in elevated positions, away from towns or cities where light pollution may interfere with visibility and atmospheric clarity. The location should be safe, and accessible to emergency vehicles. It is a good idea to be in position well before sundown in case you need to familiarize yourself with the area. Fires should not be lit, for two reasons: first, they can crucify your night vision, and second, they can get out of hand, and if you are holding your skywatch on private land you could end up facing a lawsuit. Some landowners, such as the National Trust in the UK, allow free access on to their land but impose bylaws, and these generally include the prohibition of fire-lighting.

The location should preferably be away from main roads, as passing car headlights can also play havoc with night vision, and once lost it may take around half an hour to recover it fully. On back roads or along tracks, keep away from the road itself, as speeding vehicles or drivers who have had one drink too many may be using them to avoid the local police after a night out. This is particularly important when there are youngsters in your group, who may become bored and wander off in search of adventure: what we don't want is misadventure. Keep them safe by insisting they wear reflective armbands or something similar. If group members do wander off, then make sure they have a torch with them – a red lens filter will light their way without impairing night vision.

Larger events have their own special considerations. A first-aid kit is a must, and a chemical toilet is desirable.

Once on-site, what equipment will you need? Deckchairs are useful because of the various reclining positions that they offer, from which to observe the sky without developing 'whiplash' or ailments caused by lying on hard, damp ground. Items like kip-mats, sleeping bags or even quilts can all help to make the evening a more enjoyable experience. Even in summer, temperatures can plummet once a clear night has set in, and warmth is essential to a successful event.

Talking of weather, there's nothing more disheartening than setting up for an evening skywatch only to have the heavens open upon you, so have your waterproofs handy. Give me a frost any time: I've held a skywatch at −15°C (5°F) – albeit without seeing anything unusual – but a good sleeping bag, warm jacket and trousers, flask of hot coffee, woolly hat and handwarmer can do a lot to alleviate any anticipated discomfort. However, if you don't fancy waking up with ice covering your sleeping bag, check the weather reports before you set out.

Apart from a full flask or at least the means to make a hot drink, food is another important consideration. When we are cold, we shiver. This is the body's way of generating heat, but it uses energy. Rations such as Kendal mint cake, chocolate, glucose tablets or biscuits will help to replenish energy levels and thus to keep you warm. If you are consuming high-protein foods, however, remember that the body requires extra fluids in order to break them down, so you are likely to get thirsty later on.

Tents are handy but difficult to see through, although they have their uses as a base, or as somewhere to retire to for a nap during long skywatches. If your car is nearby, then by all means use that. It has the advantage of a heater, but don't poison your colleagues with exhaust fumes as you run the engine to keep the heater going.

Once night has descended, topographical horizons can be lost against the backdrop of a dark sky. Familiarization with the terrain is therefore important so that you do not misidentify distant car headlights, outdoor security lights turning on and off, or people with torches as UFOs. Using a compass, set out twigs or markers denoting the cardinal points, emphasizing north. This makes things easier during sightings and the ensuing chaos as excitement takes over and details get overlooked.

Equipment for the skywatch should be selected from the list in Chapter 1; radios, stereos or musical instruments make useful diversions during quiet or inactive spells. Alcohol may be permitted, but don't expect anyone to believe you if you have a major sighting while under the influence!

Once you are up and running, you should keep a written record or taped account of the evening's activities – a log, if you like. At least one person should be nominated for this, or two if one anticipates taking a nap during the night. If there is an incident during your skywatch, it should not be discussed by the witnesses until such time as the details of the events have been duly logged and written down. Each witness should write down their own version of events, without discussion, as soon after the event as is practicable. In this way, the result will be a truer and more accurate picture of events, and the information can be analysed and disseminated when appropriate.

Details of national skywatches are published in the UFO literature, along with instructions on how to contact the organizers during the event. By doing this, your group effectively becomes a participant in a much larger event, and indeed may be able to provide input into the bigger picture, especially if you are called upon to track an object or phenomenon that is headed your way. Conversely, you can register your own sightings with the national organizers immediately by telephone, and then hopefully others will pick up the threads and continue to track your sighting. Remember that the more witnesses there are to an event, the more credible it becomes.

Finally, suppose it is your group that witnesses a UFO – what then? There are in fact certain 'rules of engagement' that should be adhered to, if only for your own safety, and it's as well to be aware of them before the event actually happens. These 'rules', listed below, presuppose that you will witness a landed, crashed or close-by UFO; if not, simply fill out your report form, or better still, have someone else – from a neighbouring group if at all possible – fill it out with you. This limits the 'fudge factor' and removes the personal value judgements and prejudices from the final report.

Close encounters: rules of engagement
It should be fairly obvious that if you witness a landed UFO for yourselves, you should not approach it. This might seem an odd warning, considering that you are supposed to be UFO investigators, but you would be surprised at how easy it becomes to throw caution to the wind and get carried away by the excitement and the desire to see more. This is not a good idea. Hopefully, you will go the other way. In most cases, abductees aren't so lucky and do not have an option. You do – use it. The following 'rules of engagement' were first published in an official US government publication (although I forget exactly which), and I present them here in an expanded form because I believe they are reasonable, largely common sense, and should not be ignored.

- Do not touch, or even attempt to touch, a UFO that has landed or is hovering on or close to the ground. It has probably passed through the Earth's atmospheric envelope and at the very least will have a heated hull due to friction. There is also a risk of radiation, and radiation sickness cannot be cured. There may be a discharge of steam from contact with the ground, or other gases or substances ejected or vented from the ship itself. Electromagnetic effects are also likely, and quite possibly incidental infrasound or ultrasound – and don't forget what happened to Travis Walton when he got a little too close...

○ Do not stand underneath a hovering UFO either – there are risks from radiation, electromagnetic effects or beam technology, and again, the possible threat of abduction.

○ Do not try to be a hero and attempt contact with any extraterrestrials you witness. They may perceive any movement on your part as an act of aggression, so make no gestures whatsoever and back away slowly, retreating to a safe distance. The chances are that you are no diplomat, and you are unlikely to speak their language anyway. Remember that you have no idea of what their agenda might be, and equally, they may have no idea of yours.

○ If you can, make a note of the date, time and location of your sighting, and note down any details regarding the craft, its effects and the activities of the occupants. If you have a camera handy, take some photographs, but don't expect them to turn out well if you are in close proximity to the craft. Fill out any incident report forms as appropriate – ideally, an investigator from another group should do this with you, as I have said, to avoid your personal bias or subconscious influences affecting the final analysis.

○ Do not attempt to pick up any artefacts or substances that the craft leaves behind. You may need specialized equipment in order to do so, and should at the very least verify the safety of the site with regards to radiation, time distortion, etc. You might also be in danger of damaging any on-site evidence by trampling over the site, and may be sued by the landowner for trespass, or tried for theft or criminal damage. Undertake any appropriate tests prior to touching anything of suspected extraterrestrial origin – there may be extraterrestrial microbes on it, which once inside your system may cause you a painful and horrible death, not to mention any epidemics you could inadvertently trigger once the organisms have had time to incubate and reproduce. It would be an extreme irony if, after travelling light years in peaceful intent, the ETs inadvertently wiped us out through the ill-advised contraction of the extraterrestrial equivalent of a cold.

○ Leave the area quickly, and inform the authorities as appropriate: they have all the specialized equipment that you might not. Besides this, you might have to consider that what you have witnessed could in fact be a classified military project. Always remember that it may be necessary to balance the needs of your own safety against the need to investigate.

10 Crop Circles

Crop circles are closely associated with UFO activity, and so we need to take a brief look at the background to this phenomenon and some identifying criteria. If you want to pursue the topic in more detail, a number of specialist books are available (see Bibliography).

Crop circles have appeared in many cereal crops including corn, barley, wheat, oilseed rape, oats and rye. They have even appeared in long grass. In the UK, they usually appear in the southern counties of England, with many occurrences in or around Wiltshire, Hampshire and the areas surrounding Avebury and Stonehenge, as well as at the foot of the White Horse and Silbury Hill. Similar phenomena are reported to have appeared on polar ice and in the open sea, one of which is known as 'marine lightwheels' (see pages 154–155). More recently, the phenomenon has become more widespread internationally, with many more reports coming out of European countries and the US than in previous years.

Contrary to popular opinion, crop circles are nothing new. Historical records date back to 1663, when a Mr Hart in Wiltshire recorded seeing many small creatures dancing round and round inside such a circle. In a woodcut of 1678 there is a depiction of the 'Mowing Devil' of Hertfordshire, showing a very exactly laid circle which appeared in a crop of oats. In 1946, two circles appeared on top of Pepperbox Hill, near Salisbury in Wiltshire. Near Winchester in Hampshire, every year for 28 years prior to 1986 crop circles would appear on a farm owned by Simon Brown. His father used to point them out to him when he was a child, and so he was not surprised when they started appearing elsewhere. In Whiteparish, Wiltshire, another farmer remembered seeing them for many of the 29 years during which he was farming.

Crop circles have increased in number since the late 1970s. Aerial photographic records of the phenomenon for the Wessex area go back more than 50 years. On 10 August 1965, a crop circle was found just off the Warminster–Westbury road in Wiltshire, following a UFO encounter. Then, on 7 September, another close encounter was followed by the discovery of another circle nearby. At this time, the press sensationalized the issue by referring to them as 'UFO nests', as they were believed to be UFO landing sites. In 1987, 40 circles were discovered in the Hampshire environs alone.

George Wingfield (a graduate of Trinity College, Dublin, with a Master's degree in natural sciences) and others have described the characteristics of crop circles and pictograms (the more elaborate designs which include linear and geometrical features) thus:

- A geometric form, but with the imperfect precision of most circles (+/−2 per cent perfectly round).
- Circular, ring, elliptical, rectangular or triangular-shaped designs.
- Sharp edge demarcation between the upright and the flatly laid crop, with a clearly defined, sometimes notched, serrated or interlaced edge. These features alone, because of their accuracy and complexity, go against the arguments for hoaxing.
- Very few circles cross field boundaries.
- Usually found in wheat or barley crops, but circles have appeared in other crops including grass.
- Usually appear between late spring and early autumn, once the crop is mature.
- Stems are bent (often at 90 degrees) but not broken or damaged when found, and they continue to grow and mature while in the new positions. On occasion, some stems have been torn from the soil and deposited outside the circle, while other stems have been braided together.
- Circles or pictograms often have several layers, with the lower layers pointing in different directions to the ones above them.
- The same circle may exhibit various laying directions – clockwise, anti-clockwise, away from centre, straight, swastika shaped, complex, etc. – but always with near-perfect geometrical precision.
- Crop circles are often formed parallel to ground structures and/or tram-lines (lines made by the wheels of farm vehicles).
- The phenomenon often appears overnight, usually without eyewitnesses, although a few have appeared during the hours of daylight.
- Fields with circles are often revisited, with new circles appearing in the same field or with new additions to existing circles, as if to complete them.
- There are extraordinarily diverse patterns and formations.
- The diameter of the circles varies between 1.5m (5ft) and 60m (200ft), with pictogram lengths of 14–200m (45–650ft).
- Crop circle complexity has increased between 1978 and 1997.
- The phenomenon often appears in close proximity to prehistoric mounds, sites and monuments.
- There are frequent UFO sightings prior to the discovery of crop circles.

- Unusual noises are often heard inside crop circles, and a 5kHz buzzing has been recorded within them.

- Dowsing rods seem able to detect long-lasting energy patterns found within and around crop circles and pictograms.

- There appears to be an intelligent reaction by the circle makers to researchers' discussions and theories regarding the phenomenon, apparently in an attempt to communicate and lead us in their desired direction.

- Recent studies have shown that there are changes in the molecular structure of the affected plants, which is consistent with the application of intense heat for very short duration, possibly at microwave frequencies.

- Atmospheric conditions do not seem to be significant, and circles have appeared in all weathers.

- Circles would appear to be created in seconds rather than hours, since the longer it takes to bend the stalks into position, the greater the chance of damage occurring to them.

Famous crop circle researcher Pat Delgado believes that all the crop-flattening, swirling, whorling and swathing takes place at the same time, on the basis that there must be a maximum upper time limit for the transformation of the crop stems from vertical to horizontal positions, beyond which the stems would suffer from whiplash. He suggests that all the stems move in a steady, regular manner, and, once moving, would be formed into a circle or pictogram within about 20 seconds.

It is all too easy for the sceptics to maintain that all crop circles are hoaxes, particularly in view of the publicity given to two gentlemen known as 'Doug and Dave', who created their own crop circles in order to perpetrate a deliberate hoax and then went public with it a long time after the event. In the meantime, a lot of well-meaning investigators, scientists and others had formed their own pet theories, and even went on record on radio, television and in the newspapers saying that these hoaxed circles were the genuine article because of this, that or the other criterion. Naturally, they all ended up mightily embarrassed once the truth was discovered, and the immediate result was that the phenomenon and its adherents lost all credibility in the eyes of both the media and the public.

Some researchers have highlighted the continuing interest in circles and pictograms shown by the military, even suggesting and providing circumstantial evidence to the effect that the discrediting of researchers and the phenomenon itself was a deliberate ploy by the military and intelligence agencies to divert interest and attention away from it and effectively kill it stone dead. Many reasons have been put forward for this and can be found in the specialist books, but remember that for Doug and Dave to be responsible for all the crop circles that are reported they must have been very busy indeed, given that several circles have appeared on the same dates, often at great distances from each other and close to roads and habitations, and that someone, somewhere, would have seen them at some point in their several-year hoaxing career. Furthermore, their wives apparently knew nothing of these activities – and I'm sure my wife would wonder where I was if I was out all night for months on end wielding ladders, ropes, bits of wire and so on. The simple fact is that it would be impossible for all the circles created in any one season to be the result of hoaxers, although I have no doubt that other successful hoaxers do exist.

The upshot is that is beyond question that the crop circle phenomenon does exist, but as to whether this is as a direct result of extraterrestrial activity – the jury is still out, and the debate is far from over.

11 Identified Flying Objects

Identified Flying Objects (IFOs) are likely to represent the larger percentage of sightings that are reported to you (estimates of misidentified phenomena reported as UFOs vary between 90 and 98 per cent), and it is as well to be aware of the kind of things that may be reported as UFOs when in fact they are anything but. A little time and care in investigating the likelihood of a mundane explanation for a report can do a lot to ameliorate the negative press that ufology tends to receive at the hands of the popular media and the sceptics, which often results from a reporter or sceptic doing a better job of investigating a report than some UFO investigators.

It seems that most UFO sightings (up to 75 per cent) take place during the hours of darkness, between 9pm and 7am, with a peak at around 3am. (Some researchers believe that there is another, smaller peak in sightings at around 5am, but this may have more to do with early workers being up and about and hence potential witnesses.) It has been suggested that this is because we are generally more alert at night, and strange lights in the sky are more likely to attract our attention, even while driving. It makes good logistical sense, too, from any visiting ETs' viewpoint, as most of us with diurnal rhythms are safely tucked up in bed, and only our nocturnal brethren such as shift workers, astronomers or those with an active social life are likely to be around. For the same reasons, our own military are likely to test-fly new or exotic aircraft during these hours, when there are fewer accidental ground-based witnesses likely to make embarrassing observations.

The well-known British researcher Jenny Randles believes that there are over 200 mundane explanations that could account for the vast majority of UFO sightings – and therein lies half the fun of ufology, as just because a UFO is reported to you, you cannot automatically assume that it is an extraterrestrial craft. To misquote Sherlock Holmes: 'Eliminate the obvious, and whatever remains, however improbable, must be the truth.' The flowchart on page 184 might help you to eliminate the obvious, but it should, if possible, be used in conjunction with other methods, such as a computer loaded with appropriate software. There are several very good and relatively cheap astronomical packages available (Skyglobe is a good example), plus assorted professional packages relating to various disciplines. Of course, if you have the relevant fields of expertise among your group members – such as meteorologists, astronomers, aircraft experts, etc. – so much the better.

SATELLITES

Some of the most frequently reported nocturnal UFOs turn out to be satellites: artificial structures that orbit the Earth at varying heights, usually several hundred kilometres. Most of them can be seen with the naked eye, and can be observed to be moving quite quickly. I do not wish to embark on a full discourse on orbital mechanics, but it is useful to study the behaviour of satellites, as they are not all the same and do not all behave in the same way. However, once the flight pattern and behaviour of a satellite is understood, it is a fairly simple matter to determine what kind of satellite you are faced with, and its role. This can provide a new avenue of study in its own right.

Most satellites travel from west to east along their orbital paths (the usual direction of launch), and the speed at which they travel varies with the orbital height. At the very lowest orbits, a satellite must travel at around 8km (5 miles) per second (assuming a circular orbit) simply to stay aloft against the gravitational pull of the Earth. With higher orbits, the speed decreases, quickly to start with and then more slowly. At a distance of 60 Earth radii (the distance between the Earth and the moon), the required orbital velocity is down to 1km (⅝ mile) per second.

To complicate matters further, there are two other orbits worth considering: elliptical and geosynchronous. In the former, launch speed is over and above that necessary to achieve a circular orbit, the reason being that at certain latitudes the satellite payload may be unable to function effectively, as orbital mechanics dictate that a satellite's orbital diameter must pass through the centre of the Earth, and this can limit 'line of sight' of the satellite towards more northerly or southerly latitudes in relation to the angle of inclination of the satellite ('inclination' is the angle between the satellite's orbit and the Earth's equator, as shown in the diagram). To overcome this, an elliptical orbit is initiated, wherein to all intents and purposes the satellite's altitude increases during part of its orbital phase; then, by placing three or more satellites with the same function in inclined elliptical orbits, global coverage may be obtained over a full orbital period (the time taken to complete one full orbit). This is one problem that the Russians were forced to overcome with their own communication satellites, because of the latitude variations on the (former) Soviet Union land mass.

The point at which such a satellite passes closest to the Earth is called the perigee, the most distant point of its orbit is called the apogee (a simple mnemonic to remember these terms is 'perigee is paired, apogee is apart' – see diagram), while the line joining these two points is called the major axis. The speed of a satellite with an elliptical orbit varies according to its position along the orbital path and the length of the major axis: it travels fastest at the perigee, and can appear almost stationary at the apogee. Some surveillance satellites

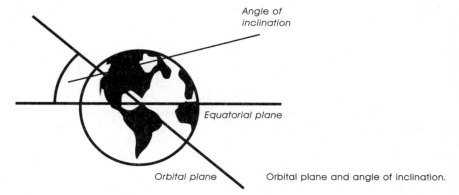

Angle of inclination

Equatorial plane

Orbital plane

Orbital plane and angle of inclination.

have only slightly elliptical orbits in order to dip low and fast over the horizon and/or their target areas.

Geosynchronous, or geostationary, orbits are not simply hovering over the Earth, although this is exactly what appears to be happening. The shortest orbital period that a satellite is able to sustain without giving way to atmospheric drag and consequent orbital decay is about 89 minutes, and occurs at an altitude of 240km (150 miles). As stated previously, the greater the altitude of a satellite, the more slowly it travels, and consequently the greater the orbital period. At an orbital height of 35,875km (22,420 miles), a satellite's orbital period will be 1,436 minutes (23.9333 hours), and is thus in synchronization with the rotation of the Earth on its polar axis – and we have a geosynchronous orbit. With a zero-degree angle of inclination (above the equator, in other words), such satellites appear to hang motionless in the night sky. However, in reality all geosynchronous satellites do have a very small angle of inclination, which is caused by the gravitational effects of the sun and the moon. Consequently, these satellites appear to describe a figure of eight over a 24-hour period, known as 'north–south station keeping', and the size of this figure of

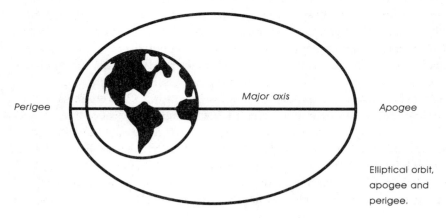

Perigee

Major axis

Apogee

Elliptical orbit, apogee and perigee.

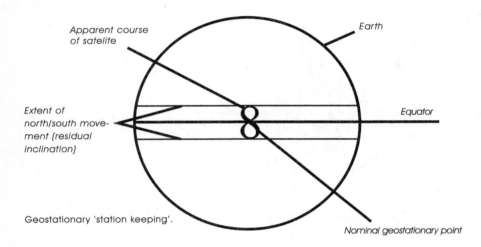

eight will depend on the actual angle of residual inclination of the perturbed orbit, but it will none the less be symmetrical (see diagram).

Satellites shine because they reflect sunlight, so brightness will depend upon the satellite's altitude, and its dimensions. Objects in lower orbits, such as the Mir space station or the Space Shuttle (Space Transportation System, to give it its proper name), often appear very bright. There are a few satellites that have angles of inclination of 90 degrees, and these may be seen moving north to south or vice versa in polar orbits. Satellites can suddenly appear, disappear, or fade in and out of view as they move into or out of eclipse – that is, leave or enter the Earth's shadow. Occasionally, it is reported that single star-like flashes of up to a few seconds' duration have been observed. This may be the result of sunlight glinting off the satellites that are too distant to see otherwise with the naked eye, or of objects passing out of and then into eclipse (the Earth's shadow). In the latter instance, this will of course depend upon the object's angle of inclination, direction of travel and apparent speed.

A useful piece of (cheaply available) software for tracking satellites is STS Orbit plus, and although it comes complete with a database in .TXT format of 170 older satellites, it explains where and how to obtain the necessary two-line element data on more recent satellites. Several astronomy and space-related magazines carry this type of information, plus advertisements for similar software. Such software usually makes pass predictions or offers graphical representations of satellite positions, ground tracks and circles of visibility, and offers a whole host of other useful features. If used in conjunction with radio-frequency monitoring on the UHF (300MHz–3GHz), SHF (3–30GHz) and EHF (30–300GHz) wavebands, a fairly detailed picture of a satellite event can be built up. Explanations and uses for these wavebands, along with full explanations of satellite and orbital mechanics, can be found in Brasseys' *Military*

Space. Your local library may have a shareware library (such as the Ramesis data bank) that can be accessed for a fee, but if you do obtain and use software in this manner, then do the decent thing and register it. There are also plenty of computer magazines advertising a wealth of available programs, plus, of course, the small ads in the relevant UFO-related publications.

Local astronomy societies and groups may be able to advise you of 'satellite' occurrences, as perhaps will any local radio amateurs, who may even be able to identify the object for you. If you have a tracking station or radar establishment nearby, they too will often be willing to help you, although it's a good idea to approach them first in writing, before you actually need their assistance, in order to establish initial contact and rapport.

SPACE DEBRIS

This can take the form of virtually anything that we care to chuck up into space, including satellites, and gravity is no respecter of political or geographical boundaries. Satellites have finite lifetimes, and sooner or later usually fall to Earth in spectacular fashion. Even at orbital altitudes, our atmosphere still exerts a drag on orbiting objects, which lowers velocity, and gravity kicks in to lower the object's orbit further. At some point, increasing atmospheric density, drag, gravity and orbital speed will take their toll, particularly at the orbital perigee, the site of maximum drag. The following apogee is subsequently lower, in ever-decreasing circles so to speak, until ultimately the friction and kinetic energy suffered by the unfortunate object cause it to break up and fall to Earth. The majority of fragments will burn up as they scream down through the upper atmosphere, but some larger fragments may actually impact upon the Earth's surface. According to the MoD's Nick Pope, RAF Fylingdales tracks approximately 7,000 items of space debris daily.

Many such fragments will end up in the sea, especially as water covers two-thirds of the world's surface. It is possible to predict the likely impact sites for such events, even if not very accurately in the early stages. The media prophets of doom usually end up looking rather silly when they pronounce that such-and-such an object is going to impact on such-and-such a place in a certain number of weeks – it's just too early to tell at that point, but as the event nears it becomes easier to predict within reasonable margins of accuracy. The relevant experts usually pinpoint final impact sites to within 80km (50 miles), and if there's a threat of impact over populated sites, warnings are usually given on radio and television.

Of course, defunct satellites are not the only objects to be classified as space junk: objects with greater mass and atmospheric resistance have a tendency to fall to Earth more slowly, but with alarming regularity. Rocket boosters, failed missiles and a whole host of other nasties, including space stations (remember Skylab?), all come down eventually, and naturally take longer to burn up than, say, the ice or dust particles that we witness as shooting stars. Many of these objects appear to flash as they tumble and fall through our atmosphere, often breaking apart in a final multi-object, multicolour display of pyrotechnics – many are ultimately destined to find their way into the UFO reports which wind up on your desk.

Again, tracking stations and radar establishments might be your first point of contact – unless, of course, the event has been publicized in the press – but remember that they may have obligations under the various secrecy laws of your nation. However, do not let that deter you.

RADAR RETURNS

We have mentioned radar several times now, without clarifying what it actually does, how it works, or how radar returns themselves can be mistaken for UFOs. 'Radar' is an acronym for RAdio Detection And Rangefinding, and it works by transmitting a beam of short-wavelength (usually 1–100cm), short-pulse radio waves which travel at light speed, and then listening for the 'echo' as the wave is reflected back to the transmitting and receiving station. The time taken for the return is then used to calculate the distance of the object from the radar position. The rotating antenna's horizontal direction in degrees (the azimuth) is measured and combined with the return signal distance to give the familiar target image, or plan position indicator (PPI), on the screen. Occasionally, the transmitted signal may 'hit' an aircraft or object beyond the normal working range of the visual indicator; although possibly hundreds of kilometres distant, this will appear electronically on the PPI, and thus give the impression of being local, due to the timing of the antenna sweep. The net effect of this is that an apparently ranged object appears on the screen, and may jump from one side to the other and disappear as quickly as it appeared. Radar operators sometimes refer to this phenomenon as a 'second-time-around' target, and they have a tendency not to report it. It is therefore worth cultivating your friendly local radar operators – you never know when they'll come in handy.

Funny thing, radar: it is capable of sensing almost anything within its area of sweep and yet, contrary to popular belief, not all reported UFOs are spotted on radar. When air traffic controllers sit in front of the radar screen to monitor air traffic, they do, in effect, 'squelch' out unwanted returns, in much the same way that CB radio operators 'squelch' out unwanted radio interference from other, possibly more distant, users. The analogy may be oversimplifying things a little, but it should be emphasized that many UFO investigators have little or no idea of how radar actually works, or indeed of how many different kinds there are.

Radar comes in all shapes, sizes and flavours, starting with small hand-held units, such as UFO-detecting 'passive radars' and Vascar, beloved of so many local police forces for assessing the speed of passing motorists. Then there are those available for use on boats for navigational purposes, right up to those covering acres of land with long arrays of antennas used for monitoring space vehicles or for astronomical measurements and surveys. The one with which we are most concerned, however, is the common or garden ATC dish, the rotating antenna of the airports. These may vary in size from 3m (10ft) to 9m (28ft) across.

Those radars designed mainly to determine the presence and position of a reflecting target within the circle of sweep around the antenna are called search radars. Another radar may then examine the reflected signal to determine height by undertaking a vertical sweep in the direction of the source of the reflection. Tracking radars are aimed at and follow a moving target to obtain accurate details regarding its motion. In some systems, these search and track-ing functions may be combined into one unit and computer controlled. Some radar establishments may have their transmitters and receiving dishes located several kilometres apart and these are called bistatic radars, as opposed to the more conventional monostatic radars. Passive radar (or, to give it its proper title, radiometer or Signal Intercept System) transmits no signal at all, but is designed to measure, in a radar-like fashion, signals from the targets them-selves.

Primary radar is a system in which the received signal is reflected by the target, while secondary radar is that in which the transmitted signal causes a transponder (a contraction of transmitter–responder) that is carried aboard the target vessel to transmit an identifying signal back to the radar establishment. Most ATC towers utilize both primary and secondary radars. Small private air-craft may not necessarily carry transponders, but while airborne they still need to be identified for reasons of air safety. Provided the pilot follows the estab-lished aviation laws and 'rules of the road' there should not be a problem, given that there is still likely to be radio communication between the tower and the aircraft.

At most major airports, radar and tracking operations are tape recorded and stored for a period before being recycled and used again. The frequency at which these tapes are reused may vary, not only from country to country but also from airport to airport, and it is these radar tapes that most often interest UFO investigators when an anomalous object is seen close to an airport, or when there is reason to suspect that an airport or radar facility may have reg-istered it on their screens. Generally it would seem that a period of at least a few days is favoured. Nevertheless, don't make the mistake of assuming that just because an airport has a radar dish it will automatically have picked up any and all UFOs and will have them faithfully recorded on tape. It will certainly not be worth approaching radar establishments or ATC personnel later than 30 days after a UFO is witnessed, as the tape is highly likely to have been reused. However, if you can get access to these recordings, it is possible to verify or establish airspeed, location, bearing, height and an indication of size. A radar operator will also be able to determine what is 'clutter' (such as ground scatter) and what are moving nuts and bolts. Remember also that radar-absorbing materials are now available and may be used by the military for Stealth technology or on remotely piloted vehicles (RPVs).

AIRCRAFT, AIRCRAFT LIGHTS AND GROUND-BASED BEACONS

Another often misperceived UFO is the humble (or not so humble) aircraft, and I use the term generically. Under international law, all aircraft are required to display a configuration of navigation lights, usually red (flashing, on the port or left wing); white (tail light, constant); and green (flashing, on the starboard or right wing). The wing-tip lights should be visible from a distance of five nautical miles on a clear night, and the tail light should be visible from at least three. Remember also that occasionally these lights do fail, but under aviation law pilots are required to rectify the problem as soon as possible. Civil aircraft may also have a flashing red light under the fuselage near the rear of the plane, and another one on top of the tail fin. From underneath a civil aircraft, you may also see two brilliant flashing and/or constant white lights (one to each wing tip), particularly on a landing approach.

Apart from the lights, many aircraft are now using quieter engines, in deference to restrictions regarding noise pollution over conurbations and built-up areas, particularly during final approaches and take-offs along known flightpaths, when the noise can sometimes be deafening. Of course, what happens now is that with these quieter engines an aeroplane can creep up on your blind side, slow down as it throttles back for landing, and give you a major fright when it is suddenly on top of you. The situation is compounded if you are travelling in a car, as you may have the radio on and thus be unable to hear it early enough; or you may be moving in a direction relative to the aircraft that gives the illusion that it is hovering. If the aircraft is on final approach, it will have its xenon floodlights on for landing, and when such an object looms out at you from a foggy night at low altitude... Equally unnerving is when the witness sees the aircraft from different angles – head on, for example. In this instance, the landing lights swamp out the flashing navigation lights, and until the aircraft turns these last may not be seen at all, so the witness sees only parallel beams of high intensity. As landing lights are usually turned on some distance and altitude away from the landing site, they may illuminate the clouds from within, which can be an eerie sight indeed. Such landing lights can be visible from over 65km (40 miles) away with good visibility.

During adverse weather conditions, both military and civilian airfields used to display beacons to aid their location and identity, and this still happens occasionally. With some witnesses reporting incidents while far from home, it is worth checking their routes to determine the proximity of any such airfields and associated beacons.

Where used, location beacons at military airfields (Royal Air Force and Royal Navy) in the UK flash alternately red and white, while at civilian aerodromes the location beacons flash alternately green and white.

Where used, identification beacons at military airfields may flash a two-letter Morse character in red every 12 seconds, while at civilian airfields, a two-letter Morse character is flashed in green at the same interval.

Sometimes, airfields and aerodromes might use light signals to regulate aircraft movement. Under certain conditions, such as fog, these can easily be misinterpreted as UFOs.

From the aerodrome to an aircraft on the ground:

- Intermittent green beam – taxi within the confines of the manoeuvring area.
- Constant green beam – take off.
- Intermittent red beam – taxi clear of the landing path immediately.
- Constant red beam – remain stationary within the confines of the manoeuvring area.
- Intermittent white beam – return to allocated parking position.

From the aerodrome to an aircraft in flight near it:

- Intermittent green beam – wait for permission to land.
- Constant green beam or a green Very flare – permission to land.
- Intermittent red beam – landing permission denied, go to another airfield.
- Constant red beam or a red Very flare – please wait, landing temporarily suspended.

From the airfield to an aircraft on a cross-country flight:

- Several black or white puff-smoke signals, or white stars bursting at ten-second intervals, or an intermittent white beam aimed at the aircraft –

aircraft is approaching a prohibited area, change course immediately.

○ Several bursting green flares or stars – prohibited area has been violated, make distress signals and land at nearest airfield.

From an aircraft in flight to the airfield or aerodrome (not usually used where the aircraft is in radio communications with the ground):

○ Series of red Very flares – aircraft in distress.

○ Series of white Very flares and/or irregular flashing of navigation lights – aircraft in need of assistance.

○ Series of green Very flares or green flashes on an Aldis lamp – aircraft wishes to transmit urgent message.

○ Constant white light underneath the aircraft – aircraft is acknowledging the given permission to land.

Occasionally, a flashing amber beacon on or near the control tower is used to indicate that 'instrument flight rules' are in force. These are to be found in airfields within the perimeters of 'control zones' – areas of special protection around large airports, where there may be heavy air traffic travelling at varying speeds. These control zones vary in size, and in the UK there are 12 of them, the 'walls' of which usually extend up to 3,400m (11,000ft), and they vary in shape. The control zones are (roughly north to south): Scottish (Prestwick), Edinburgh, Belfast, Ronaldsway (Isle of Man), Manchester, Birmingham, London, Lyneham, Southend, Southampton, Gatwick and the Channel Islands.

Control zones are connected by a series of 'air corridors', known as airways; these can extend vertically from a base of 920m (3,000ft) upwards to 7,500m (25,000ft), and are 10 nautical miles in width. Pilots not wishing or unable to fly through these airways may apply to fly under the base of them (topography clearance permitting), over them or around them. The bases of these airways may be 'stepped down' and thus be lower as they come closer to the airport. In countries where the air traffic is relatively light, 'advisory routes' only may be established instead. In the UK some of the major air corridors over British territory are numbered thus:

Alpha One From Prestwick, through Manchester, Birmingham, between the London and Southampton fringes, and then out over the south coast towards France.

Alpha Two From north-east London, over Essex, Kent and the Channel towards Paris.

Bravo One A short airway, with a north-west to south-east alignment over Sussex.

Bravo Two Another short airway, between Belfast and Prestwick.

Golf One From the southern Irish Sea, over south Wales, the northernmost part of the Bristol Channel, and on to join Alpha One on the outskirts of London. It later leaves (and joins) Romeo One off the Kent coast and heads off over Belgium.

Golf Two From Dublin, over Anglesey, Merseyside, Manchester, then turning slightly north-east to head out over Yorkshire, Humberside, and out to the North Sea off the east coast.

Romeo One From the Channel Islands, over Poole, then turning east over Hampshire, Sussex and Kent, and out to sea over Dover towards Belgium.

Romeo Three From Belfast, over Merseyside to Manchester, where it joins Alpha One.

Romeo Five A connecting corridor between Bravo Two and Alpha One, over Prestwick.

These air corridors were formerly designated with colours and numbers, such as Amber One, Red Two, Red Five, etc., but these were changed to the current system in 1987 because of the increasing traffic and the need to control it effectively and safely. There are many others, of course, and an excellent guide to air traffic control, the use and designations of airspace, and the use of radios to monitor that airspace is the *International Air Band Radio Handbook* by David J. Smith.

When instrument flight rules are in force, in cloudy weather or in darkness, inconsiderate flying by private pilots can seriously jeopardize civilian air traffic, and generally most private aircraft are prohibited from flying in control zones and airways under these conditions. There are exceptions to this, of course, but flight rules and regulations are very complex, and if you believe that an aircraft might be responsible for a UFO report you should enlist the advice of an expert. However, there are certain rules that it is worth bearing in mind when you are considering an initial report, particularly with regard to the behaviour of an anomalous aircraft.

- Powered aircraft are required to give way to airships, balloons and gliders, and this may require a course change to avoid collision and then a realignment with the original flight path.

- Where two aircraft's courses will converge, the aircraft with the other on its starboard (right) side must give way, and again a course change is more or less inevitable.

- When two aircraft approach each other head on, then both must change course to starboard.

- Likewise, when one aircraft overtakes another, it must pass on the starboard (right) side.
- When following linear landmarks such as railways, canals, power lines, roads or coastlines, aircraft must fly at least 280m (300yd) to starboard of them (landmarks on the left or port side).
- When an aircraft is coming in to land, it automatically gets right of way, although when two or more are coming in to land, the lowest one gets priority, then the second lowest, and so on.

It might also be useful here to look at what is known as the 'quadrantal rule' (for which all heights are currently given in feet, not metres). This is the civil aviation regulation stating that when flying below 24,500ft under adverse weather conditions, or on instruments alone, an aircraft must fly within one of four separate height bands, or 'quadrants', particularly where two or more aircraft are flying on diverse magnetic bearings to each other. It effectively divides the compass into four sectors, and within these, aircraft are confined to certain levels. These quadrants and their cruising heights are as follows:

Magnetic track	Cruising height
000–089 degrees inclusive	Odd thousands of feet
090–179 degrees inclusive	Odd thousands of feet + 500ft
180–269 degrees inclusive	Even thousands of feet
270–359 degrees inclusive	Even thousands of feet + 500ft

When flying under the same conditions but above 24,500 feet, another, 'semi-circular' rule applies:

Magnetic track	Cruising height
Less than 180 degrees	25,000ft
	27,000ft
	29,000ft or higher at intervals of 4,000ft
180 degrees, but less than 360 degrees	26,000ft
	28,000ft
	31,000ft or higher at intervals of 4,000ft

Remember that nearby airports or airfields may be able to confirm aircraft presence within the area of a reported UFO sighting.

Anyone not familiar with the above 'rules of the road' may be forgiven for misinterpreting aircraft activity for a UFO's aerial manoeuvres. During daylight hours, aircraft lights may not be so apparent, but none the less aircraft are still mistaken for UFOs. Sunlight reflecting off the fuselage can cause the aircraft to flash brilliantly, particularly when the sun is low on the horizon at sunrise and sunset. Wings may not be seen, depending on the angle at which the witness sees the aircraft, so they may report a long cylindrical craft, flashing intermittently. High-flying commercial aircraft usually fly at between 6,000m (20,000ft) and 9,000m (30,000ft).

Low-flying regulations may also be considered during the initial analysis of UFO reports (again, heights are currently specified in feet).

- In the main, no aircraft should endanger property, people or animals (wildlife included) by approaching within 1,000ft or less of any such incidence on the ground or on the sea.

- Over urban areas, an aircraft must maintain a height of at least 1,500ft above the highest obstacle that is within 2,000ft of the aircraft, and a height should be maintained that is sufficient to enable a forced or crash landing well outside such urban areas.

- No aircraft may fly near an open-air public gathering without prior consent from the relevant authorities.

Restricted areas where anomalies might occur include 'nolite' areas (where military aircraft carry out night manoeuvres and exercises with navigation lights extinguished), explosive sites, searchlight training zones, some shooting ranges, and balloon centres. Restricted areas on flight hazard maps are marked thus:

Solid red outline Firing, bombing, permanently active, day and night.

Broken red outline Inactive unless notified appropriately (so possibly active at the time of a UFO event).

Solid blue outline Permanently active by daylight only.

Broken blue outline Inactive unless notified appropriately (again, possibly active during a UFO event).

In the UK, the Civil Aviation Authority (CAA) publishes flight hazard maps detailing areas that are restricted or dangerous to aviation, and these may be available in your local library, or by writing to the CAA. Notifications of activity are given in *Notams*, the monthly supplement to *Air Pilot*, which is available from HMSO. (For both, see Useful Addresses.)

As a first point of contact, though, try the nearest civil airports: they are often only too keen to help, as UFO reports do little for public confidence in the airlines. Mind you, given a real encounter scenario they can be extremely tight-lipped. When you've exhausted the possibilities there, try nearby airfields and military bases; the latter usually have an information desk, but don't expect full explanations of military movements. They may, however, confirm or deny that they had aircraft in the vicinity at the time in question. In coastal areas, don't forget that there may be a naval base or coastguard station nearby.

When dealing with these official authorities, if you don't get any joy from a telephone call, put your request for information in writing, as they generally have a policy of responding to official communications. If it's written, it has to be acted upon, and they are, after all, civil servants and therefore work for you, the public. Including return postage acts as a sweetener, but still guarantees nothing.

HELICOPTERS

Helicopters are seen more and more in our skies these days, often flying low for reasons such as crop spraying, power-line checking, policing, road traffic control, bracken control in upland areas, etc. From a distance, a crop- or bracken-spraying helicopter with outstretched booms attached appears to behave irrationally – swooping, climbing, turning, hovering and the like – and it looks a little odd, too. Like aircraft, many modern helicopters have quieter engines than some of their predecessors, so they may not be heard initially, especially if the wind is against the listener.

At night, the effects of a helicopter can be a little more alarming. Police or Search & Rescue helicopters carry 'nightsun' searchlights slung underneath them, which when illuminated throw out somewhere in the vicinity of 40,000,000 candlepower. These searchlights can often be focused into a narrow beam, and during a search such a helicopter may hover for several minutes, so all the witness might see is a narrow beam of light shining down on to the ground from a stationary craft. This is a commonly reported 'UFO'.

For information, try the usual sources such as airports and military bases. Don't forget the coastguard and police, the latter particularly in large metro-politan areas. They may not give you operational details, but they may well confirm any aerial activity. Other organizations that fly helicopters include radio stations, power companies, Search & Rescue teams, and even some farmers and large country estates.

BALLOONS

That old chestnut. Roswell notwithstanding, it is a fact that balloons of various shapes and sizes do get mistaken for extraterrestrial craft, sometimes quite understandably. They do also occasionally go awry, and may quite disturb a witness if, in fading light, they are seen bobbing up and down among the trees as they drift down and become snagged on foliage. There is even a balloon owned by Richard Branson that is deliberately modelled on a flying saucer! As if we didn't have enough to do.

Balloons come in a variety of types: hot air, helium, weather – even, I'm told, ones used to detect the fallout from Russian nuclear testing.

Helium balloons released from fêtes and fairgrounds may climb to quite a height before external air pressure and the balloon's internal pressure even out and the balloon's altitude stabilizes. These balloons may be coated with highly reflective surfaces which catch the sunlight and cause them to glint or flash. Such balloons usually travel in straight lines and at a constant speed, depending upon the windspeed at the balloon's altitude. They may thus move very slowly, or at speed.

There is not really much you can do to discover the balloon's point of origin in this instance, unless there is a fair or fête being held near you on the day of the sighting. Balloons can cover quite a distance in a short space of time, and so in the face of no conclusive evidence, the most you could offer a witness is a best guess, although your local meteorological office, airfield or airport might be able to shed some light on local wind conditions. Remember to ask for windspeeds and directions at various heights, such as 300m, 1,500m, 3,000m, 4,500m, 6,000m (1,000ft, 5,000ft, 10,000ft, 15,000ft and 20,000ft), as well as at ground level, as a reported object might be travelling against the wind flow.

Hot-air balloons are only slightly different and are usually only misidentified at night, when the flare from the inflater unit can be seen for miles as it illuminates the inside of the balloon. However, during daylight hours they are fairly easy to distinguish, unless seen at a distance, especially if there is a rally in progress, when several may be seen at once, possibly appearing to fly at the same speed and in formation. There are several balloon flying clubs in the UK; in other countries, the number of clubs will obviously depend on the popularity of the sport. Nevertheless, these should be the first port of call if such a balloon is suspected of triggering a UFO report.

Weather balloons are usually made from a very lightweight and reflective material, and may have a metal radar reflector suspended underneath them. At their launch, they appear under-inflated – rather long and pathetic, like a Christmas Day balloon on 10 January. As they gain altitude, however, the internal gas pressure equalizes with external air pressure and they take on a different shape entirely, as if they have miraculously inflated themselves. These balloons can appear egg- or disc-shaped, and account for a high percentage of UFO reports. When they do finally come to Earth, they often have a tag with an address on them for you to contact. If you suspect a weather balloon is responsible for a reported UFO, check with your meteorological office to see if this is likely.

AIRSHIPS AND BLIMPS

Airships are growing in popularity as an advertising and leisure medium, due largely to the developments of safer gases and construction materials. Some serious consideration has also been given to commercial passenger-carrying airships, but memories of the Hindenburg and R101 disasters still haunt the backers.

Many airships or 'blimps' used for advertising have message boards that carry flashing lights or LEDs to spread the appropriate message, while later 'lightships' are actually lit up from inside. From some angles, it is not always possible to read the messages, but a witness may still see flashing lights of various colours. When tethered, blimps hover or move aimlessly in a restricted area, around the point on the ground at which they are tethered, depending on windspeeds. At night, moored blimps and balloons carry pairs of constant lights – one red, one white, spaced 4m (12ft) apart, at 300m (1,000ft) intervals along the mooring line up to the blimp. The mooring point on the ground is marked by a triangle of flashing lights, one green and two red.

Airships under way move at a steady, if fairly slow speed, usually at around 30 knots, but possibly up to 50 knots, although they are unlikely to be operating in windspeeds in excess of 25 knots. Because of their use as an advertising medium, they are unlikely to be travelling at much above 900m (3,000ft), and as low-flying regulations apply, they are equally unlikely to be much below 450m (1,500ft). Airships are also required by law to carry standard navigation lights: a constant red light on the port side, a green one on the starboard side, and a flashing strobe atop the airship. Around conurbations, airfields, airports and major airways they will be in contact with air traffic controllers, and have the same responsibilities and requirements as other air traffic, therefore contact your local ATC tower for advice.

There are likely to be multiple witnesses to blimps and airships, at least one of whom should be able to confirm the craft's identity as an IFO. Failing that, contact your local planning department with regard to blimps, as permission may be needed to advertise in such a fashion. Civil aviation authorities and radar establishments are likely to be aware of any powered airships in the area.

REMOTELY PILOTED VEHICLES (RPVs)

Also known as unmanned aerial vehicles, these are usually secret military projects, weapons or reconnaissance drones. Many of them look very bizarre and as if they shouldn't be able to fly at all – but then, so does the bumblebee. RPVs come in a variety of shapes and sizes, including disc, spherical, winged, unwinged, triangular, etc. There is usually an operator nearby, and the chances are that if you are seeing one, then you are probably not far from military terri-tory or activity. There will always be exceptions, though, and as is the way with many such projects, especially prototypes, they are sometimes inclined to go AWOL, and thus you receive another UFO report. I wouldn't hold out much hope of receiving a satisfactory response from the military authorities, how-ever. The project may well be classified, and you may be required to sign the Official Secrets Act (or your nation's equivalent).

STARS AND PLANETS

Even the most obvious astronomical occurrences can be reported as UFOs, and we should not be too quick to condemn those who do misidentify them. It's easily done, and sometimes understandably so. One of the most frequently misidentified objects is the planet Venus, and 'eight out of ten debunkers who expressed a preference said their lobby preferred Venus' as an explanation for any and all UFOs.

Much depends upon the 'magnitude' of the stars and planets. This is a scale of values for brightness, and a star's magnitude may have a positive or negative value. A difference of five magnitudes equals a difference in bright-ness of 100 times, and the lower the number, the brighter the object, right down through zero and into the negative numbers. To illustrate, a magnitude 1 object is 100 times brighter than a magnitude 6 object. The brightest star in the night sky is Sirius, with a magnitude of −1.46, while the brightest planet, Venus, can peak at −4.7. Jupiter, another often misidentified object, can reach magnitude −2.9. The full moon reaches −12.7, while the sun remains at −26.8. Even Mars can reach −2.8. Of course, with the addition of chemical and/or light pollution in towns, these magnitudes may appear to be far less.

Stars do move across the night sky east to west, but they do not change their positions in relation to each other, while planets do, but only over fairly long periods of time, particularly the outer planets (Jupiter, Saturn and so on). However, for our purposes, these more distant planets are of too low a magni-tude and travel far too slowly to be mistaken seriously for UFOs. Venus usu-ally makes its appearance in the eastern winter skies shortly before dawn, or in the western summer skies shortly before sunset, hence its popular names of the 'morning' or 'evening' star.

Whether a planet is actually visible in the night sky depends upon where it is along its orbital path around the sun, and it is here that the appropriate computer software comes into its own. It is usually possible to pinpoint the exact position in the sky, night or otherwise, of any given star, planet, comet or other heavenly body, on any date, at any time and at any location, plot its movement and print it out as a starchart. So next time your favourite debunker claims that a reported UFO is the planet Venus (or Jupiter or Mars, two more of their favourite standbys), you might be able to check and, if appropriate, persuade them to think again.

AUTOKINESIS

Really an extension of mistakenly identifying stars or planets as UFOs, autokinesis is a visual illusion caused by a bright light, such as a star, *appearing* to move against a dark sky simply because there are no other visual reference points. This can be witnessed by looking at a star when there is moderate cloud cover which is being moved quickly by high winds in the upper atmosphere, and especially where such cloud cover is backlit by the moon. The star seems to move in and out of this cloud cover quite quickly, and it will appear that its rate of movement is quite profound. Verification of meteorological conditions, combined with consultation of an appropriate astronomy software package, could highlight autokinesis as a possible explanation for a UFO sighting.

COMETS

There can be few people who didn't witness the comets Halley or Hale-Bopp during their recent visits to our part of the galaxy. The latter in particular was widely reported in the press and on television, and triggered several millennium-fever events, including the tragic deaths of many members of the Heaven's Gate cult in the US, who died believing that the tail of the comet carried with it a great spaceship that would take their mortal souls to another planet. This unfortunate event greatly damaged the cause of serious ufology, and while sympathy must be extended to the families of the people concerned, the incident serves to highlight the kind of thing that can happen on the fringes of ufology, especially where comets are concerned. They are traditionally associated with death, destruction and catastrophe, and are considered to be harbingers of great changes in the affairs of man. However, comets which are visible to the naked eye are in fact quite rare, but as billions are believed to exist in a vast cloud out beyond the edge of our solar system, previously unknown comets could approach the sun at any time and from any direction.

Basically, a comet is little more than a dirty snowball, but as it approaches the sun, gas and dust are vaporized to form an 'atmosphere' around the nucleus – called the coma – the diameter of which might reach 100,000km (62,500 miles), and a long tail, which may diverge into two, with dust in one tail and gas in another. The tail of the comet always points away from the sun, as it is impelled by the solar wind.

METEORS OR SHOOTING STARS

Again often reported as UFOs, meteors or shooting stars are the result of dust or small particles of debris burning up in the upper atmosphere. They are a common occurrence, and you may see several on a clear night. They are usually seen at a height of 80–100km (50–65 miles). The nucleus – usually dust particles from comets – is usually not much greater than a few microns across, about the size of a grain of sand. Occasionally larger particles may reach the Earth to land as meteorites, but even so, they are still only visible for a few seconds, however brightly they burn.

At regular times throughout the year, the Earth is prone to meteor showers as its orbit enters the trail left behind by a comet. During these showers, it is often possible to watch many meteors per hour, and these showers seem to originate in well-defined areas of the sky, known as the radiant. This radiant gives these meteor showers their names, according to where in the sky they appear from; thus, those appearing in the constellation Orion are named the Orionids, those from Perseus are called the Perseids, and so on. Current scientific estimates are that as much as 10,000 tonnes of meteoric debris falls on Earth annually.

The main meteor showers that can be seen throughout the year are as follows:

Aquarids (Aquarius) Appearing between 1 and 8 May, peaking around 6 May, with approximately 20–35 meteors per hour. Generally very fast with persistent trails, and appearing in the early morning.

Geminids (Gemini) Appearing between 9 and 14 December, peaking on 13 December, with around 75 meteors per hour. A bright shower, many having prolonged trails.

Leonids (Leo) Appearing between 15 and 19 November, peaking on 17/18 November, with approximately 10 meteors per hour. A generally unreliable shower, but produced an awesome show in 1966.

Lyrids (Lyrus) Active from 20–23 April, peaking on 22 April, with about 10 meteors per hour.

Lyrids (June Lyrids) (Lyrus) Appearing between 10 and 21 June, peaking around 15 June, to a maximum of eight meteors per hour. Usually bluish in colour and to be seen directly overhead.

Ophiuchids (Ophiuchus) Appearing between 17 and 26 June, peaking around 20 June with a maximum 20 per hour, although many will appear below the southern horizon.

Orionids (Orion) Peaking on 22 October, with approximately 25 meteors per hour.

Perseids (Perseus) Appearing from late July through to mid-August, peaking on 12/13 August, with around 60–75 meteors per hour, often with flaring trails.

Quadrantids (between Boötes and Draco) Appearing between 1 and 6 January, peaking on 4 January (but often in daylight, with radiant very low on the eastern horizon, and hence very difficult to observe), with a very brief shower of around 60 meteors per hour. Showy electric-blue, with a mottled silver trail.

Taurids (Taurus) Appearing between 20 October and 30 November, peaking on 5 November, with approximately 10 meteors per hour. There are two radiants in close proximity to each other, and many of its meteorites are slow-moving.

Sometimes, a really bright meteor may be witnessed, possibly with a brightness between −3 and −10. These are known as 'fireballs'; they often have a tail, and may be visible for several seconds. There are also what are known as 'sporadic' meteors, which occur at random and are not usually associated with known meteor showers. Understandably, these too are sometimes reported as UFOs.

AURORA BOREALIS/AUSTRALIS

Better known by their usual names of Northern and Southern Lights, these are the result of charged atomic particles from the sun being focused by the Earth's magnetic fields toward the north and south poles. As they bombard the upper atmosphere at a height of around 100km (65 miles), they begin to glow, usually green and red, although other colours have been reported. The effect is similar to that of a curtain being blown gently by a breeze. Those inhabitants of the more extreme latitudes may witness them frequently, be familiar with them, and consequently disregard them as possible effects of UFOs. The displays become more prominent following solar flares and increased sunspot activity towards the centre of the sun's disc, when solar flares head straight for the Earth. The consequential atomic particles take a day or two to reach us, but when they do the effects can be quite dramatic, may last for several hours, and may indeed be witnessed at more distant and semi-equatorial latitudes, and under these circumstances they may give rise to some UFO reports.

Major auroral events are accompanied by disruption of the Earth's magnetic field, resulting in increased static interference of radio and television communications, burn-out of power lines and generators, and even loss of some satellite links. Although auroral predictions cannot be made with any accuracy, if the sunspot activity is still intense there may be a repeat lightshow 27 days later, once the sun has completed one revolution on its own axis. Of course, these secondary effects, coupled with the appearance of a misidentified aurora, serve to reinforce the belief that an extraterrestrial craft is behind it all. The media have a field day, people demand explanations from the government, and then, when we do get them, we don't believe them! Small wonder, then, that popular ufology is quickly discredited by more methodical debunkers. We simply have to learn to be more thorough than they are.

TEMPERATURE INVERSIONS

These are very similar to the familiar 'mirages' seen on hot road surfaces during the long summer months, which look like mirrors or pools of water on the road. Such mirages occur where light rays bend, providing the optical illusion of reflections of the sky or vehicles approaching or over the mirage. Similarly, layers of air of different temperatures cause a kind of 'elevated' mirage, or at least, the conditions under which a mirage may appear.

These are apt to occur where there is an uneven topography, such as in hilly or mountainous regions. Normally, air temperature decreases the higher one goes, but during temperature inversions, the lowest temperatures are in the valleys, while the warmer air rises up the slopes. One explanation is that as the slopes cool down at night, the air also cools, and as cold air is denser, it runs down the slopes and displaces the warmer air in the valley bottoms. This usually happens on clear and calm nights, when there is rapid radiation of surface heat into space, and there is no available wind to mix and equalize the air temperature. What happens then is that any passing aircraft which has a temperature inversion in the line of sight between the aircraft and the ground observer appears to jump, distort or disappear altogether, only to revert to its original condition once past the inversion. If there are mountains obstructing or partially obstructing the view, however, the observer may not see the reversion, and may thus believe they have witnessed a UFO.

CLOUDS

Clouds are less likely to be misinterpreted as flying saucers these days, due to a wider knowledge of the phenomenon, although certain cloud formations still occasionally give rise to UFO reports. The usual culprit is the lenticular cloud, which, like temperature inversions, generally occurs in more mountainous regions, often following a storm. Lenticular clouds may appear as disc-, cigar- or dome-shaped objects, often with a distinct 'stepped' appearance, which can make them look structured. They do not move a great deal, as their movement becomes stalled by local air-movement systems. Again, local meteorological offices may advise.

A rarer phenomenon is the noctilucent cloud, which is usually seen around northern or southern polar horizons (particularly between the latitudes of 45 and 70 degrees), generally around midnight. These are high-altitude clouds that form around meteor dust particles in the Earth's atmosphere, which reflect the sun's rays and make them appear to glow in the night sky. They often have a bluish or pearly white appearance, but as with most cloud types, they do not move quickly. Chapter 9 includes full descriptions of cloud types and the usual heights at which they may be found.

SUNDOGS/MOONDOGS

These are created when the sun or moon refracts through ice crystals high in the atmosphere, or through very thin cloud layers. The net result is either a patch of brightness (often circular, or seemingly spherical), or a patch of rainbow hues. I personally have watched a small diamond-shaped patch of vivid rainbow high up in an otherwise clear blue summer sky for about 45 minutes, before it eventually faded. Jenny Randles states that sundogs are usually short-lived and appear nearer to sunset, and may manifest as rings around the sun. These phenomena are also known as parhelia (sun-related) and parselenae (moon-related).

BIRDS

Even wildlife is not immune to being misidentified or mistaken for flying saucers, especially when flying in formation. When at high altitude, birds can reflect sunlight and be misidentified as UFOs because of slow movement. Unfortunately for the witness, real UFOs rarely put in an appearance in any numbers. A tightly packed flock, however, may give a blip on a radar screen. Birds are not usually a very credible explanation for an observed UFO, but might be the culprit on photographic or video footage presented as UFO evidence.

MARINE LIGHTWHEELS

A somewhat obscure phenomenon, marine lightwheels are considered to be the oceanic equivalent of crop circles. They seem to appear around the latitude of 19.5 degrees in the Persian Gulf, the Indian Ocean and the South China Sea. The phenomenon has been attributed to bioluminescent life-forms such as certain types of plankton. These circles or wheels usually appear just below the surface, and seem to spin or oscillate, often at great speeds. It is likely that they could be responsible for many USO (Unidentified Submarine Object) reports. Oceanographic institutes or coastguards may be able to put you in touch with research vessels in the vicinity of such occurrences, who might be able to add further details or explanations. There are also stories of similar phenomena to crop circles appearing on ice caps.

LIGHTS ON OR NEAR WATER, INLAND AND COASTAL

These are likely candidates for mundane explanations of UFOs and include emergency flares, which may be red, white or green. These may ascend into the air suddenly and at speed, and burn briefly, sometimes suspended from a small parachute. Emergency miniflares, carried by backpackers in remote areas and on small sailing craft, have a burn time of around six seconds, and two or three may be sent up in tandem. A single green or white flare is the usual response to two or more emergency red flares. Other flares may have a longer burn time, or may present smoke, and some may stay aloft longer through being suspended beneath a small parachute. Local Search & Rescue teams, the police and the coastguard will be able to advise you of any activities on the date of a suspect UFO report, but should you witness such flare activity yourself, please don't assume that someone else has telephoned the emergency services. Do it yourself: you could save a life.

Lighthouses and navigation buoys have distinct flash patterns as aids to identification and navigation, and coastguards and harbourmasters should be able to advise you as to these patterns and their originators. A lighthouse was held to be partly accountable for the infamous Rendlesham Forest Incident, seen shining through the trees. It couldn't, however, account for all the other phenomena reported that night, and the soldiers on the base should have seen it frequently enough and thus have been familiar with it. On coastal waters, the cause of a UFO alarm might be nothing more than a navigation buoy, although unless one has come adrift from its anchorage, buoys are unlikely to drift or move very far.

Where lights are witnessed close to the ground, particularly in rural areas, do not discount the possibility of boats on rivers and canal systems. Although it is unusual for boats to travel at night, it is not unknown. In the UK, such inland craft are required to display anti-collision lights according to International Collision Regulations. These are a red light on the port (left) side, visible from dead ahead to 22.5 degrees abaft the beam (width), with a green light with the same conditions on the starboard (right) side – remember that port and starboard are the left and right sides respectively when viewed from the aft, or back, of the boat looking forward. There should also be a white light on the masthead, which covers the areas not covered by the sidelights. Most river and canal craft also have a white spotlight, especially for use in tunnels or when under way at night, and this may be extremely bright. Do not forget that these lights may appear to be higher up than the witness if such a boat is crossing an aqueduct – in which case, during darkness they may appear to be either hovering or moving very slowly through the air. The maximum permitted speed on rivers for pleasure craft is 11kph (7mph), while on canals it is 6.5kph (4mph) or less. At night, speeds may be necessarily slower.

LASER LIGHTSHOWS/CEILOMETERS

Laser lightshows, popular with some entertainment complexes and usually roof-mounted, can cast beams on to the base of the cloud layer, where they may appear as discs of light. In clear or only partly clouded skies, these beams are easily misinterpreted as UFOs. In some instances they can actually pierce the clouds, and beams of red, green and other colours have been reported. A quick check with the local planning department, and then with the suspected complex, may provide you with verification of such a display on the dates in question.

Ceilometers are devices used by airports, with which a light beam is focused on the cloudbase and the reflected light measured in order to determine the height of an aircraft's visual ceiling. The beams may manifest as discs of light, and when seen from a distance at an oblique angle may be misinterpreted as UFOs, in much the same way as laser lightshows. Check with local airports and airfields for the times and dates in question.

CERENKOV RADIATION

Cerenkov radiation is a bluish light emitted by particles travelling at almost the speed of light, when they enter a substance or material in which the velocity of light is less than the particles' speed. Although plausible as an IFO, Cerenkov radiation is not very likely to be cause for investigation by most ufologists, even though it is believed to be responsible for reported flashes of light witnessed by astronauts in space (even when their eyes are closed). Scientists favour three explanations for this Cerenkov radiation:

- That cosmic rays actually pass through the retina of the eye and ionize a few molecules on the way, thus transmitting a signal to the brain that a flash of light has been seen.

- That 'HZE' particles produce Cerenkov radiation inside the eyeball, which is then registered by the retina. (HZE particles are very energetic atomic nuclei from cosmic rays which leave energy in their tracks as they pass through a substance; this energy then ionizes the atoms of the substance they have passed through and disrupts their molecular bonds.)

o That alpha particles from energetic collisions caused by protons emitted from the Van Allen Belt again produce ionization in the retina, causing a signal to be registered and an image seen. Astronauts have reportedly seen many such light flashes in a variety of shapes and sizes.

OTHER POSSIBLE CAUSES

Reflections on glass windows, such as might be found on board vehicles, may easily be misinterpreted as UFOs as they dance around on the glass with the motion of the vehicle, and are only one such instance of misidentification. There are, of course, other explanations for many UFO sightings, but to detail all of them would take an entire volume of its own if the job were to be done thoroughly. However, you should by now have some idea of how simple it is to mistake a perfectly innocuous event or natural phenomenon for something a little more out of this world.

12 Background Research and Lobbying

It is generally acknowledged among the UFO fraternity that the eternal 'they', the powers in authority, know a damn sight more about what goes on in our skies than they are prepared to let on. Government denials of knowledge of and interest in UFOs and extraterrestrials continue apace, along with the number of sightings. So, just what does go on behind closed doors, and is there anything we can do to find out about it? Well, yes, there is actually, particularly if you think that there is a UFO cover-up in force.

All countries have their security services, police forces and politicians, and to a greater or lesser degree it is possible to discover what decisions are made that can affect us all, beyond those you read about in the newspapers (or see on television – in most western countries, the television set is no longer considered a luxury household item, as it is the medium through which the elected government maintains contact with its people).

What follows is primarily concerned with how to go about things in the UK, but there should be enough pointers for readers from other countries to help you look in the right directions and undertake investigations of your own. When you have 'picked up a tail', or your mail is tampered with, or your telephone is tapped, then you know you are looking in the right direction, because it's the direction in which someone doesn't want you to look. It is estimated that the UK's Special Branch holds over two million files on members of the public, and as a UFO investigator you could be among them.

FREEDOM OF INFORMATION?

As I write, there are plans afoot to lift part of the veil of secrecy that pervades the British political system. According to the *Guardian* newspaper, a white paper on a British Freedom of Information Act was published on 11 December 1997. Under the proposed Act, ministers, government departments, quangos (quasi-autonomous non-governmental organizations) and other such bodies will be required to open their files upon request within 20 days of such a request being made. An Information Commissioner will be appointed who will have the power to regulate any charges that may be levied for the provision of information, and this must be limited to 'reasonable costs'. He will also be able to order disclosure of information. The Act will include a list of exemptions to disclosure, among which are those relating to defence issues and foreign policy, and a blanket exemption regarding the activities of the security and intelligence services. However, the Act will introduce a test of 'substantial harm', which will itself have to be balanced against the public interest. Likewise, commercially sensitive information will also be exempted, which in essence means that government contractors and privatized public utilities will be outside the Act. So, all in all, it will probably not be a great deal of use to UFO investigators. *Plus ça change...*

What the British government does propose to do with this Act is to make it a criminal offence to shred documents that are requested by members of the public, although it supports only limited disclosure of advice given to ministers by civil servants. The government will, however, have to justify why certain documents or information will remain suppressed. Of course, there currently appears to be nothing to prevent individuals shredding certain sensitive documents long before the Act becomes law (originally proposed for late 1999). The Act will not fulfil the obligations that UFO campaigners had hoped for, but in other areas it appears to be acceptable to the Campaign for the Freedom of Information. It will certainly be interesting to see what embarrassing questions are subsequently answered in Parliament without all the chasing about, stonewalling and general avoidance techniques that we have all become so used to.

If you are interested in digging a little deeper, try to get hold of a copy of David Northmore's excellent *Freedom of Information Handbook*. It's a mine of useful information and could prove immensely valuable to UFO researchers and conspiracy theorists alike. Much of it is relevant to getting the information you want while undertaking UFO or cover-up investigations.

The UK is probably the most secretive country in the developed world, with over 90 pieces of legislation buried in assorted Acts of Parliament which make the disclosure of certain sensitive data or information illegal – although to be fair, some of it quite legitimately so. Sometimes, unearthing the information you want requires a little lateral thinking. If certain information is for restricted circulation to particular quarters of the population, such as the catering industry (I'm serious: Northmore quotes such an instance!), then simply pretend to be in the industry and the information will very often be yours for the asking. However, there are only four kinds of personal information that you, as a citizen, are actually entitled to see. These are:

○ Information held about you on computers (and any organization holding such information *must* be registered under the Data Protection Act 1984).

○ Credit reference files.

○ Certain social work and housing files.

○ Some (but not all) of your medical files.

Under the terms of the Data Protection Act, you are entitled to find out if any organization has files on you and what exactly that information is, examine some of those files, and have the information corrected if necessary. If any computer errors have caused you to lose out in some way, then you are entitled to recompense or redress. However, you can only see such files about *yourself* and some data will be withheld, such as sensitive social work files or information regarding crime detection and prevention, national security issues, or data for tax assessment and collection. There is a fee for looking at these files, which to some may be prohibitive, and there are many complex forms to fill in beforehand. Your local library will either have a copy of the Data Protection Register or know where to find one; they should be your first point of contact. Getting the information can be a lengthy business, and your library or Citizens' Advice Bureau will be able to help you initiate the process.

It can sometimes be useful to investigate an individual when undertaking an evaluation of conspiracy or cover-up, and much of the information about them will be openly published and therefore a matter of public record. Investigating an individual is not illegal, and indeed, the more powerful the person, the more information you will be likely to discover within the public domain. A little cross-checking could highlight a great deal about what might or might not be going on, professional relationships, business interests, agendas and so on. Just be careful not to go about things in such a way as to compromise yourself or end up with a libel or slander lawsuit against you. You need proof, not hearsay or circumstantial evidence.

POLITICIANS

It might become necessary to lobby your MP with your favourite cause, or to investigate what they are up to when they suddenly change tack or if they have an axe to grind regarding the UFO issue. So how should you go about the necessary background research?

You may be looking at some of the following questions: Does the MP have Masonic or aristocratic connections that put them under pressure to trade or to keep quiet, for example? Are they on the board of any major defence contractors, perhaps, meaning that they suddenly have to disavow any interest in or knowledge of UFOs and connected issues? What Parliamentary committees or subcommittees do they sit on, and are any of these pulling their strings? Are you likewise in a position to pull any of these strings? All these questions and more will help you build up a profile of the person you wish to approach.

The more you know, the easier it should be to word your approach, and establish contact and rapport. In an ever-changing political climate, most MPs are quite prepared to listen and respond appropriately to a well-argued and well-presented case. Think of 'the system' like a computer: rubbish in, rubbish out. Program your computer properly, and you should get a result – even if it's not the one you want to hear. By being well prepared, respectful of these individuals and not invading their privacy, you are likely to get further than you would if you went in poorly informed and with all guns blazing. Sometimes, a little sympathy doesn't go amiss: they are likely to be in as difficult a position as you are, and are bound by the same regulations and laws that hold the system together. Nor are your results likely to be as spectacular as you had hoped, or as quick in coming. Take the softly, softly approach.

The following are all good places to start when compiling background data on a politician or councillor:

- *Who's Who* (all MPs are listed)
- *Dod's Parliamentary Companion*
- *Register of Members' Interests*
- *Debrett's Peerage and Baronetage*
- *Burke's Peerage*
- *The Times' Guide to the House of Commons* (published following each general election)
- *Vachers* (a guide to the key select committees and backbench committees, and their members, plus addresses of peers and MPs)
- Andrew Roth's *Parliamentary Profiles* (contains biographies of MPs and the subjects on which they have made statements, some of which have attracted media attention)

Don't forget newspaper indexes, press cuttings agencies, and *Hansard*, which lists all the questions asked in the House and the responses to those questions. This latter is bulky, and may not be carried by all reference libraries.

The House of Commons and the House of Lords both have an information office which you can telephone for information (see Useful Addresses). From the end of July to the middle of October, Parliament is in recess (i.e. on summer holiday); other recesses take place at Christmas (three weeks), Easter (two weeks) and Whitsun (one week).

Des Wilson's *Citizen Action* gives good advice on reaching and dealing with MPs, and should not be overlooked if this kind of action is necessary.

Councillors' backgrounds and data should be available at local libraries and, of course, from the council itself, through its own publications. *The Municipal Yearbook* covers the entire UK, including the Channel Islands, the Isle of Man and the Scilly Isles, and contains complete information on local government.

Lobbying your MP

This guide to lobbying your MP was originally compiled by Dr Colin Ridyard, and I have have edited and expanded it for our current purposes.

If a wider acceptance of the UFO issue is to be achieved in public, sooner or later a wide-ranging political debate on the subject will have to be precipitated. A number of UFO-related issues will no doubt continue to arise on television or through the press and news agencies, and you may wish to express your concern to your local MP. If you are unsure as to who that is, contact your local Electoral Registration Office. Whether you have been inspired by a national campaign or prompted by a purely local problem, when writing to your MP you should bear the following points in mind:

- Writing to MPs should be a last resort, and should only be done once all other avenues have been explored and have proved fruitless. Failure to follow other options may mean your MP is unwilling to be very helpful, considering the volume of mail that they receive. If you disagree with their political ideology, don't mention the fact.

- The majority of MPs are not government ministers, and are therefore limited to what they can achieve. They are not empowered to change or alter policies or decisions made by government departments, although they do have considerable influence and may help to put you in touch with those in a better position to be of more practical help. They may even write to these people themselves and include a copy of your letter. This does not guarantee results, of course, but it does imply that such people will be more willing to oblige because of the official referral.

- Peers within the House of Lords are not obliged to take up your case, and so a respectful and polite approach is doubly important in the first instance. They may, however, be interested if your concern is already one of theirs.

- Should you write in longhand or use a word processor? There are no hard-and-fast rules, although MPs say they almost always reply to handwritten letters from constituents.

- When writing in unison with others on an issue, be careful not to mass-produce duplicate letters, as this will be seen as a lack of conviction on the part of the writers, particularly if the original letter does not fulfil the required criteria as outlined here. MPs' secretaries, and others, can easily spot the word-processed circular, and might file it accordingly. Better by far under these circumstances is a signed petition.

- Keep your letter short and organized. Present your case as concisely and accurately as you can. Don't send reams of paper: MPs are busy people and their attention threshold may therefore be shorter than you would like. Take care over spelling and layout, as a sloppy approach is not appreciated.

- Press only the facts, not your opinion. Don't generalize, and don't criticize. Specify your concerns, and set out your reasons for them. If you have professional memberships or qualifications relevant to your concerns, then emphasize them.

- Offer seriously considered and reasoned proposals for how the situation could be tackled. If you perceive genuine alternatives to actions or policies currently in force that are realistically achievable, then by all means include them.

- Don't use techno-babble. Your MP may not have a clue what you're on about, and is thus unlikely to be of much help. If you have documentary evidence to back up your argument, then append copies to the letter, with your name, address and any reference details written clearly on them. Equally, don't overdo the documents: one or two key elements will suffice.

- Many people make the mistake of giving their MPs titles they do not possess. If you are unsure, check with the press, the local constituency party, or publications such as *Who's Who* or *Debrett's Peerage and Baronetage.* It is more difficult to establish whether they are a Rt Hon (Right Honourable) or Hon (Honourable). Again, the above sources should help to clarify the position.

- Correspondence can be sent to all MPs at either their constituency office or at the House of Commons (see Useful Addresses). If your MP is a member of the government (i.e. a Minister or Secretary of State) it is generally still better to think of them as your constituency MP rather than to address your letter to the relevant government department. Grassroots pressure can best be applied at a constituency level.

- Always ask for your MP's comments on your letter, to make it clear that you are expecting a response. It might be worth enclosing a stamped addressed envelope to oil the wheels.

- If you have not received a reply within a reasonable length of time, then write again, enclosing a copy of the original correspondence and also informing the local constituency chairman. You can always phone the MP's secretary at the House of Commons (see Useful Addresses) or the constituency surgery to ascertain whether the correspondence has gone astray.

Effect of your letters

Monitoring campaigns in London has made it apparent that MPs are very much aware of the pressure that letters from constituents can bring. Mention was made earlier of the need to be careful when duplicating parts of letters to the same MP. However, when organizing a written lobby on an issue it is useful to get as many people as possible to combine their efforts through writing letters to an MP. Some MPs regard six letters from constituents as relevant warning on an issue of concern, while others say that 20 or 30 similar letters prompt extreme concern.

Meeting your MP

It is always useful to meet your local MP face to face in order to establish a rapport. There are a number of ways in which this can be done.

Most, if not all, MPs hold a 'surgery' in their constituencies when they are available to talk to local constituents on any problem or issue. Surgeries are usually held on Fridays and/or Saturdays, as MPs are generally engaged in Westminster from Monday to Thursday. Check with your local constituency office as to when your MP is available and whether it is necessary to make an appointment. Times may vary during the Parliamentary recesses. Constituency surgeries are an opportunity to lobby your MP with any UFO-related concerns.

It might be a good idea to invite your local MP to regional or branch meetings of your UFO group to hear people's grievances firsthand. Whether or not your MP is a member of the governing party, it is always useful to explain your concerns to them and, if possible, get them to lobby the relevant government department(s) on your behalf.

You may also lobby your MP in person at the House of Commons. You should always write to your MP in advance to forewarn them of a visit from yourself or others, and explain why you particularly wish to speak to them at the House. This advance notification may achieve one of two things: first, it can lead to swift correspondence from your MP, attempting to stall your visit by suggesting other arrangements; or second, it can lead to an appointment with a specific time and date (which you should keep).

You should then decide who will be attending the meeting and inform your MP's secretary accordingly. If you are contemplating organizing a 'mass lobby' of more than one MP, the rules and guidelines governing such tactics are available from the House of Commons. Many MPs are antagonistic towards mass lobbying but they do, however, respect and welcome small numbers of constituents on a well-organized and meaningful visit.

When making arrangements for your visit, be aware of the times when the Commons is sitting and obtain other times when your MP will be unavailable from their secretary. The Commons sits on Monday, Tuesday and Thursday between 2.30pm and 10.30pm, sometimes later; on Wednesday between 10am and 10.30pm; and on Friday between 9.30am and 2.30pm. Your MP may well have another occupation or profession which means that they may be working elsewhere during the morning, when most MPs deal with constituency matters. Some MPs reserve Fridays for constituencies, while others from far-flung places also travel late on Thursday. Many MPs prefer later afternoon meetings, between 4pm and 6pm, but those who are on committees which sit in the morning and afternoon are constrained by those activities.

Attending the meeting

Most people in London should be able to direct you to the House of Commons, and all 'black cab' taxi drivers will know where to drop you. The nearest Underground station is Westminster, which is on the District and Circle Lines. Directions are available from there. If you are lobbying your MP, you will want the St Stephen's Gate of the Commons, while the entrance to the Lords is further along the Embankment, situated at the centre of the Peers' car park.

At the St Stephen's Gate you will see railings separating off those people waiting to go into the Public Gallery to listen to proceedings in the Commons. Those with appointments do not have to queue. On reaching the entrance, you should inform the duty policeman of the name of the MP with whom you have an appointment. You will then be shown through the security machinery and will proceed towards the Central Lobby. If you have arranged to meet your MP there (which is the most popular meeting place in the House), you may recognize them immediately. However, MPs can be late and it is worth informing the staff at the desk in the Central Lobby that you are there to see your MP. Your name or names will be called when your MP turns up.

What you say at your meeting is up to you, although if there are several people attending you should rehearse beforehand and plan what you are going to say. Establish a spokesperson for your group and then present a united message. If you are dealing with a complicated issue, or one that is difficult to get over in a limited amount of time, take with you prepared information on the subject which you can leave with your MP for them to consider after the meeting.

There can be a variety of different reasons why politicians suddenly cancel meetings or fail to turn up even on the day of the appointment. Most should have informed the desk at the Central Lobby, and requested that they let you know once you arrive. If, however, they are unavoidably delayed and cannot get a message to you, then you can get a message to them by filling in a Green Card at the desk in the Central Lobby. This will be given to your MP in due course wherever they are, so that they will at least know you are in the building and can arrange to see you at a later time, or at least get a message to you.

Hopefully, you will have conducted a useful meeting with your MP and should therefore have prepared follow-up proceedings. These should include a courteous thank-you letter, as well as notification of any appropriate action that needs to be taken as a result of the meeting.

Finally, your local media may want to be kept informed of events. Appoint a spokesperson from within your group to let the media know after the meeting what took place. With this in mind, it is useful to have in your delegation somebody who is prepared to take minutes of the meeting.

Other useful information

Some other ideas you might find useful include the following:

- Send copies of UFO reports/witness statements/completed incident report forms/newspaper clippings of incidents in the locality to your local MP. Also, urge all UFO witnesses to write to their local MPs, either directly or via your group's offices, respectfully requesting that the MP investigate matters on the witnesses' behalf.

- Write to your MP to inform them that you are interested to hear that questions referring to unidentified craft have been raised in the Commons, and request transcripts (*Hansard* 1996: 24 July, 423–4 and 16 October, 921; 1982: 17 October, 1091–5, 5 November, 409, 25, 111, and 18 December 169–70, 173, 176, 246 and 249). Although you may already have these in your possession, it should alert the MP to the fact that questions are already being asked.

- Try to prepare Commons questions according to the text and format as seen in the *Hansard* Commons transcripts (see below). This will make it easier for the MP if their workload is heavy.

- Try to think of questions that can be asked of departments other than the MoD, such as Transport (air near-misses or other incidents witnessed by pilots); Agriculture, Fisheries and Food (crop circles, cattle mutilations); and the Home Office (police involvement, civil defence issues).

Finally, Dr Ridyard would be happy to assist anyone or any group who wish to lobby their MP, especially with the initial paperwork (see Useful Addresses).

Commons questions

Once you have persuaded your MP to table questions in the House on your behalf, they will be asked in the format given in the four sample questions below, which were actually passed to MPs to ask in Parliament.

> To ask the Secretary of State for Defence, does his Department accept that based on evidence such as that given by Lt Colonel Charles Halt on The Rendlesham Forest Incident, material contained in Joint Airmiss Working Group Report No 1/95 and the fact that his Department receives up to five hundred reports a year relating to unidentified craft that (i) the UK airspace has been penetrated on one or more occasions by unidentified craft whose performance characteristics far exceed cutting edge technology and (ii) that the best available evidence supports the hypothesis that these craft are of extraterrestrial origin; and if he will make a statement.

To ask the Secretary of State for Defence to explain why his Department feels it unnecessary to adopt a policy referred to in his answer of 18 December (*Hansard*, Col 628) to Mr Ieuan Wyn Jones, MP for Ynys Mon, on the reporting of unidentified craft and releasing to the Press details of (i) shape, flight-pattern, colour and size of craft, (ii) where and when the craft was seen, (iii) what action his Department took and (iv) the radar profile of the craft when such details are clearly in the public interest and his Department consistently take the view that such incidents are of no defence significance; and if he will make a statement.

To ask the Secretary of State for Defence, why did paragraph 5 of Earl Frederick Howe's response of the 28 October 1996 to questions tabled by The Late Mr Martin Redmond MP on 17 October 1996 (*Hansard*, 1091–94) state that discussions with foreign governments had not extended to 'UFO/flying saucers' despite the existence of a document released by the Public Record Office (AIR 2/17527) which clearly shows consultations with the US government; and if he will make a statement.

To ask the Secretary of State for Defence, why did paragraph 7 of Earl Frederick Howe's response of the 28 October 1996 to questions tabled by The Late Mr Martin Redmond MP on 17 October 1996 (*Hansard*, 1091–94) state that RAF Rudloe Manor has never been involved in UFO investigations yet in a letter dated 27 September 1996 his Department clearly states in Paragraph 5 that 'until 1992, The Flying Complaints Flight (FCF) part of the HQ Provost and Security Services (UK) based at RAF Rudloe Manor was the central co-ordination point for any "UFO" reports made to RAF stations.'; and if he will make a statement.

These are just examples of the many questions that have been asked in Parliament, but should help you get the idea. The Resources section includes a template for a petition to your MP (see page 192), requesting that they table official questions in the House on your behalf. Readers from other countries will need to modify it slightly, but it should still be valid. Lastly, should you wish to contact your Euro-MP, you can write to them care of The European Parliament, BEL 4135, 97–113 Rue Belliarb, B-1047 Brussels, Belgium.

A note for US citizens

The Resources section includes a template for a letter that you can write to your Congressman to request that they sponsor Open Hearings in Congress to return the whole UFO argument to the public arena, where it belongs (see page 193). It was generated by Dr Steven Greer's CSETI (Center for the Search for Extraterrestrial Intelligence), and is included even though according to CSETI every member of Congress had already received a direct invitation to attend a recent CSETI briefing regarding the UFO and extraterrestrial phenomenon – many Congressmen chose not to attend the event or even to reply to their invitations. Open Hearings on the subject were previously held in 1966 and 1968, but the body of evidence is far more overwhelming now. If you do not know who your Congressman is, then try the following Internet website: http://www.visi.com/juan/congress/ziptoit.html. This will list your Senators and Members of the House of Representatives. Go to their homepages, and their mailing addresses will be listed.

Regular postal mail is the recommended medium rather than e-mail, as it seems to be recognized as more official, is less likely to be lost or overlooked, and can sit in an in-tray looking menacing until dealt with. Be sure that your return address is listed so that your Congressman will know that you are a constituent; otherwise, they may ignore you. When writing to your Congressman to request hearings, you should make reference to the fact that you are approaching them in their official capacity as a member of whatever committee they sit on. It is suggested that you head the letter 'Request for Open Congressional Hearings'. CSETI advise that according to a House staff member, the letters that find their way most quickly to the waste bin are those headed 'UFOs' or 'Animal Rights'. Be warned.

The CSETI website (see Useful Addresses) regularly updates the current position regarding their lobbying efforts. The Resources section also contains some useful FOIA addresses for you to try, and an example of a covering letter.

POLICE

Despite the uniforms, and the bad press they tend to receive, the police are by and large not a bad lot. True, their policies and powers are sometimes open to abuse, but it seems that on the whole it is only a few individuals who ruin it for the rest of them. They have their uses for UFO investigators, too: I registered our local UFO group with the constabulary headquarters via their public relations officer, and we were duly placed on their database of useful addresses. In theory, any reports that reach the police regarding UFO sightings should ultimately come to us via their press office. In practice, I've yet to receive anything from them. Keep at it, especially if you have received a local report and they have not contacted you – ask them if they have received a report on or around the day in question. The officer with whom I communicated was quite keen on the idea, but I suspect that any reports they do receive go straight off to the MoD instead – which is odd, as UFOs apparently have 'no defence significance'.

From time to time, however, your activities as a UFO investigator may attract their attention. This could simply be because you have trespassed on to

private land during the course of an investigation, and while in the UK trespass is not a criminal offence (it's a civil offence – you can't be prosecuted, but
you can be sued), criminal damage *is* an offence, for which you can be sued by
the land- or property owner and prosecuted by the police. The prosecution
lawyers must, however, be able to demonstrate that any such damage was
either deliberate or 'reckless'. The penalties can be anywhere between a fine,
and ten years' imprisonment and an unlimited fine. You can now see why it is
important to obtain permission to venture on to private land prior to conduct-
ing of an investigation.

On the other hand, you might be looking into something that the police
would rather you didn't, for whatever reason, and I have fond memories of
playing cat and mouse with a white Ford Sierra Cosworth for about three
weeks some time ago, following certain questions being asked of a certain individual. Of course, if you are daft enough to wander around the perimeter fences
of sensitive military or government installations at the dead of night, you
shouldn't be too surprised when you end up spending several uncomfortable
hours being questioned, cajoled or otherwise bullied by mod-plod (MoD police),
soldiers, officials or other police – and in this case you have only yourself to
blame. It can sometimes pay off, if it's part of a well-thought-out strategy, but
otherwise this approach is generally more trouble than it's worth.

Another startling tactic to come to the fore recently is police use of their
broadcast waveband to entrap scanner users. In a recent case, the police set up
a bogus UFO sighting in order to attract investigators to the scene. Using the
airwaves, they gave out the location of the sighting and many people flocked
to the scene. Two UFO investigators were arrested and their scanners confiscated. In fact, the possession of a scanner is not in itself a criminal offence, nor,
contrary to popular belief, is monitoring police wavebands. What *is* illegal is to
act upon police data or information received by means of a scanner or other listening device. Arriving at such a scene following a disclosure, bogus or otherwise,
is acting upon information received, and consequently an offence. Be warned.

Your local constabulary is answerable to the local Police Authority, who
in turn are a subcommittee of your local County Council, and as such are
required to register certain information and data under the terms of the Data
Protection Act 1984, the Local Government (Access to Information) Act 1972,
and the Local Government Act 1972. Under section 228 (2) of the latter, you
are entitled to '...Make a copy of, or extract from, an order for the payment of
money made by the local authority.' Although poorly defined, such 'orders'
are usually taken to mean written requests by senior officers or council representatives to the finance department for the funds to pay for certain items,
requirements or transactions. This should at least enable you to see where a
police authority is spending taxpayers' money – such as on overtime on the

night of a major UFO incident, military liaison requirements, and so on.

Data held on police computers has to be registered with the Data Protection Register under the terms and conditions of the Data Protection Act 1984, and information about individuals is gleaned from a wide range of sources, including the Driving & Vehicle Licensing Centre, HM Customs & Excise, the Department of Social Security, the MoD, and even banks and insurance companies. The type of information held on individuals is equally wide and includes their habits, criminal intelligence, personal details, movement details and even possessions.

The best source of information about the police is the *Police and Constabulary Almanac*, which apart from listing every constabulary in the UK, also details such oddities as the Royal Naval Provost, all the Military Police forces, the UK Atomic Energy Authority Constabulary, British Rail police, the various Home Office police departments such as C5 Division, the Forensic Science Service, the Scientific Research & Development Branch, and lots more besides.

MILITARY TECHNOLOGY AND THE ARMED SERVICES

Information on armed forces personnel and military technology is understandably (and probably quite rightly) a little more difficult to get hold of, and what is available is generally expensive to obtain. However, the Jane's Information Group is as good a place to start as any. They list among their publications such things as military catalogues of equipment, market intelligence reports, newsletters and magazines such as *Jane's Defence Weekly*, electronic databases, and the like.

Brassey's publish an annual text called *The British Defence Directory*, which lists all senior military and civilian personnel working for the MoD, the armed services and NATO (North Atlantic Treaty Organization), including intelligence staff direct line telephone numbers, defence liaison staff, service attachés in British embassies around the world, and other in-service diplomatic posts.

The International Institute of Strategic Studies publishes details of military capacity for each NATO and Warsaw Pact country in *The Military Balance*, which is handy if you need to discover whether military hardware such as RPVs might be in their possession and behind a recent spate of UFO sightings.

Many larger reference libraries will have these publications on their shelves, or should be able to get them for you. Do not overlook the Patents Office as a source of data on new developments – sooner or later, even the military will register new technology, especially if they intend to generate revenue from it through foreign sales.

Once you have the information you require, or alternatively if you find that you can't get hold of it, try looking on the Internet, or enlisting the help of the media. Of course, it's only worth approaching the latter if you are dealing with a UFO issue of considerable importance: a simple UFO story might warrant just a paragraph on the middle pages, but something more tangible with potential for a wider audience might justify front-page news, especially if there is some skulduggery in the background. It could happen that such a story arises as a side-issue from an investigation into something only mildly related. I am not promoting character assassination here, or indeed the toppling of those in positions of power: that's not what ufology is about. We are investigators, not anarchists.

Remember, though, that the press can be 'gagged', as allegedly happened at Roswell, where reporting radio stations were threatened with closure and loss of their broadcasting licence, and more recently with the British government's 'D-noticing' of the BBC over reports of the 'flying triangle' phenomenon. This effectively barred the BBC from issuing news reports regarding this phenomenon, long held by some researchers to be either extraterrestrial craft or a new generation of Stealth aircraft. A D-notice is a formal government request that is circulated to newspaper editors and news agencies, advising them that reporting a particular topic or subject may bring them into conflict with the Official Secrets Act, or that the topic is considered a matter of national security or to be against the national interest. While a D-notice is not legally enforceable, it would be an unwise editor or agency boss who disregarded one.

FREEMASONS

It is true that Freemasons come from all walks of life, but it will come as no surprise to learn that many high-ranking military, police and government personnel are also members of the 'craft'. Seen by many as a sinister organization, Freemasons are certainly more than simply the 'funny handshake brigade'. There are a lot of fingers in a lot of pies, and as an international organization they probably have the greatest private intelligence network anywhere on the planet. If you have them in your corner, all to the good, but equally, they can utterly destroy your professional and social standing if you cross them. They seem to be able to obtain any information, on any individual or organization anywhere in the world, simply by tapping into the huge network of contacts that is available to them – a network that includes solicitors, doctors, military staff, senior police officers, bankers, accountants, computer operators, publishers, company directors, prominent clergymen, High Court judges... However, most Freemasons with whom I have come into contact have been sincere, well-intentioned individuals and, as with any other organization, not all members should be tarred with the same brush.

As with many large organizations, much of their information will be stored on the Data Protection Register, and it is probably my own paranoia that makes me wonder just how much Masonic information *isn't* on there! Although it is not widely available, you might be lucky enough to lay your hands on a copy of *The Masonic Yearbook*, which lists over 12,500 separate lodges and chapters, with information on over 6,000 prominent Freemasons, and gives some insight into the power and influence that they hold in or over our society.

PUTTING IT ALL TOGETHER

Once all the background research and investigative work on a UFO incident has been done, all that remains is to put it all together into some sort of coherent and cohesive final report.

What follows is Dr Colin Ridyard's final report and summing up of a UFO incident involving several objects witnessed and radar traced on Thursday, 4 April 1957 in the area of Stranraer in south-west Scotland. If you can produce final reports or summaries of a similar or even higher calibre, you will be doing ufology a favour by raising our professional profile, while at the same time performing a service for the public by presenting them with the facts, educating and enlightening them, and raising awareness of the UFO problem. Remember the Agenda 21 philosophy: 'Think globally, act locally.' It goes without saying that the finished product should be placed in the public domain for dissemination and discussion, and how you do this is a matter of choice. Apart from the local press, you could try the nationals, radio, newsletters, the Internet and so on. However, do not allow the press to muddy the waters or distort the facts. This is where having a friendly reporter sympathetic to ufology can be extremely useful, so cultivate one if you can.

Of course, with recent or new sightings you will not be able to access some of the data or records, but a little lateral thinking will take you a long way. Speed is often of the essence: get the story from source before the familiar blanket of secrecy and denial has a chance to descend, and before the witness has had a chance to forget anything or become thoroughly fed up with all the attention. And if you still get no joy from the authorities, approach your MP and ask them to table questions in the House on your behalf. Now on to Dr Ridyard's report.

> On the morning of the 4 April 1957, radar operators at the Ministry of Supply, Bomb Trials Unit, West Freugh, picked up an unusual response from an almost stationary object. The first return was picked up on the screen of a radar at Balscalloch. Although its range remained appreciably uniform for about ten minutes, its height appeared to alter from about 50,000ft to 70,000ft. A second radar was switched on and validated this return as the unidentified flying object was detected at the same range and height. The radar sets used were capable of tracking the objects automatically and the information was obtained in the form of polar coordinates. These could then be converted to give plan position indication and were printed out on to a

plotting board via an electronic pen; the heights were read off a meter. The unidentified object was tracked on the plotting table and after ten minutes, it moved in a north-easterly direction with a gradual increase in speed (70mph ground speed at 54,000 feet). Further confirmation of the unidentified object came from a radar station 20 miles away from Balscalloch which was equipped with similar height/position monitoring equipment. After the radar return had travelled about 20 miles, it did a sharp turn and proceeded in a south-easterly direction while increasing its speed. The Balscalloch radar tracked an object at 50,000ft moving at a speed of 240mph while the other station tracked four objects at 14,000ft and 4,000yd line astern from each other. The Balscalloch radar also picked up these returns. It was noted by the radar operators that the sizes of the echoes were considerably larger than would be expected from prosaic aircraft. In fact, they considered that the size was nearer a ship's echo.

In the previous December, a memo marked SECRET had been issued by RAF HQ No 11 Group (Ref 11G/S.1803/7/Air Int). Paragraph 3 of this memo stated:

> It will be appreciated that the public attach more credence to reports by Royal Air Force personnel than to those by members of the public. It is essential that the information should be examined at Air Ministry and that its release should be controlled officially. All reports are, therefore, to be classified 'CONFIDENTIAL' and personnel are to be warned that they are not to communicate to anyone other than official persons any information about phenomena they have observed, unless officially authorized to do so.

Despite these standing orders, it appears that the *Evening Standard* must have got a handle on the story as a reference was made to West Freugh in the Saturday edition (6 April). It would seem that the newspaper's Air Reporter was told by an Air Ministry spokesman that the radar returns were attributable to a weather balloon which had been sent up from Aldergrove airfield in Northern Ireland. This rather mundane explanation seems to have been accepted, the reporter had his story and the case was to all intents and purposes closed.

It would be interesting to see what the Deputy Directorate of Intelligence thought of the West Freugh Incident. In a report dated the 30 April 1957 (Ref DDI (Tech)/C.290/3/), the following observations were made:

> It is deduced from these reports that altogether five objects were detected by the three radars. At least one of these rose to an altitude of 70,000ft while remaining appreciably stationary in azimuth and range. All of these objects appeared to be capable of speeds of about 240mph. Nothing

can be said of physical construction except that they were very effective
reflectors of radar signals, and that they must have been either of
considerable size or else constructed to be especially good reflectors.

There were not known to be any aircraft in the vicinity nor were
there any meteorological balloons. Even if balloons had been in the area
these would not account for the sudden change of direction and the
movement at high speed against the prevailing wind.

Another point which has been considered is that the type of radar
used is capable of locking on to heavily charged clouds. Clouds of this
nature could extend up to the heights in question and cause abnormally
large echoes on the radar screens. It is not thought, however, that this
incident was due to such phenomena [clouds, like balloons, would also
be unlikely to move against prevailing winds at high speed – DC].

It is concluded that the incident was due to the presence of five
objects of unidentified type and origin. It is considered unlikely that they
were conventional aircraft, meteorological balloons or charged clouds.

It is interesting to note that observation two states that there were no meteorological balloons in the vicinity at the time in question, which contradicts the
version of events given to the *Evening Standard* by an Air Ministry
spokesman. Was this a blatant cover-up of the facts? Certainly the Deputy
Directorate of Intelligence were unhappy that the radar incident fell into the
hands of the press and this is alluded to in a secret memo (Ref DDI (Tech)
/S290/). However, even more damning were the draft notes prepared for Mr
George Ward, the Secretary of State for Air. A Parliamentary Question was
tabled by Mr Stan Awberry, a Labour MP for one of the Bristol constituencies
on Wednesday, 17 April 1957 (*Hansard*, col 206). The question read:

To ask the Secretary of State for Air, what recent investigations have been
made into unidentified flying objects; what photographs have been taken;
and what reports have been made on the subject.

Extracts from the Ministerial notes prepared for George Ward read:

...3 The Ministry of Supply Bombing Trials Unit at West Freugh,
Wigtownshire reported a radar sighting made on 4 April of an object
which was tracked for 36 minutes, continually increasing in speed while
losing height. Enquiries so far made reveal that no service or commercial
aircraft was in the vicinity at the time. It is possible that the object was a
private aircraft, and enquiries on this point are still being made. The
object could not have been a balloon since it was moving against the
wind.

...4 A reference to this report was contained in the *Evening News* and

Evening Standard on 6 April (cutting attached). If S of S is asked questions on this point, it is suggested that the reply should be on the following lines: 'That report is still being investigated, and the cause has not yet been established. It may well have been a private aircraft.'

You will notice from these draft notes that the Minister was not informed of:

a) The size of the object;

b) The appreciable height;

c) The fact that it was hovering.

Also, no mention was made of the number of objects, so, was there a cover-up? Certainly, if you consider the withholding of information from a Government Minister and the blatant misrepresentation of facts to the press as a cover-up then this is indeed the case. Clearly this presents a strong argument for effective legislation on the reporting of unidentified craft and it is hoped that provisions will be made for this in the forthcoming Freedom of Information Act.

It is easy to explain UFOs with everyday objects such as clouds, conventional aircraft, etc., so, let us consider the alternatives:

1 Helicopters. I agree that helicopters can hover and reach speeds in excess of 290mph; however, in 1957, helicopters were an emerging technology and I am certainly not aware of any, even today, that could reach a height of 70,000ft.

2 Clouds/weather balloons. No, these do not move against prevailing winds.

3 Powered airship. I think 290mph is a little excessive, as is 70,000ft.

4 Meteorites/bollards. These do not fly in formation or change direction and are very susceptible to the laws of gravity.

5 Flock of birds. I do not know of any birds that can fly at 70,000ft [or at the speeds stated! DC].

6 Harrier Jump Jet. There may well have been Harrier prototypes about in 1957, however, I don't think the service ceiling of the Harrier exceeds 40,000ft and it certainly would not give a radar return the size of a ship (note – in an interview with Sir Ralph Noyes, Jenny Randles was told that the West Freugh returns were more akin to battleships!).

7 Psychological delusion. Three radar sets at two separate stations? Extremely doubtful explanation.

So there you have it, a classic case of a UFO. No whiff of a down-to-earth explanation and most definitely a structured craft under intelligent control. Let us be honest about this, any powered craft that hovers from 50,000ft to

70,000ft, changes direction and speed has to be under intelligent control. Otherwise, the object would fall down to Earth with a resounding thud. I understand the laws of gravity are very stringent on this point. In conclusion, there were clearly several craft at West Freugh with design and performance parameters way in excess of the technology of the day. Even now with modern aircraft capabilities, it would be very difficult to emulate the conditions witnessed on that day in 1957.

Source material Files AIR 20/9320, AIR 20/9321 and AIR 20/9444 obtained from Public Record Office, Kew. Telephone 0181 876 3444.

See how it all dovetails together? Talk to witnesses. Check with the local papers. Verify the weather conditions for the date in question. Examine released documents at the Public Record Office (see Useful Addresses), and get a reader's ticket for a nominal fee from your local Archives and Record Office (your local library or town hall will advise on its whereabouts) – this allows you to access the entire British Archives and Record Office network. Check *Hansard*.

There is only one point on which I am at odds with Dr Ridyard, and I raise it not to disprove or discredit his point (I applaud his findings), but purely to demonstrate how a little lateral thinking or another mind may be brought to bear. In fact, the point I refer to could have been best used by the authorities, as it would have been more plausible than the aircraft scenario they present us with as an explanation. The point is this: it is true that clouds and weather balloons do not move against prevailing winds, but Dr Ridyard has not stated whether he or the authorities had obtained meteorological reports regarding windspeed and directions at varying heights for the day and time in question. At heights of 14,000ft, 50,000ft, 54,000ft and 70,000ft, there may indeed have been varying windspeeds and directions. Allied to this, weather balloons do carry powerful radar reflectors. Of course, the size of the radar returns alone would preclude weather balloons as a viable option, but none the less (and as this point was omitted from the ministerial notes anyway) this would seem to have provided a more satisfactory explanation for the anomaly than the one that was offered. The mere fact that the authorities overlooked this salient point regarding radar returns implies that they probably knew more than they were letting on. A radar operator should certainly have understood the meteorological implications of varying windspeeds and directions at different heights, temperature inversions and so on, and given that, the case should (as far as the authorities were concerned) have been put to bed there and then: 'Weather balloon(s). Case closed. That's our story and we're sticking to it.'

So then, the authorities do make mistakes, and when they do, we should be prepared to jump on them from a great height. After all, they do on us when we give them the opportunity!

Resources

UFO Group Constitution and Membership

The following is merely a suggestion of how your group's remit may be established. A professional approach to your undertaking may raise your profile with the public, the media, and with those you wish to involve in some of the broader issues of ufology. You may need alter or modify it as you see fit, but as a template, I hope it will be useful, if a little idealistic.

(Name of group) is a non-profit-making organization. Contact with and membership of other groups, national and international, is actively encouraged in the interests of dissemination of data, and the sharing of information and alternative viewpoints. There is a nominal 'joining fee' of (state amount), and it is envisaged that any fees or costs incurred during investigations, where not covered by available funds or from assistance donations by witnesses, will be shared by the membership and possibly recovered by the members' involvement with lectures, sales from regular newsletters, voluntary contributions from outside agencies and individuals, etc. Funds will be held in a separate bank account and will be used to purchase research equipment, service outside professional fees, etc. Responsibility for such an account will be shared by two elected members, and will be subject to annual review.

(Name of group)'s aims are to:

- Receive reports, and investigate claims to see if any mundane causes can explain the reported sighting.
- Send out field investigators on close encounter, landing and abduction reports.
- Have soil and plant analysis done; conduct time anomaly tests, photographic analysis and background radiation tests (where appropriate); interview observers and draw conclusions, if possible, in final reports on cases; send these to other UFO groups and other such authorities (who may request them if considered to be of national defence or security significance).
- Adhere to our code of ethics.
- Maintain a healthy scepticism and adherence to scientific method.
- Prepare and assist with the delivery of lectures on various aspects of ufology.
- Liaise with other appropriate agencies.

(Name of group) invites all reputable UFO groups and independent researchers to establish contact with (name of group) or arrange affiliation.

Incident report forms will be sent to those non-members who ask for them. All completed forms must be sent to (name of group) immediately after completion of an investigation, where appropriate. Blank forms may be freely photocopied for use by (name of group) investigators and affiliated members only.

Members with the following qualifications are particularly welcomed:

O Minimum of three years' intensive UFO research/study, including reading at least five books on the subject.

O University or college degree.

O Experience or training in any of the following: any scientific discipline (including medicine), insurance investigation, media reporting, astronomy, aeronautics, computer technology, electronics, photography, law enforcement (military or civilian), public relations, psychology/psychiatry (including nursing), military/intelligence, theology, plus those having the necessary training in observation skills along with the sensitivity, tact and diplomacy essential to dealing with contactees, witnesses and authorities on a personal level.

Researchers from other disciplines (occult, parapsychology, etc.) are not precluded from membership, likewise those with close encounter experiences of their own.

Members will be expected to submit articles and reports (where appropriate) to the (name of group) newsletter, and assist with publication/distribution if possible. Members will be expected to exercise the utmost discretion and confidentiality in their dealings with witnesses, and to acknowledge and respect the privacy, feelings, views and opinions of those witnesses, without prejudice, to the extent of *not* publishing or otherwise broadcasting witnesses' details in any form without their written consent. Any infraction of this directive will result in the immediate and irrevocable expulsion of the member from the group and withdrawal of access to data and equipment, and may result in legal proceedings under provisions of the Data Protection Act 1984 (UK), as due to the nature of personal details that may be held in a database, we will be required to register with the Data Protection Agency.

It is further desirable that (name of group) maintains the highest standards of professionalism in all its dealings with the public and private sector, including those brought in as outside consultants. Members will be encouraged to share resources and data not only with other (name of group) members, but also with other UFO organizations and external agencies, and military or civilian authorities where possible or practical. Scepticism will not be discouraged, with the caveat that views expressed by individual members will not necessarily reflect the views held by (name of group) as a research/ investigative body.

Any member involved with the misuse of funds, data or equipment, or theft, or other action undertaken while operating on behalf or under the auspices of (name of group) which renders the incumbent liable to criminal prosecution, thus bringing (name of group) into disrepute, will immediately be suspended from membership. Upon conviction for such offences in a court of law, this suspension becomes irrevocable, and said individual will be excluded from membership permanently.

UFO Incident Report Form

(Your group's name and logo)

INVESTIGATOR: **DATE OF REPORT:**   **CASE NO:**

WITNESS DETAILS

Name: Address:

Telephone No: Occupation:

SIGHTING DETAILS

Date of sighting: Time (24 hour):   Location (including OS grid ref):

Duration of sighting: Encounter type (Hynek System): CE 1   2   3   4

Circle one or more of the following as appropriate:

Radar-visual   Daylight disc   EBE   Nocturnal lights   Alleged abduction

If other phenomenon, please specify:

BRIEF DESCRIPTION OF OBJECT(S) (and how it/they came to be noticed)

OBJECT(S) SEEN WITH (circle as appropriate)

Binoculars   Naked Eye   Telescope   Other (specify):

PHOTOGRAPHS? Y/N   If Yes, are photographs: Colour   B/W

If Yes, camera type: Film type: Shutter speed (if known):

VIDEO FOOTAGE? Y/N

Are photographs/video footage available for computer analysis? Y/N

ESTIMATE OF OBJECT'S POSITION

Height: Speed: Approximate size:

Azimuth (angle above horizon, 0–90 degrees):

Direction object first seen in: Direction of object's trajectory:

Distance from observer (including landmarks for reference):

Pattern of flightpath (zigzag, linear, climb, etc.):

Flight characteristics (wobbling, pulsing, hovering, landed, fluttering, etc.):

OTHER RELEVANT DETAILS

Did object or perceived occupants display any:
Curiosity or inquisitiveness? Y/N   Hostility or aggression? Y/N

Avoidance or similar tactics? Y/N   Give details:

ASSOCIATED EFFECTS (SPECIFY)

EMP effect (ignition, compass, etc.)? Y/N

Radiation (burns, induced radioactivity, etc.)? Y/N

Ground disturbances (dust cloud, standing wave, etc.)? Y/N

Sound (thunder, roaring, hiss, hum, etc.)? Y/N

Vibration (weak, slow, strong, fast, etc.)? Y/N

Smell (ozone, ammonia, chlorine, etc.)? Y/N

Smoke/cloud (amount, colour, persistence, etc.)? Y/N

Flames (quantity, where from, colour, etc.)? Y/N

Debris (amount, colour, properties, etc.)? Y/N

Lights (number, flashing, constant, colour, etc.)? Y/N

Sorensen effect (black cone under craft)? Y/N

Any inhibition of voluntary movement during encounter? Y/N   Duration:

Were crew observed? Y/N   Where:

If Yes, specify type (grey, humanoid, exotic, etc.):

Were there, or have there been since the encounter, any observable after-effects (physical traces; 'missing' time; mutilated or missing animals or items; mental disturbance; etc.)? Y/N

NEARBY TERRESTRIAL OBJECTS (including telephone or electricity wires or poles, pylons, dams, rivers, lakes, radio/TV masts, steeples, floodlights, etc.)

PREVAILING WEATHER CONDITIONS (attach meteorological office data as appropriate)

NEAREST AIRFIELDS

Civilian: Military:

ANY ADDITIONAL DETAILS
(Please continue on separate sheet if necessary, and attach with any sketches, charts, notes, etc.)

INVESTIGATIVE RESULTS

VERIFY PROXIMITY OF

Police helicopter   Military aircraft

Civilian air traffic   Weather/science balloon

METEOROLOGICAL DATA (including source)

ASTRONOMICAL DATA (attach starchart if appropriate)

MEDICAL DATA (including medication, X-ray results, etc. – with witness's permission only)

ON-SITE FIELD ANALYSIS (attach data as appropriate)

Time anomaly test: Y/N

Soil sample: Y/N

Vegetation analysis: Y/N

Geiger counter/dosimeter readings: Y/N

OTHER NOTIFIED AUTHORITIES

MoD (local): Y/N   Sec (AS) 2a: Y/N   Civil Aviation Authority: Y/N

Coastguard : Y/N   Air traffic control: Y/N   Radar establishment: Y/N

Police (specify station/officer): Y/N

(Please attach any supporting statements or reports from the above, signed if possible)

VALLÉE CLASSIFICATION OF SIGHTING REPORT

AN-   MA-   FB-   CE-

SVP rating: Source credibility: Site visit:

Possible explanation:

Date received:

Further action required: *Signature:*

Anomalous Object Flowchart

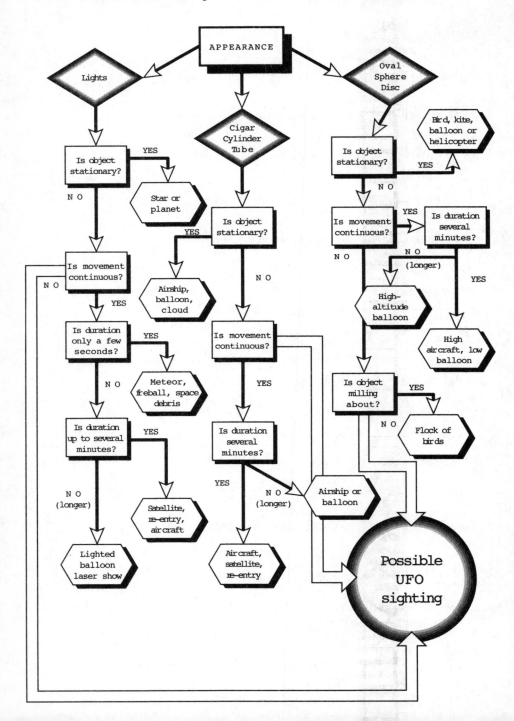

UFO Landing-Site Time Anomaly Test Form

WATCH INSPECTION DATA SHEET
(This page is only for data taken before and after field testing)

LOCATION:

INITIAL DATA		Watch 1	Watch 2	Watch 3	Watch 4
Date:	Reading:				
Local time:	Ref watch:				
Air temp (°C):	Difference:				

FINAL DATA		Watch 1	Watch 2	Watch 3	Watch 4
Date:	Reading:				
Local time:	Ref watch:				
Air temp (°C):	Difference:				

COMMENTS

I hereby certify as a (group name) field investigator that the above data is true and accurate to the best of my knowledge and belief.

Signed: *Date signed:*   *Print name:*

FIELD DATA SHEET

LOCATION:

1ST VISIT		Watch 1	Watch 2	Watch 3	Watch 4
Date:	Reading:				
Local time:	Ref watch:				
Air temp (°C):	Difference:				

2ND VISIT		Watch 1	Watch 2	Watch 3	Watch 4
Date:	Reading:				
Local time:	Ref watch:				
Air temp (°C):	Difference:				

3RD VISIT		Watch 1	Watch 2	Watch 3	Watch 4
Date:	Reading:				
Local time:	Ref watch:				
Air temp (°C):	Difference:				

4TH VISIT   Watch 1   Watch 2   Watch 3   Watch 4

Date: Reading:

Local time: Ref watch:

Air temp (°C): Difference:

5TH VISIT   Watch 1   Watch 2   Watch 3   Watch 4

Date: Reading:

Local time: Ref watch:

Air temp (°C): Difference:

COMMENTS

I hereby certify as a (group name) field investigator that the above data is true and accurate to the best of my knowledge and belief.

Signed: *Date signed:*   *Print name:*

(This form may be duplicated as appropriate for subsequent visits, but each visit must be numbered accordingly, and statemented and signed, as above.)

MAGNETISM DATA SHEET

LOCATION:

INITIAL DATA	Watch 1	Watch 2	Watch 3	Watch 4	Watch 5
Date: Local time:					
Magnetism? Y/N					

ON-SITE TEST	Watch 1	Watch 2	Watch 3	Watch 4	Watch 5
Date: Local time:					
Magnetism? Y/N					

ON-SITE TEST	Watch 1	Watch 2	Watch 3	Watch 4	Watch 5
Date: Local time:					
Magnetism? Y/N					

ON-SITE TEST	Watch 1	Watch 2	Watch 3	Watch 4	Watch 5
Date: Local time:					
Magnetism? Y/N					

ON-SITE TEST	Watch 1	Watch 2	Watch 3	Watch 4	Watch 5
Date: Local time:					
Magnetism? Y/N					

FINAL DATA	Watch 1	Watch 2	Watch 3	Watch 4	Watch 5
Date: Local time:					
Magnetism? Y/N					

I hereby certify as a (group name) field investigator that the above data is true and accurate to the best of my knowledge and belief.

Signed: *Date signed:*   *Print name:*

Aircraft Designations

When you are reading a document, book or UFO report from an official source, an aircraft's operational role may be discovered by noting its official designation. This will mean nothing to you unless you know what these designations signify, particularly where aircraft are referred to by designation only.

Designations generally follow the aircraft's name, and are usually a mixture of letters and numbers. For example, an RAF Tornado GR-1 is a Tornado aircraft used by the RAF for Ground Attack Reconnaissance purposes. The digit '1' simply denotes the particular aircraft model, with or without later modifications (e.g. GR-1A). These designations are not to be confused with the registration letters to be found on the aircraft's fuselage – the latter denote the airfield, tactical wing or squadron, etc. from which it comes. Naturally, these will vary from country to country, from air force to air force, but designations will usually remain the same, or at least along the same lines. Many other countries have designations of their own, however, and these include Spain, Korea, Japan and China, to name but a few.

A good 'field guide' is useful, and you should obtain one if possible. Nevertheless, the following should provide a useful source of reference.

UK

AEW Airborne Early Warning
AH Army Helicopter
AL Army Liaison
AS Anti-submarine
B Bomber
B(I) Bomber (Interdictor)
B(PR) Bomber (Photo Reconnaissance)
B(T) Bomber (Tanker)
C Transport/Cargo
CC Transport and Communication
D Drone or unmanned
E Electronic or flight check
F Fighter
FG or **FGA** Fighter Ground Attack

FGR Fighter Ground Attack Reconnaissance
FR Fighter Reconnaissance
FRS Fighter Reconnaissance Strike
GA Ground Attack
GR Ground Attack Reconnaissance
HAR Helicopter Air Rescue
HAS Helicopter Anti-Submarine
HC Helicopter Cargo
HT Helicopter Training
HU Helicopter Utility
K Tanker
MR Maritime Reconnaissance
PR Photo Reconnaissance
R Reconnaissance
S Strike

T Trainer

TT Target Towing

TX Training Glider

W Weather Reconnaissance

US

Type designations

A Tactical support or Attack

B Bomber

C Transport

E Electronic aircraft

F Fighter

H Helicopter

O Observation

P Patrol

S Anti-Submarine

T Trainer

U Utility

V Vertical or short take-off and landing

X Experimental

These initial designations can be seen in such aircraft as Tomcat F-14, Hercules C-130, X-29 (Experimental Aircraft), A-10 Thunderbolt and so on. However, some USAF aircraft have a special status and thus have a prefix to the designation, such as DC-130, which might represent, for example, a transport aircraft currently used for research and development with UAVs (Unmanned Aerial Vehicles).

Role prefixes

D Drone director

E Electronic equipment

G Permanently grounded

H Search & Rescue

J Special test (temporary)

K Tanker

L Cold weather ops

M Permanently Modified

N Special test (permanent)

Q Drone, targeting or unmanned

R Reconnaissance

V Staff transport

W Weather reconnaissance

Y Service test, or prototype

Z Project, or in planning and development

Commonwealth of Independent States (formerly the Soviet Union)

Most of the names and designations that we in the west tend to associate with Soviet aircraft are no more than a legacy from the days of the Cold War. True designations were not usually known to NATO until the aircraft had been in service for some years, and so it became necessary to give 'reporting names' to these aircraft in order that they might be identified. Hence, the standard designations were applied as the initial letter of the names given: F for Fighter (Flanker, Flogger, Foxbat, etc.), B for Bomber (Backfire, Badger, Beagle, etc.), C for Transporters (Cossack, Crate, Condor, etc.), M for Miscellaneous, H for Helicopters, and so on. As any new variants or modifications came along, they were given suffix letters. The numbers, or combinations of numbers and letters, that are sometimes seen quoted inform us that Mi-24 Hind is a Mil model 24 Helicopter, and Su-27 Flanker is a Sukhoi model 27 Fighter. What follows is a list of major Soviet manufacturers and their abbreviated designations, and examples of their aircraft with NATO reporting names.

Antonov An- (An-30 Clank; An-8 Camp; An-72 AEW Madcap, etc.)

Beriev Be- (Be-12; Mail)

Ilyushin Il- (Il-28 Beagle; Il-86 Camber; Il-78 Midas)

Kamov Ka- (Ka-34 Hokum; Ka-26 Hoodlum)

Let L- (L-29 Delfin Maya)

Mikoyan MiG- (MiG-23/-27 Flogger; MiG-25 Foxbat; MiG-15UTI Midget)

Mil Mi- (Mi-24/-25 Hind; Mi-28 Havoc)

Myasischev M- (M-4 Bison; M-17 Mystic)

Sukhoi Su- (Su-24 Fencer; Su-25 Frogfoot; Su-7U Moujik)

Tupolev Tu- (Tu-95/-142 Bear; Tu-16 Badger; Tu-124 Cookpot; Tu-28 Fiddler)

Yakovlev Yak- (Yak-28P Firebar; Yak-11 Moose; Yak-12 Creek)

The vast majority of the world's governments actually obtain their aircraft from a very few controlling suppliers and manufacturers. Thus what becomes available to an interested government will largely depend upon arms embargoes, political climates, international trade agreements, and the like. Consequently, many of the same aircraft will be found on both sides of the ideological fence, with many low-defence-budget countries buying-in secondhand. Naturally, the liveries (flight colours and markings) will change, but the operational designations will mostly remain unaltered. A good guide to aircraft markings, serial numbers and designations that the ufologist might find useful is *Modern Aircraft Markings* by Mike Spick & Barry Wheeler.

Example Petitions/Letters

To British MPs

To (*MP's name*) MP

The petition of a number of the residents of the city/town of (name of your city/town), in the county of (name of your home county) and elsewhere declares that there are a number of sightings of aircraft or unexplained objects in the sky in or around the said county and elsewhere.

The petitioners therefore request that the Honourable [or Right Honourable, if appropriate] (MP's name) MP table formal, written Parliamentary questions as requested by (your name) of (your address) and others to make enquiries with respect to the full relevance of the Unidentified Flying Object phenomenon in the UK.

And the petitioners remain, etc.

Names   *Signatures*   *Addresses*

Freedom of Information Request

Dear Sir or Madam

I am writing to request a copy, under the terms and regulations of the Freedom of Information Act (or whichever legislation applies in your country), of any document(s) relating to (state issue and any relevant information). If your department is unable to fulfil this request, I would be grateful if you could transfer my request to the appropriate department or office on my behalf.

Yours faithfully, etc.

To United States Congressmen/women

Dear Congressman (*Congressman's name*)

You were recently invited to attend an event sponsored by CSETI (Center for the Study of Extraterrestrial Intelligence) regarding Project Starlight (9/10 April 1997). Project Starlight is an international coalition effort that includes current and former government personnel, aerospace executives, military officials, intelligence operatives, American astronauts, Russian cosmonauts, UFO/ET researchers, civilians and others. Over 50 per cent of the US population believe in the reality of UFOs, and this is more people than voted for President Clinton in the last two elections. You are strongly requested by the undersigned to take the initiative and sponsor Open Hearings in Congress so that the whole matter can be placed back into the public domain.

Your immediate action on this matter is requested.

Yours truly, etc.

Names   *Signatures*   *Addresses*

Local Contacts

For all entries in your investigator's address book, you will need to include the following information:

Location: Contact (including rank, if applicable):   Tel: Ext: Notes:

IMPORTANT LOCAL CONTACTS

Civil airfield/airport

Military airfield

Meteorological office

Ballooning club

Police station

Police air support unit

Air ambulance base

Mountain rescue helicopter support

Coastguard station

Harbourmaster

Fire station

Park rangers/wardens stations

Radar establishment

Radio telescope establishment

Radio/television station

MP/Congressman/Other political representative
(home and surgery/office details)

OTHER USEFUL CONTACTS

Name:

Address:

Tel:

Notes:

Who's Who in Ufology

From time to time, particularly when looking through the UFO-related press, names crop up that either we are familiar with but can't remember where from, or are altogether unfamiliar. Again, you may see an advertisement for a lecture or UFO conference, and wonder who the speakers are and what they are likely to be talking about. Wonder no more: I have compiled a brief 'who's who' to help you. I recognize, of course, that lecturers come and go, die, lose credibility (and/or their marbles), etc., and so the following list is not intended to be exhaustive, and not 'everyone who is anyone' will be on it.

Exclusion from this list does not imply that any particular speaker is no good – it's simply that I've included only the more widely known ones, or have overlooked others who perhaps ought to be listed. Likewise, inclusion below is not meant to suggest any kind of excellence: indeed, some of those listed are sadly no longer with us, but are included here because their names are well known. I also have no doubt that there are some brilliant up-and-coming local and regional experts who write, lecture and put in the odd television or radio appearance, but space is limited.

Alford, Alan F. Former accountant turned author. Has travelled extensively to study ancient historical precedents for alien contact with mankind, and seems to have found some...

Andrus, Walter H. Jr American head honcho at MUFON. Lecturer and author.

Arnold, Kenneth The man who started it all with that famous UFO sighting over the Cascade Mountains way back in 1947. The press misinterpreted his statement and coined the term 'flying saucers' – and the rest is history.

Ashpole, Edward SETI scientist, and author of many books and articles on the biological aspects of SETI, astronomy and space science.

Azhaza, Vladimir Former deputy director of the Underwater Research Section of the Soviet Academy of Sciences, who established the first officially approved civilian research association in the former Soviet Union. Lecturer.

Birdsall, Graham W. Long-time UFO researcher, and editor of the UK's premier UFO-related publication, *UFO Magazine*. Author and lecturer.

Blackmore, Dr Susan British clinical psychologist, and lecturer on same. One of the UK's arch-sceptics regarding abductions, and proponent of the 'temporal lobe lability' explanation for the abduction experience. Several infamous television appearances to her credit, but often treated unfairly by ufologists as a result.

Boylan, Richard, PhD American clinical psychologist and counsellor. Founding director of the Academy of Clinical Close Encounter Therapists. Researcher into the alien–human contact experience. Author and lecturer.

Brookesmith, Peter Former editor of *The Unexplained* partworks, regular contributor to *Fortean Times*, and consultant on the paranormal for the *Readers' Digest*. Author and occasional lecturer.

Brown, Courtney, PhD American author and associate professor of Political Science at Emory University. Remote-viewer, trained by ex-military RVers.

Cannon, Dolores American regressional therapist, and teacher of same. Has spent many years working with UFO researchers and abductees, and is a long-time consultant with MUFON. Author.

Carpenter, John Leading American abduction researcher and well-known MUFON figure. Internationally known personality and lecturer.

Chalker, William 'Bill' Well-known Australian UFO researcher. Industrial chemist, author and lecturer.

Corso, Philip, Lt Col (Retired) Former head of US Army's Research & Development branch at the Pentagon and former career intelligence officer. Dealt with the Roswell debris in his official capacity. Author.

Creighton, Gordon Former diplomat, linguist and editor of the UK's oldest regular UFO magazine, *Flying Saucer Review*. Author.

Dean, Sgt Major Robert 'Bob' American. Former career intelligence officer who defected to ufology with his disclosures regarding official views about UFOs and extraterrestrials known as 'The Assessment'. Impressive background in covert operations and intelligence services. Author and lecturer. Married to **Celia**, also a lecturer.

Delcour-Min, Pauline British regression expert, therapist, writer and lecturer. Several radio and television appearances.

Delgado, Pat Pilot and the UK's foremost crop circle researcher. Co-authored two books on the subject.

Devereux, Paul British writer and lecturer in Earth Mysteries, and proposer of the 'Earthlight' hypothesis for some UFO activity.

Dodd, Tony British former career police officer, UFO witness, and now director of investigations for the UK's Quest International. Author and lecturer.

Drake, Professor Frank American Professor of Astronomy and Astrophysics at the University of California, Santa Cruz, and former Dean of Natural Sciences. Considered to be the father of modern SETI, Professor Drake is currently head of the SETI Institute. Author and lecturer.

Fowler, Omar British researcher and 'flying triangle' specialist. Author and lecturer.

Friedman, Stanton T. Nuclear physicist, very highly qualified. Long-established UFO researcher and promoter of the 'Majestic 12' documents as the real McCoy. Original Roswell researcher. Has written and lectured extensively, nationally (in the US) and internationally, and has made several international television and radio appearances.

Garza, Santiago Yturria Reputed to be Mexico's top UFO expert. Lecturer.

Gevaerd, A.J. Possibly Brazil's leading UFO researcher, and Brazilian representative for MUFON. Editor of *Revista UFO*, and co-ordinator of leading Brazilian UFO research group. Lecturer.

Good, Timothy Prolific British author and lecturer on many aspects of the UFO phenomenon, particularly cover-ups and covert alien/government agendas. Internationally known figure on radio and television.

Greer, Dr Steven Director of CSETI who has briefed senior CIA officials, US Joint Chiefs of Staff, Congress, White House personnel, UN leadership and delegates, and also senior UK and other European cabinet-level staff on the UFO phenomenon, and has approached the American Congress 'head on'. CSETI promote a more passive and spiritual response to UFOs and their occupants. Writer and lecturer.

Harris, Harry British solicitor and UFO researcher. Abduction research specialist, especially regarding mass abductions. Has locked horns publicly with Dr Susan Blackmore on more than one occasion. Lecturer.

Hesseman, Michael Respected German UFO and crop circle researcher. Editor of *Magazin 2000*, and director of Germany's largest UFO organization. Has briefed government staff in San Marino, the Vatican and the UN on the UFO phenomenon.

Hind, Cynthia R. Well-recognized South African ufologist, and Africa representative for MUFON. Draws comparisons with westernized UFO experiences that might be viewed as spiritual occurrences in many African cultures.

Holden, William 'Bill' Former USAF officer and crewman on Airforce One. Lecturer.

Hopkins, Budd Abduction expert. Promotes the 'genetic experimentation' aspect of the phenomenon. Author and lecturer.

Hough, Peter Prolific British author writing on many aspects of the paranormal, including ufology.

Hynek, Dr J. Allen Former Director of the US government's Project Blue Book. Astronomer. Devised 'close encounter' classification system. Did not subscribe to the ET Hypothesis, but realized that there was at least something very real to the UFO phenomenon. Author.

Jacobs, David M. American Associate Professor of History at Pennsylvania's Temple University. Acknowledged authority on the abduction phenomenon. Founder of the Intruders Foundation. Author and lecturer.

Keel, John A. Well-known and respected American researcher who publicized the Mothman sightings of the 1960s. Prolific writer and internationally recognized figure.

Keyhoe, Donald E. Former Major in the US Marine Corps and director of the National Investigations Committee on Aerial Phenomena (NICAP). Proponent of government cover-ups.

Klass, Philip American arch-sceptic and aviation expert. Believes all UFOs are the result of hoaxes, misidentified natural phenomena, delusion or psychological disturbance. Author and lecturer. The debunker that ufologists love to hate.

Knapp, George Las Vegas television anchorman and UFO researcher. Has investigated Area 51, and aired some excellent Russian research. Lecturer.

Mack, Dr John Former Chairman of the Department of Psychiatry at Harvard Medical School. Pulitzer prizewinner and expert on the abduction phenomenon. Author and lecturer.

Mantle, Philip British former director of investigations with BUFORA. Author and lecturer.

Martin, Jorge Puerto Rico's top ufologist. Author and lecturer.

Matthews, Tim Director of the Lancashire UFO Society and possibly the UK's foremost researcher of the 'flying triangle' phenomenon. Author and lecturer.

Menzel, Donald Arch-sceptic, astronomer and professional debunker who, it turned out, had known CIA and NSA connections. Many believe his explanations for some UFO phenomena (which included hoaxes, delusions and mirages) to be downright laughable. Even so, some are still used and quoted today. Alleged before his death to be a former member of 'Majestic 12'.

Michel, Aimé French ufologist and expert on radio and acoustics. Author and lecturer.

Morris, Eric British psychiatric nurse and abduction expert. Founder of the British UFO Studies Centre and the Abduction Research & Counselling Centre, although his stance on abductions has changed recently. Author and lecturer, with several television and radio appearances.

Moulton-Howe, Linda American television producer and well-known researcher into UFO involvement with animal mutilations. Author and lecturer, with many television and radio appearances.

Oberg, James NASA computer expert. Sceptical of the ET Hypothesis.

Pope, Nick Higher Executive Officer within the British MoD, formerly on the UFO desk. Author and lecturer. Several television and radio appearances.

Randles, Jenny Former director of BUFORA and the UK's foremost professional UFO researcher. Consultant to *International UFO Reporter* (published by the J. Allen Hynek Center for UFO Studies in the US) and several television programmes. Prolific author and lecturer. Many national and international radio and television appearances.

Redfern, Nick Leading British expert on the MoD's UFO cover-up. Has secured the release of many documents from CIA, FBI and MoD UFO files. Author and lecturer.

Sagan, Carl Former Professor of Astronomy & Space Sciences at Cornell University, and internationally acclaimed space scientist. Co-author (with Iosef Shklovskii) of *Intelligent Life in the Universe*.

Sims, Derrel Former CIA operative. Director of Physical Investigations for the Houston UFO Network. Known as the 'Alien Hunter' because of his stance of believing in fighting back against abductions. Claims to have several 'implants' in his possession, obtained from witnesses or by surgical removal. Writer and lecturer.

Stacy, Dennis Editor of *MUFON Journal*. Writer and lecturer.

Stevens, Wendelle, Lt-Col (Retired) Former test pilot and Air Technical Intelligence Center operative, with an impressive military history and background. Writer and lecturer. Claims to have received death threats as a result of his disclosures.

Streiber, Whitley Author and famous alleged abductee who wrote a series of books about his own abduction experiences. Lecturer. Several television and radio appearances. Author of *Communion*, which was made into a Hollywood film.

Stringfield, Leonard H. American PR executive and expert on UFO crashes and their retrievals. Author.

Vallée, Jacques French computer scientist with a Master's degree in astrophysics, and world authority on the UFO phenomenon. Proponent of 'cultural tracking'. Prolific writer. It is rumoured that the French ufologist in Steven Spielberg's *Close Encounters of the Third Kind* was based on him. That he has advised several governments on the UFO phenomenon does not seem to be in dispute. Devised an Anomaly Classification System that in many places has superseded that of Hynek.

Walton, Travis Woodsman and famous alleged abductee, whose experiences effectively drove him into becoming a recluse. Author of *Fire in the Sky*, which detailed his experiences and was ultimately made into an (inaccurate) Hollywood film. Lectures on his experiences occasionally.

Warren, Larry Former USAF security policeman. Leading witness in the British RAF/USAF Woodbridge/Bentwaters encounter case. Co-author of *Left at East Gate*, which detailed the account. Lectures occasionally.

Wingfield, George British UFO and crop circle researcher. Author and lecturer.

Useful Addresses

UFO RESEARCH GROUPS

Although details are believed to be correct at the time of going to press, the following listings are not intended to be exhaustive, nor are they meant to imply that any one individual, group or organization is any better or worse than another. Groups fold, and others spring up to fill the vacuum; people move, change their telephone numbers, establish websites, etc., so it is likely that some of the details given here will sooner or later become out of date. None the less, many of the larger or well-known groups or organizations listed here are likely to remain for a good while yet.

UK

West Midlands

BIRMINGHAM UFO STUDIES *Tel* 0956 140998 *Contact* Rob

BRITISH EARTH AND AERIAL MYSTERIES SOCIETY Chris Harris (Birmingham Branch), 37 Oakthorpe Drive, Kingshurst, Birmingham B37 6JD

CIRCULAR FORUM Cheltenham *Tel* 01242 577629 *Contact* Robin Cole *24-hour local hotline* 0973 778 906

NORTHANTS UFO FORUM (NUFORUM) *Tel* 01604 756153 *Contact* Diane Shepherd

PHENOMENON RESEARCH ASSOCIATION Derby *Tel* 01332 761464
Contact Omar Fowler

RESEARCHERS OF ALIEN MYSTERIES & RECOVERIES Stuart Hunt, 27 Shaws Lane, Great Wyrley, Walsall WS6 6EQ

SPI (STAFFS PARANORMAL INVESTIGATION) Stoke-on-Trent *Tel* 01782 522620
Contact David Pointon

STAFFORDSHIRE UFO GROUP 11, Sandy Lane, Rugeley, Staffordshire WF15 2LB

UNITED KINGDOM UFO NETWORK D. Somen, 6 Aspbury Croft, Castle Bromwich, Birmingham B36 9TD *E-mail* ufo@holodeck.demon.co.uk

UNITED UFO RESEARCH & INVESTIGATION NETWORK Matthew Aldridge, 5 Bramble Close, New Invention, Willenhall WV12 5AH *Tel* 0839 609881

Bristol Area

BRITISH FLYING SAUCER BUREAU Dennis Plunkett, 10 Branksome Drive, Winterbourne, Bristol BS36 1LY

Northern England

BRITISH UFO STUDIES CENTRE Eric Morris, 52 Dart Walk, Winsford, Cheshire CW7 3JE
Tel 01606 552175 *Mobile* 0374 639089

HATFIELD UFO RESEARCH ASSOCIATION John Ball, 18 Lichfield Road, Dunscroft,
Doncaster DN7 4NF

LANCASTER UFO MARSH NETWORK Steve Johnson, 6 Lime Grove, Marsh, Lancaster
LA1 5RZ

LAPIS 293 Devonshire Road, Blackpool, Lancashire FY2 0TW

MACCLESFIELD UFO RESEARCH 17 Long Row, Lowerhouse, Bollington, Cheshire
SK10 5HN *Tel* 01625 572875

MERSEYSIDE ANOMALIES RESEARCH ASSOCIATION Tony Eccles, 52 Hawthorn
Avenue, Halewood, Liverpool L26 9XD *Tel* 0151 486 6087
or Tel 01695 729410 *Contact* Paul Rogers
or Tel 0151 476 0356 *Contact* Mark Glover

NORTHERN AERIAL PHENOMENA STUDIES
Paul Earl/Steven Stratton, 21 Daisy Lane, Lathom, Ormskirk, Lancashire WF15 2LB

NORTHERN ANOMALIES RESEARCH ORGANIZATION (NARO) Andrew P. Blunn,
41 Somerset Road, Droylsden, Manchester M43 7PX *Tel* 0161 3705694
E-mail andrew.p.blunn@stud.umist.ac.uk

NORTHERN UFO NETWORK 37 Heathbank Road, Stockport, Cheshire SK3 0UP

QUEST INTERNATIONAL 18 Hardy Meadows, Grassington, North Yorkshire BD23 5DL

QUEST INTERNATIONAL (DERBYSHIRE) *Tel* 01246 471742 *Contact* Ian Taylor

SHEFFIELD UFO RESEARCH ASSOCIATION 87 Hawley Street, Sheffield S1 2EA

SOCIETY FOR PARANORMAL & UFO RESEARCH Graham Wilson, 26 Cardigan Close,
Batley, West Yorkshire WF17 6PR

UFO RESEARCH NETWORK Russell Kellet, 29 Springfield Avenue, Lidgett Green,
Bradford BD7 2PL

WIGAN AREA SOCIETY FOR PARANORMAL INVESTIGATIONS (WASPI) Ian Hawthorn,
467 Gidlow Lane, Beech Hill, Wigan, Lancashire WN6 8RJ *Tel/fax* 01942 493761
Pager 01426 669350

Eastern England

EAST MIDLANDS UFO RESEARCH ASSOCIATION 8 Roosa Close, Hempshill Vale,
Bulwell, Nottingham NG6 7BL *Website* http://www.logicnet.co.uk/EMUFORA

ENIGMA RESEARCH SOCIETY Nottingham *Tel* 01949 836375 (24 hours)
Contact Martyn Carrol *Abduction regressionist*

NORTHAMPTONSHIRE UFO RESEARCH GROUP 38 Portland Road, Rushden,
Northamptonshire NN10 0DJ

Southern England

BRITISH UFO RESEARCH ASSOCIATION (BUFORA) London WC1N 3XX
E-mail bufora@stairway.co.uk
Website http://www.citadel.co.uk/citadel/eclipse/futura/bufora/bufora.htm

BRITISH UFO RESEARCH SOCIETY 16 Southway, Burgess Hill, West Sussex RH15 9ST

BUREAU OF LOCAL INVESTIGATION OF PARANORMAL PHENOMENA Tony Stubley,
'La Folie', 49 Mark Close, Bexleyheath, Kent DA7 5JX

CONTACT INTERNATIONAL PO Box 23, Wheatley, Oxford OX33 1FL
Contact Brian James or Frances Copeland
or 11 Ousley Close, New Marston, Oxford OX3 0JS *Tel* 01865 726908 *UFO hotline* 01689
320989 *E-mail* 93015501@cs3.brookes.ac.uk

ENIGMA RESEARCH SOCIETY 16 Clare Close, East Finchley, London N2 0UY
Tel 0181 343 3910 *Fax* 0181 346 8277 *E-mail* Raskew1042@aol.com *Contact* Richard Askew

ESSEX UFO RESEARCH GROUP 95 Chilburn Road, Great Clacton, Essex CO15 4PE

GLOBAL UFO INVESTIGATION SYSTEMS 4 Coronation Buildings, Ham Road, East
Worthing, Surrey

HARLOW UFO GROUP Alan Kirby, 70 Great Brays, Harlow, Essex CM18 6DW

HASTINGS UFO RESEARCH GROUP D.G. Soanes, 7 Arundel Court, Edwin Road, Hastings,
East Sussex TN35 5JX

MI'RAJ EXTRATERRESTRIAL RESEARCH ASSOCIATION Waseem Iqbal, 15 Tyndall Road,
Leyton, London E10 6QJ *Muslim researcher on UFOs*

SKYSEARCH UFO RESEARCH ORGANIZATION PO Box 2507, Saltdean, Brighton BN2 8NE

UFO MONITORS EAST KENT Chris Rolfe, 23 Brabner Close, Folkestone, Kent CT19 6LW
Tel 01303 254774 *Pager* 01523 401224
or Tel 01227 728480 *Contact* Jerry Anderson

South West England

ASSOCIATION FOR THE SCIENTIFIC STUDY OF ANOMALOUS PHENOMENA
20 Paul Street, Frome, Somerset BA11 1DX

CORNWALL UFO RESEARCH GROUP David Gillham, 24 Carrine Road, Truro, Cornwall
TR1 3XB *Tel* 01872 276381

COSMIC RESEARCH Ian Gould, 4a Adcombe View, Fly Boat Lane, Corfe, Taunton,
Somerset TA3 7AW *Tel* 01823 421815

Wales

BANGOR UFO GROUP 1 Llys Bedwyr, Tan-y-Bryn, Bangor, Gwynedd LL57 1SF

RUFORG Daniel Lewis, 109 High Street, Clydach Vale, Tonypandy, Rhondda, Mid
Glamorgan CF40 2BJ

WALES FEDERATION OF INDEPENDENT UFOLOGISTS
Mid-Wales *Tel* 01766 780665 *Contact* Mike Orton
North Wales *Tel* 0145 860537 Margaret Fry
South Wales *Tel* 01443 431841 Matthew Williams
Angelsey *Tel* 01248 811580 Dr Colin Ridyard
Young people's section *Tel* 01686 688301 *Contact* Max Baines *Open to all young people
from any area*

WEST WALES UFO GROUP Richard Alexander, Cwm Gwen Hall, Pencader, Dyfed
SA39 9HA *Tel* 01559 384574
or Tel 01545 560164 *Contact* Adam Whaley

Scotland and Borders

INDEPENDENT NORTHWEST CUMBRIA UFO RESEARCH & INVESTIGATIONS
1 Richmond Close, Workington, Cumbria

OBAN UFO SOCIETY Oban *Tel* 01631 720 434 *Contact* Dennis or Tony Hartley

SCOTTISH EARTH MYSTERIES RESEARCH John Morrison, PO Box 16370, Glasgow
G20 8PX *Tel* 01786 832 480 *E-mail* morrison@psy.gla.ac.uk

SCOTTISH UFO RESEARCH 129 Langton View, East Calder, West Lothian EH53 0RE

SCOTTISH UFO RESEARCH ORGANIZATION Allan Brown, 5 Old Church Road, Torry, Aberdeen AB11 8DS *Tel* 01224 879979

SCOTTISH UNEXPLAINED PHENOMENA RESEARCH *Tel* 01506 635 184
E-mail supr@cablenet.co.uk *Contact* Dave Colman

STRANGE PHENOMENA INVESTIGATIONS 41 The Braes, Tullibody, Alloa FK10 2TT
Tel 01259 210714 *Contact* Malcolm Robinson

Northern Ireland

BRITISH EARTH AERIAL MYSTERIES SOCIETY (IRELAND) Alan Sewell,
156 Meadowbank, Craigavon, Co Armagh BT65 5AA *Tel* 01762 349014

NORTHERN IRELAND PARANORMAL RESEARCH ASSOCIATION *Tel* 04100 32276
Contact Warren *E-mail* warren@pagan.thegap.com

EIRE

GOLDEN UFO INVESTIGATIONS Derek Vesey, Cloon-fad, Carrick on Shannon,
Co Roscommon

IRISH UFO & PARANORMAL RESEARCH ASSOCIATION Box 3070, Whitehall, Dublin 9
E-mail iufopra@indgio.ie

JERSEY (Channel Islands)

JERSEY UFO RESEARCH TEAM Kevin Giannoni, 14 John le Quesne Close, St Clements
JE2 6NJ *Tel* 01534 878839/0979 716839

US

CIRCLES PHENOMENA RESEARCH (CPR-USA) PO Box 3378, Branford, Connecticut 06405

CITIZENS AGAINST UFO SECRECY (CAUS) 3518 Martha Cutis Avenue, Alexandria,
Virginia 22302
or PO Box 218, Coventry, Connecticut 06238

ED & KRIS SHERWOOD MILLENNIUM RESEARCH PO Box 2084, Santa Monica, California
90406

FUND FOR UFO RESEARCH PO Box 277, Mount Rainier, Maryland 20712

INTRUDERS FOUNDATION PO Box 30223, New York, NY 10011 *Contact* Budd Hopkins

J. ALLEN HYNEK CENTER FOR UFO STUDIES 2547 W. Peterson Avenue, Chicago, Illinois
60659

MUTUAL UFO NETWORK (MUFON) 103 Oldtowne Road, Seguin, Texas 78155-4099
Tel 512 379 9216 *Hotline* 813 595 7964 *Fax* 813 596 2038
E-mail 73521.3045@compuserve.com

PENNSYLVANIA ASSOCIATION FOR THE UNEXPLAINED 6 Oak Hill Avenue,
Greensburg, Pennsylvania 15601

UFO REPORTING AND INFORMATION SERVICE PO Box 382, Mercer Island, Washington
98040

CANADA

ALBERTA UFO RESEARCH ASSOCIATION 162 Pumpridge Place, SW, Calgary, Alberta
T2V 5E6 *Website* http://www.aufora.org

CANADIAN UFO RESEARCH NETWORK PO Box 15, Station A, Willowdale, Ontario M2N 5S7

CENTRALE DE COMPILATION UFOLOGIQUE DE QUEBEC CP 103, Drummondville, Quebec J2B 2V6

MUFON (CANADA) 3058 Fifth Line West No 7, Mississauga, Ontario L5L 5W4
Website http://www.interlog.com/~epona/mufonont.html

SOS OVNI (QUEBEC) PO Box 143, St-Jean-sur-Richleau, Quebec J3B 6Z1, *Tel* 514 349 4437 (English spoken) *Contact* Christian Page *E-mail* ocipe@chucara.hexacom.com *Website* http://www.cam.org/~martinc/ (French version) *Director* Jacques Poulet

UFOLOGY RESEARCH OF MANITOBA PO Box 1918, Winnipeg, Manitoba R3C 3R2

UFO RESEARCH INSTITUTE OF CANADA Dept 25, 1665 Robson Street, Vancouver, British Columbia V6G 3C2

AUSTRALIA AND NEW ZEALAND

AUSTRALIAN CENTRE FOR UFO STUDIES Martin Gottcha, 11109 Curragundi Road, Jindalee, Queensland 4074

AUSTRALIAN UFO ABDUCTION STUDY CENTRE Keith Basterfield, GPO 1894, Adelaide, South Australia 5001

NEW ZEALAND UFO STUDIES CENTRE 168 Brooklands Road, New Plymouth
Tel 6 7533968 *Director* Dr J.F. De Bock

MUFON Australia Continental PO Box 1894, Adelaide, South Australia

MUFON New Zealand PO Box 27117, Mt Roskill, Auckland 1030
Tel 9 6315825 *E-mail* murrayb@kiwi.gen.nz *Contact* Murray Bott

TASMANIAN UFO INVESTIGATION CENTRE PO Box 174, South Hobart, Tasmania 7004

UFO EXPERIENCE SUPPORT ASSOCIATION Peter Khoury, PO Box 191, Regents Park, New South Wales 2143 *Tel* 0412 649428 (mobile) *E-mail* ufoesa@giga.net.au

UFOIC Bill Chalker, PO Box W42, West Pennant Hills, New South Wales 2125

UFO RESEARCH AUSTRALIA PO Box 229, Prospect, South Australia 5082

UFO RESEARCH FAR NORTH QUEENSLAND c/o Russel Boundy, PO Box 1585, Cairns, Queensland 4870

UFO RESEARCH NEW SOUTH WALES PO Box Q95, Queen Victoria Building, Sydney, New South Wales *Website* http://www.ufor.asn.au

UFO RESEARCH QUEENSLAND PO Box 111, North Quay, Queensland 4002

UFO RESEARCH SOUTH AUSTRALIA Jim Atwell, PO Box 281, Blair Athol, South Australia 5084

VICTORIAN UFO RESEARCH SOCIETY PO Box 43, Moorabbin, Victoria 3189
Tel 03 9506 7080 *E-mail* vufors@ozemail.com.au/ *Website* http://www.ozemail.com.au/~vufors

BELGIUM

BELGIUM UFO GROUP Gino Ratinckx, Lodewijk de Koninkstraat, 17 2600 Berchem, Antwerp *Tel* 03230 6811

NUFOC Jodenstraat 66/102, B-3800 St Truiden

SOBEPS 74 Avenue Paul Jansen, B-1070 Brussels

SOS OVNI PO Box 148, 1950 Kraainem *Tel* 2 772 21 80 (English spoken)
E-mail 100531.3521@compuserve.com *Director* Vincent de Baeremaeker

SVL Oever 28, B-2000 Antwerp

DENMARK

JYSK UFO CENTRE Carsten Jakobsen, Kloevervej 33, 13 MF, 6000 Kolding

SUFOI Peter Noergaard, Box 6, DK-2820 Gentofte *Tel* 70 20 11 22

FINLAND

HELSINKI UFO SOCIETY (INTERPLANETIST) Urpo Hayrinen, Mannerheimintie 59 B 25, 00250 Helsinki

UFO RESEARCH OF FINLAND (SUOMEN UFOTUTKIJAT) PO Box 34, 24101 Salo
Tel 400 823 350 *Fax* 41 618 889 *E-mail* pob41@sci.fi
Website http://www.sci.fi/~pob41/sufotute.htm

FRANCE

AERO 28 Rue Claude Monet, 66000 Perpignan *E-mail* bernard@lagare.fr
Website: http://www.mygale.org/11/ibanez

AESV BP 324, 13611 Aix-en-Provence

SOS OVNI (FRANCE) BP 324, 13611 Aix-en-Provence, Cedex 1 *Tel* 42 20 18 19 *24-hour hotline* (33) 42 12 30 59 *E-mail* sosovni@pacwan.mm-soft.fr *Director* Perry Petrakis

GERMANY

CENAP Eisenachenweg 16, D-6800 Mannheim 31

DEGUFO eV (DEUTSCHSPRACHIGE GESELLSCHAFT FÜR UFO-FORSCHUNG) PO Box 2831, D-55516 Bad Kreuznach

MUFON CES (GERMANY) Illobrand von Ludwiger, Gerhard-Hauptmann-Str. 5, W-8152 Feldkirchen-Westerham *Tel* 8063 7065

ITALY

CISU Corso Vittorio, Emmanuelle 108, 10121 Torino
Websites http://www.oasi.shiny.it/Homes/CISU/ufo1.htm (Italian version)
http://www.oasi.shiny.it/Homes/CISU/english/ufo1bis.htm (English version)

NORWAY

UFO-HEDEMARKEN Gaedveien 9, 2332 Asvang *Tel* 62 58 64 31

UFO I NORD v/Reiel Pedersen, Rubbeldalsveien 8, 990 Batsfjord

UFO-NORGE Odd Gunnar Roed, Postboks 24, N-3133 Duken
Tel 33 38 65 00 *Mobile* 941 81 800 *Fax* 33 38 33 68

UFO-ROGALAND Postboks 786, Krossen, 4301 Sandnes *Tel* 51 42 57 07

UFO-SANDEFJORD Osteroyveien 1, 3234 Sandefjord *Tel* 33 45 07 26

UFO-STAVANGER Postboks 550, 4040 Madla *Tel* 51 55 08 08

SPAIN

V-J Ballester Olmos, Guardia Civil 9, D-16, 46020 Valencia

SWEDEN

AFJ PO Box 11027, S-60011 Norrköping

UFO SVERIGE PO Box 175, 733 23 SALA *Tel* 0224/ 867 71 *E-mail* info@ufo.se, *or*
clas.svahn@online.dextel.se *Contact* Clas Svahn *Websites* http://www.ufo.se (Swedish version) http://www.ufo.se/english.html (English version)

AFRICA

Cynthia Hind, Box MP 49, Mount Pleasant, Harare, Zimbabwe *Tel* 4 744 770
E-mail gemini@samara.co.zw *Cynthia Hind is also the South African state representative for the Mutual UFO Network, based in Texas. MUFON-SA address as above.*

JAPAN

JAPAN SPACE PHENOMENA SOCIETY 5–2, Kamiyama-cho, Shibuya-ku, Tokyo 150

MALTA

MALTA UFO RESEARCH PO Box 14, Rabat RBT 01
Fax 456729 *E-mail* mufor@maltanet.omnes.net
or mufor@waldonet.net.mt/ *Website* http://www.waldonet.net.mt/~mufor

RUSSIA

INTERNATIONAL INFORMATION CENTRE FOR UFO INVESTIGATION Valery Uvarov, Karpinskogo Str. 36-7-58, Sankt Petersburg 195252 *Tel/fax* 812 5381994
E-mail iicufi@glas.apc.org

RUSSIAN UFOLOGY RESEARCH CENTRE c/o Paul Stonehill (Co-ordinator), 5700 Etiwanda Avenue, Suite 215, Tarzana, California 91356

RUSSIAN UFO RESEARCH STATION (RUFORS) Nikolay Subbotin, PO Box 6303, Perm 614010 *Tel/fax* 3422 450184 *E-mail* norsa@psu.ac.ru
Website http://www.psu.ru/perm/ufo/index.html (in English, and worth a visit)

URAL UFO Valery Yakimov, Komvuzovskaya 21 'G' – 104, Ekaterinburg 620066
Tels 3432 492 020/3432 492 092/3432 608 145 *E-mail* root@ufo.nu.x-atom.net
Contact Nathaly Borzenko *Website* http://www.wic.net/page/rusweb.htm

SOUTH AMERICA AND THE CARIBBEAN

CADIU Casilla de Correo 218, Córdoba, Argentina

SBEDV CP 10-017, Correio do largo Machado, Rio de Janeiro, Brazil

UFO INVESTIGATION CENTER OF PUERTO RICO INC RD 845, Building No 662, Villas De Cupey, San Juan 00926, Puerto Rico *Tel* 809 760 5661 *Fax* 809 761 8689)

OTHER USEFUL ADDRESSES

BRITISH AIRPORTS AUTHORITY Masefield House, Gatwick Airport, Gatwick, West Sussex RH6 0HZ

CENTRE FOR CROP CIRCLE STUDIES 20 Paul Street, Frome, Somerset BA11 1DX

CIRCLE EFFECTS RESEARCH SOCIETY (CERES) 3 Selbourne Court, Tavistock Close, Romsey, Hampshire SO51 7TY

CIRCULAR FORUM 22 Stow Court, Gloucester Road, Cheltenham, Gloucestershire GL51 8ND *24-hour hotline* 01973 778906

CIVIL AVIATION AUTHORITY/NATIONAL AIR TRAFFIC SERVICES CAA House, 45–59 Kingsway, London WC2B 6TE
Note *A copy of the* Flight International Directory *should be available from most public libraries. It lists addresses and telephone numbers of both national and international airline companies, airports and airport services.*

TORNADO AND STORM RESEARCH 54 Frome Road, Bradford-on-Avon, Wiltshire BA15 1LD

UFO MAGAZINE Quest Publications International Ltd, Lloyds Bank Chambers, West Street, Ilkley, West Yorkshire LS29 9DW *Tel* 01943 816611 *Fax* 01943 816622

Brian Lucas B.M. Lucas Electronic Resources, PO Box 694, St Helier, Jersey, Channel Islands *Manufacturer and supplier of a range of UFO detectors and passive radars*

Courtney Brown PhD Farsight Institute, PO Box 49243, Atlanta, Georgia, GA 30359, US *Remote viewing issues, including training courses*

Dr Colin Ridyard 13 Lon Lwyd Isaf, Pentraeth, Anglesey LL75 8LN, Wales

Dr David M. Jacobs Dept of History, Temple University, Philadelphia PA 19122, US *Abduction research specialist*

Dr Susan Blackmore Dept of Psychology, University of the West of England, St Matthias College, Bristol BS16 5JP

Nicholas Reiter 541 W. Stone St, Gibsonburg, Ohio 43431, US *Supplier of 'anti-abduction' equipment*

Stanton T. Friedman 79 Pembrook Crescent, Fredericton, New Brunswick, Canada E3B 2V1

LOBBYING, RESEARCH AND FREEDOM OF INFORMATION ACT REQUEST ADDRESSES

US

CENTRAL INTELLIGENCE AGENCY (CIA) Information and Privacy Co-ordinator, PO Box 1925, Washington, DC 20013 *Do* not *mention CIA in the address!*

DEFENSE INTELLIGENCE AGENCY Chief: Freedom of Information Staff, Washington, DC 20340

DEPARTMENT OF JUSTICE Office of Information and Privacy, FOIA Officer, Washington, DC 20530

DEPARTMENT OF THE AIR FORCE 11 MSS/IMS (FOIA), Room 4A1088C, 1000 Airforce Pentagon, Washington, DC 20330-1000

DEPARTMENT OF THE ARMY Chief: FOIA/PA Division, US Army Information Systems Command, Crystal Square 2, Suite 201, 1725 Jefferson David Highway, Arlington, Virginia 20350-2000

DEPARTMENT OF THE NAVY Head, PA/FOIA Branch, Chief of Naval Operations, 2000 Navy Pentagon, Washington, DC 20350-2000

FEDERAL BUREAU OF INVESTIGATION Department of Justice, FOIA Officer, Washington, DC 20535

NATIONAL SECURITY AGENCY (NSA) Central Security Sevice, FOIA Officer, Fort George G. Meade, Maryland 20755-6000

UK

CIVIL AVIATION AUTHORITY PRINTING AND PUBLISHING Greville House, 37 Gratton Road, Cheltenham, Gloucestershire GL50 2BN

COMPANIES HOUSE (UK)
England 55 City Road, London EC1Y 1BB *Tel* 0171 253 9393
Wales Crown Way, Cardiff CF4 3UZ *Tel* 01222 388588
Scotland 100–102 George Street, Edinburgh EH2 3DJ *Tel* 0131 225 5774
Northern Ireland Companies Registration Office, IDB House, Chichester Street, Belfast BT1 4JX *Tel* 01232 234488

DATA PROTECTION REGISTRAR (UK) Springfield House, Water Lane, Wilmslow, Cheshire SK9 5AX

EUROPEAN PARLIAMENT (LONDON OFFICE) 2 Queen Anne's Gate, London SW1H 9AA *Tel* 0171 222 0411

HOUSE OF COMMONS London SW1A 0AA *Tel* 0171 219 3000 *Information office* 0171 219 4272

HOUSE OF LORDS *Tel* 0171 219 3107

MINISTRY OF DEFENCE (MoD) Secretariat (Air Staff) 2a, Room 8245, Main Building, Whitehall, London SW1A 2HB *Tel* 0171 218 2140 (direct)/0171 218 9000 (switchboard) *Fax* 0171 218 2680

OPERATION RIGHT TO KNOW (GREAT BRITAIN) Paul Vigay, 104 Manners Road, Southsea, Hampshire PO4 0BG *E-mail* pvigay@cix.compulink.co.uk *Website* http://www.interalpha.net/customer/pvigay (good site, with relevant links)

PUBLIC RECORD OFFICE Ruskin Avenue, Kew, Richmond, Surrey TW9 4DU *Tel* 0181 876 3444

THE STATIONERY OFFICE (formerly HMSO) Publications Centre, PO Box 276, London SW8 5DT

OTHER USEFUL INTERNET SITES, FTPs AND NEWSGROUPS

Black triangle sightings/pics http://www.ufomind.com/place/be/triangle/

Bob Lazar/Area 51 http://www.serve.com/mahood/lazar/lazarmn.htm http://www.banzai-net.com/tridot/s4.htm http://www.ufo-mind.com/ (Glenn Campbell's site; for 'Groom Lake Desert Rat' e-zine, *see also* http://www.ufomind.com/rat/1997/38)

British UFO Research Association (BUFORA) http://www.bufora.org.uk/. http://www.citadel.co.uk/citadel/eclipse/futura/bufora/bufora.htm

BUFOD Space, Above and Beyond http://www.abcfield.force9.co.uk

Crop circle newsgroups http://www.tpoint.net/mchorost/circles_biblio.html. http://www.primenet.com/cosmic/circle.html.

Dr Bruce Macabee/Kenneth Arnold http://ourworld.compuserve.com/homepages/pulsar/arnold.htm

Dr Steven Greer (CSETI) http://www.cseti.org *E-mail* 103275.1472@compuserve.com

Ed Walters/Gulf Breeze http://www.skiesare.demon.co.uk/intro.htm http://wwwgarlic.com/ufo/txt3/2609.ufo http://www.deleree.com/skywatch-diary/

Institute for the Study of Non-Human Intelligence http://www.CNINEWS.com

Major Bob Dean's 'Stargate Project' http://www.sisna.com/stargate

Men in Black (MIB) http://meninblack.com/meninblackmag/index.html

Mexican wave photos http://www.pufori.org

Mutual UFO Network (MUFON) http://www.rutgers.edu/~mcgrew/mufon/index.html

Newsgroups http://alt.ufo.reports http://alt.paranet.ufo

Parascope http://www.parascope.com/nebula.htm

Roswell http://www.iufomrc.com/fiufomrc.htm (International UFO Museum & Research Centre site) http://www.parascope.com/articles/0697/roswell1.htm

Santilli alien autopsy footage http://wwwexecpc.com/vjentpr/rfilmimg.html *See also* Parascope.

Sci-Fi channel's 'sightings' site http://www.scifi.com/sightings/

SETI Institute http://www.seti-inst.edu/seti-top.html

Space missions http://www.yahoo.com/Science/Space/Missions (note upper-case letters; an interesting site)

UK UFO Network Bulletin http://www.holodeck.demon.co.uk/

UFO Info http://www.digiserve.com/ufoinfo

UFO Magazine (UK's Quest Publications) http://www.ufomag.co.uk

UFO Search Engine http://www.yahoo.com (good one!)

'Ultimate Ufologist's Site'
http://ntd-wwaab.compuserve.com/homepages/AndyPage/WWWUFO.htm

UFO-related anonymous ftp sites *Phoenix UFO pics*
phoenix.oulu.fi (130.231.240.17) In /pub/ufo_and_space_pics

NASA PICS SITES

Note The material at these sites is voluminous to say the least, and the original compiler of this list of ftps suggests acquiring the CD-ROMs instead of attempting to transfer many gigabytes of material. However, to access the online catalogue of NASA material, CD-ROMS, etc.: telnet nssdca.gsfc.nasa.gov (log in as 'NODIS'; no password).

Anonymous ftp sites nssdca.gsfc.nasa.gov [128.183.10.4] (this is a VAX/VMS box, so you must ftp-log in as 'anonymous') To get a direct listing into a file on your system: ftp> dir [...] (file on your system) vab02.larc.nasa.gov (lots of information, including aliens and UFO pictures) ames.arc.nasa.gov (online copies of what appears to be all NASA's CD-ROMs, and lots of gifs, *.img and *.jpg from most (if not all) missions since the Apollo flights) archive.umich.edu (appears to be popular, and slow as a result; this site is said to have many NASA and Voyager data files)

NASA *Historical archives* http://www.ksc.nasa.gov/history/history/html
Spacelink (Telnet) Spacelink.MSFC.nasa.gov
Research labs http://www.yahoo.com/Government/Research_Labs/NASA/ (note upper-case letters)

NASA/NORAD (US Space Command) satellite 2-line elements
RPV Astronomy BBS: (310) 541 7299 @ 14400 / 9600 / 2400 BAUD
RPV Hotline BBS: (310) 544 8977 @ 2400 / 1200 BAUD
Note These are the numbers for those requiring the necessary 2-line elements for satellite, Hubble, Space Shuttle and Mir tracking programs such as David H. Ransom Jr's STSORBIT PLUS, and for updated versions of the program itself. The system may be busy, however, so if there is no answer after three rings, hang up and retry after two minutes. May also be downloaded directly from NASA's website (see above).

NASA Shuttle footage NASA Select on Satcom 2, Transponder 13, carries missions live, and anybody with a satellite dish can tune in. The original uplink and Shuttle audio can be found on Transponder 5. This is the raw and uncut video with Shuttle-to-ground audio communications on it.

ASTRONOMY AND SETI-RELATED ORGANIZATIONS

UK

BRITISH ASTRONOMICAL SOCIETY/ROYAL ASTRONOMICAL SOCIETY Burlington House, Piccadilly, London W1V 0NL *The former for amateur astronomy, the latter for professionals*

BRITISH INTERPLANETARY SOCIETY 27/29 South Lambeth Road, London SW8 1SZ
Promotion of astronautics, space science and related subjects

JUNIOR ASTRONOMICAL SOCIETY c/o 30 Wemyss Road, London SE3 0TG

RESEARCH COMMUNICATIONS LTD Unit 1, Aerodrome Industrial Complex, Aerodrome
Road, Hawkinge, Folkestone, Kent CT18 7AG *Tel* 01303 893631
Suppliers of amateur SETI equipment, although mainly RF equipment

US

ASTRONOMICAL SOCIETY OF THE PACIFIC 1290 24th Avenue, San Francisco, California
94112 *Professional and amateur SETI researchers*

BOB'S ELECTRONIC SERVICE 7605 Deland Avenue, Fort Pierce, Florida 34591
Tel 407 464 2118 *Suppliers of amateur SETI equipment*

INTERNATIONAL ASTRONOMICAL UNION (IAU) c/o Professor Micheal Papagiannis,
Secretary, Dept of Astronomy, Boston University, Boston, Massachusetts 02215 *Largest
international professional astronomers' organization*

NASA MAILING ADDRESSES
National Aeronautics and Space Administration (NASA) Office of Public Information,
NASA Headquarters Code L, Washington, DC 20546 *Tel* 202 358 1547
Same address for Office of Space Science and Applications

Ames Research Center Mountain View, Moffat Field, California 94035 *Tel* 415 604 9000

Jet Propulsion Laboratory 4800 Oak Grove Drive, Pasadena, California 91109
Tel 818 354 5011

Johnson Space Center Houston, Texas 77058

Kennedy Space Center Cape Canaveral, Florida 32899

PLANETARY SOCIETY PO Box 91687, Pasadena, California 91109 *Supporters of non-
governmental SETI research, and exploration of the solar system*

SETI INSTITUTE 101 First Street, No 410 Los Altos, California 94022 *Promotes activities
and research devoted to the search for intelligent extraterrestrial life*

SOCIETY OF AMATEUR RADIO ASTRONOMERS PO Box 250462, Montgomery, Alabama
36105 *For amateur radio astronomy*

SPACE STUDIES INSTITUTE PO Box 82, Princeton, New Jersey 08540 *Supports research
devoted to colonization of space*

Note Some of the addresses listed are for private individuals: please afford them their due
privacy. Approach them only with realistic and appropriate questions, concerns and
requests. Do include return postage – you may not receive a reply if you don't. If you would
like your group, website, company, etc. listed in this section in future editions of the book,
or if you would like your details withdrawn, altered or updated, then please contact me via
the publishers with your details. There is no charge for this service other than to include
first-class postage for carriage from the publisher to myself.

Bibliography

Anderson, P., *Is There Life on Other Worlds?*, Macmillan, New York, 1968

Angelo, Dr J.A., *The Extraterrestrial Encyclopedia*, Facts On File, Oxford, 1991

Ashpole, E., *The Search for Extraterrestrial Intelligence*, Blandford Press, London, 1989

Birch, N.H., & Bramson, A.E., *Flight Briefing for Pilots Vol 4.: Associated Ground Subjects*, Pitman, London, 1977

Birdsall, M.I., 'The Pennine Lights', *UFO Magazine*, May/June 1998, Quest Publications, Leeds

Blair, S., 'Aliens', *Focus*, September 1996, G&J Publications, London

Boar, R., & Blundell, N., *The World's Greatest UFO Mysteries*, Hamlyn, London, 1983

Bova, B., & Preiss, B. (eds), *First Contact*, Headline, London, 1991

Brookesmith, P., *UFO – The Complete Sightings Catalogue*, Blandford, London, 1995

Christopher, J., 'Air Ships Part 1: Identifiable Flying Objects', *UFO Magazine*, May/June 1995, Quest Publications, Leeds

Davies, P., *Are We Alone?*, Penguin, London, 1995

Devereux, P., & Brookesmith, P., *UFOs and Ufology – The First 50 Years*, Blandford, London, 1997

Digby, R.S., & Cooper, C., 'UFO Photos: Facts and Frauds' in *The Alien World* (ed. P. Brookesmith), Orbis Publishing, London, 1984

Drake, F., & Sobel, D., *Is Anyone Out There? The Scientific Search for Extraterrestrial Intelligence*, Simon & Schuster, London, 1991

Dutton, Squadron Leader L., De Garis, Wing Commander D., Winterton, Squadron Leader R., and Harding, Dr R., *Brasseys Air Power: Aircraft, Weapons Systems and Technology Series Vol. 10: Military Space*, Brasseys (UK), London, 1990

Good, T., *Alien Liaison – The Ultimate Secret*, Arrow, London, 1991

— *Beyond Top Secret – The Worldwide UFO Security Threat*, Pan, London, 1996

Goudie, A., *The Nature of the Environment*, Blackwell, Oxford, 1993

Griffiths, J., 'Listening In – Part Two', *UFO Magazine*, September/October 1997, Quest Publications, Leeds

Harbinson, W.A., *Projekt UFO*, Boxtree, London, 1996

Hedgecoe, J., *The Photographer's Handbook*, Ebury Press, London, 1977

Hessemann, M., *Cosmic Connection – Worldwide Crop Formations and Extraterrestrial Contacts*, Gateway, Bath, 1996

Hicks, R. (ed.), *Cassell Camera Wise Guides: Problem Solver – Your Questions Answered*, Cassell, London, 1994

HMSO (Her Majesty's Stationery Office), *The Outer Space Act 1986*

Hogues, J., *The Millennium Book of Prophecy*, HarperCollins, London, 1994

Jacobs, D.M., PhD, *Alien Encounters - Firsthand Accounts of UFO Abductions* (formerly published as *Secret Life*), Virgin Books, London, 1996

Kahn, J.E., DPhil (ed.), *How to Write and Speak Better*, Reader's Digest, London, 1991

King, J., & Mills, J., 'Idiot's Guide to UFO Reality', *UFO Reality Magazine*, No. 4, October/November, 1996, Arc Soundwaves of Glastonbury Ltd

Kramer, W.M. & Bahme, C.W., 'Disaster Control and UFOs' in *Fire Officer's Guide to Disaster Control*, Fire Engineering Books & Videos, Chicago, 1992

Landsburg, A. & Landsburg, S., *In Search of Ancient Mysteries*, Corgi, London, 1974

Lawson, A., 'The Aliens Within' in *UFOs, Where Do They Come From?* (ed. P. Brookesmith), Macdonald & Co, London, 1988

Lucas, B.M., letter to *UFO Magazine*, Nov/Dec 1996, Quest Publications, Leeds

Maccabee, B.S., PhD, 'Photographic Analysis and Evidence', Section xiv, *MUFON Field Investigator's Guide*, MUFON website, 1998

McClure, K., *Abduction Watch*, Newsletter No. 6 ('Recovered Memory & Hypnosis Special')

Marrs, J., *Alien Agenda*, HarperCollins, London, 1997

National Investigations Committee on Aerial Phenomena (NICAP) *The UFO Evidence* (ed. R.H. Hall), Barnes & Noble, New York, 1997

Northmore, D., *Freedom of Information Handbook*, Bloomsbury, London, 1990

Noyes, R. (ed.), *The Crop Circle Enigma*, Gateway Books, Bath, 1990

Odum, E.P., *Fundamentals of Ecology*, W.B. Saunders, Philadelphia, 1971

Parker, S.P. (ed.-in-chief), *McGraw-Hill Encyclopedia of Science & Technology*, McGraw-Hill, New York, 1992

Parsons, P., 'Turning Back the Clock', *Amateur Astronomy and Earth Sciences*, Vol. 1, No. 12, December 1996

Pike, A., 'Night Sky Guide', *UFO Magazine*, several issues 1995–1997, Quest Publications, Leeds

Pope, N., *Open Skies, Closed Minds*, Simon & Schuster, London, 1996

Randles, J., *UFOs and How to See Them*, Anaya Ltd, London, 1992

— *UFO Study – A Handbook for Enthusiasts*, Robert Hale, London, 1981

Ridge, F., writing in *UFO Intelligence Newsletter*, No. 23, June 1990

Ridpath, I., *Pocket Guide to Astronomy*, Parkgate Books Ltd, London, 1997

Rodemerk, J. & T. (eds), *A Proposal for the Scientific Study of Possible Residual Time Anomalies at UFO Landing Sites*, MUFON, Texas, 1995

Sagan, C., & Shklovskii, I.S., *Intelligent Life in the Universe*, Pan Books, London, 1966

Sainio, J., *UFO Photo and Video Analysis*, MUFON website, 1998

Saunders, D.R., 'A Spatio-temporal Invariant for Major UFO Waves', in *Proceedings of the 1976 CUFOS Conference* (ed. N. Dornbos), Center for UFO Studies, Evanston, Illinois

Smith, D.J., *International Air Band Radio Handbook*, Patrick Stephens Limited, Yeovil, 1995

Solomon, R., *ET Exposure Law Details*, alt.alien.visitors (newsgroup)

Spall, N.J., 'The Physical Appearance of Intelligent Aliens', *Journal of the British Interplanetary Society*, Vol. 32, 1978

Spencer, J., *The UFO Encyclopedia*, Headline, London, 1997

Spick, M., & Wheeler, B., *Modern Aircraft Markings*, Salamander Books, London, 1992

Stonely, J., & Lawton, A.T. (FRAS), *CETI – Communication with Extraterrestrial Intelligence*, Wyndham, London, 1976.

Sullivan, G., *Modern Fighter Aircraft (Military Aircraft Series)*, Facts On File, Oxford, 1991

Temple, R.K.G., *The Sirius Mystery*, Sidgwick & Jackson, London, 1976

Tomas, A., *On the Shores of Endless Worlds – The Search for Cosmic Life*, Sphere, London, 1975

Van Dyke, G., *The Alien Files*, Element Books Ltd, Shaftesbury, Dorset, 1997

Watts, A., *UFO Quest*, Blandford, London, 1994

Willis, T., *Inland Cruising*, Pelham Books, London, 1987

Wilson, D., *Citizen Action*, Longman, Harlow, 1986

Glossary of Ufological and SETI Terms

AAT Acquired Alien Technology. Super 'state of the art' technology allegedly obtained from extraterrestrials as part of some undisclosed human–alien agreement.

ALF Alien Life Form. Not widely used now because of its connotations with a small, furry television character of the same designation; EBE (see below) is now preferred, probably because it sounds more scientific! *See also* RDA and VOA.

Altered state of consciousness Heightened sensitivity to surrounding psychic conditions or psychic phenomena. May be present as an adjunct to a 'close encounter' (see below). *See also* Oz factor.

Angel False radar return, aka 'ghost return', or 'anomalous propagation'. May be a result of ground scatter. May also be caused by two radar systems affecting each other, or by unusual weather conditions.

Angel hair White, cobweb-like material that is sometimes said to be present on vegetation at UFO landing sites. Quickly evaporates. A similar phenomenon is associated with 'ghostly manifestations'.

Animal mutilation Mysterious fate befalling (particularly) cattle, in which certain anatomical features and internal organs are apparently 'cored out', or otherwise surgically removed. There are often very small puncture wounds in a triangular formation through which organs are removed, and a cutting and simultaneous cauterizing of tissue. There is no evidence of blood loss or vascular collapse at wound sites. In many instances, the cadavers have been completely drained of blood. No tracks or trails left by the perpetrators to or from the cadavers have ever been found, no one has ever been caught or prosecutions brought, despite rewards being offered by ranchers and cattlemen. There are recorded cases of similar instances of human victims, particularly in Brazil. Cases are usually attributed to indigenous predators, but cattlemen and many veterinarians disagree.

Antimatter Matter in which the protons are negatively charged, as opposed to matter protons, which are positively charged. Very little antimatter actually occurs in nature, as it is destroyed soon after its creation. Matter–antimatter annihilation reactions are proposed as drive mechanisms for future terrestrial starships.

Area 51 Includes the S4/Groom Lake missile proving-grounds complex, usually associated with the USAF's Nellis Air Force Base, not far from Rachel, Nevada. Much beloved of conspiracy theorists and ufologists alike, as it is rumoured that it is here, at this super-secret military base, that captured alien vehicles were back-engineered and test flown. It has restricted airspace above it, and if you overstep the perimeters you are likely to be summarily shot dead – 'use of deadly force is authorized'. Aka 'Dreamland', it does not appear on any official maps because, of course, it does not really exist...

Astronomical Unit (AU) Average distance between the sun and the Earth, generally accepted to be a mean of 149,000,000km (93,000,000 miles).

Aurora Aka Project Aurora, said to be the latest generation of Stealth technology, and consequently the cause of many UFO reports. Also known in England by the acronym HALO – High Agility, Low Observability – although it is unclear as to whether or not these may be two separate projects.

AWACS Airborne Warning And Control System. Mounted in aircraft used to monitor and give early warning of (among other things) a hostile nation's nuclear attack. Radar and other data-sensing capabilities are utilized. Characteristic of an American AWACS aircraft is the huge, often rotating 'radome' (radar dome) on top of and towards the back of the fuselage. The British RAF use Nimrod aircraft for more or less the same purposes.

Back-engineering System of taking apart an existing item of machinery piece by piece to see how it works, and then attempting to reverse the procedure and rebuild or duplicate this machinery and its capabilities based on the findings.

Bandwidth In a radio channel, the difference between the highest and lowest frequencies. If the range is small, it is said to be 'narrowband'; if wide, it is known as 'broadband'. Intentional signals are generally narrowband, while signals from natural sources such as cosmic radiation are usually broadband. Modern SETI receivers have millions of narrowband channels.

Beamship Term coined by Eduard 'Billy' Meir to describe a spacecraft or UFO capable of apparent dematerialization.

Binary code Coding system in which only two characters are used, such as yes/no, on/off, 1/0, etc. Morse code is an example (dot/dash).

Binary star Twin star system, in which two suns orbit a common centre of gravity. To Earthbound observers, they may appear to be one single star. The Zeta Reticuli system from which the greys are said to come is a binary system about 34 light years distant.

Bioastronomy Science of examining the necessary conditions for the evolution and possible structures of life on extrasolar planets.

Black budget Term used to describe military operations or projects undertaken with funding not approved by Congress, Parliament or your own country's equivalent. In the US, it is rumoured that the CIA covertly operate or manipulate the international drug cartels in order to fund their own 'black projects'.

Black helicopters Said to be Special Forces attack helicopters such as the Bell Corporation's Apache. Usually appear when you are in a place that you shouldn't be. May be operated by the Joint Military Tactical Force: black-uniformed, black-bereted, unbadged soldiers whose only purpose in life is to do exactly as they are told without question. They are used primarily to guard Stealth projects and retrieved alien craft – allegedly! However, should you have a close encounter with one, it is likely that life is about to become rather uncomfortable for a while. Black helicopters have also been seen associated with certain 'oriental' types of alien.

Black hole Extremely dense, collapsed star or other object with such an incredibly strong gravitational pull that space forms a pocket around it, into which matter and energy pour. Not even light can escape it (although X-rays usually can), and it has been suggested that the forces exerted by black holes warp space and time in such a way as to allow astronauts to use them to navigate vast interstellar distances and times, enter hyperspace, or even to come out in another universe entirely. Alternatively, it's where the money appropriated for black projects goes!

CETI Communication with Extraterrestrial Intelligence.

CIA Central Intelligence Agency. Infamous agency set up in the US by direct presidential order in 1947, shortly after the Roswell incident.

Close encounter Literally, an encounter in which a UFO comes to within 150m (500ft) of a witness. Generally, however, the term has come into common usage to describe any suspected or claimed extraterrestrial encounter. Under the Hynek Classification System, there are three types of close encounter (CE1, CE2, CE3 – close encounters of the first, second and third types respectively), and a further two (CE4 and CE5) were added later.

Collective unconscious Imagery and symbolism common to all cultures, proposed by psychologist Carl Jung as the origin for all UFO sightings and imagery.

Cosmic haystack Analogy for the universe as drawn by SETI researchers looking for an intelligent ET radio signal – the proverbial needle.

Cultural tracking The observed tendency for UFO and alien technology to be parallel to, or only just exceed, our current terrestrial technological level.

DARPA Defense and Research Projects Agency (US).

Debunker Strictly speaking, one who attempts to demystify, discredit or explain away the UFO phenomenon with mundane, everyday, easily explained terms. In bar-room reality, anyone who doggedly disagrees with a ufologist! Debunkers' arguments usually fall apart under scrutiny, as they are often ill-informed, erroneous or downright badly reasoned. When all else fails, debunkers may resort to name calling and other such infantile tactics. Funnily enough, debunkers accuse ufologists of doing exactly the same!

Declination Celestial equivalent of latitude, used for establishing positions of stars and other celestial objects. The celestial north and south poles and the celestial equator are simply projections into space of their terrestrial counterparts. *See also* Right ascension.

DEA Directed Energy Weapons.

Doppler effect Effect of a moving body upon the sound energy waves it emits. As an object approaches, the pitch of the sound emitted will rise, while as the object departs it will drop – an example is the change in tone as an ambulance approaches you and then passes by with its sirens blaring. A characteristic associated with some UFO reports.

Drake equation Named after its principal inventor, Professor Frank Drake, the equation attempts to determine the number of technologically advanced civilizations in the galaxy. It incorporates considerations such as the rate of star formation, planetary evolution, the evolution of life, technology and communication, and measures this against the expected lifespan of a civilization, to give a number representing the number of technologically advanced races in the galaxy at any one time. Current estimates put the number anywhere between one (us!) and several million.

Earthlights Balls of light said to be generated by the Earth's tectonic stresses within the planet's crust. *See also* Plasma.

EBE Extraterrestrial Biological Entity, i.e. alien.

Electromagnetic spectrum (EM spectrum or radiation) Array of packets of electrical and magnetic energy called 'photons', whose vibrational frequencies are characteristic of the type of radiation they are. At the long-wavelength end of the spectrum, those having the slowest vibrations include radio and infrared, then speed up through visible light, and accelerate with shorter wavelengths up into ultraviolet, X-rays and gamma radiation.

ESA European Space Agency.

Exobiology Scientific study of extraterrestrial life.

Extraterrestrial Hypothesis (ETH) Argument proposing that UFOs and their occupants are space vehicles and aliens from another planet.

Fermi paradox Apparent lack of concrete and indisputable evidence of extraterrestrial visitation to the Earth, given the number of civilizations likely to exist, or to have existed, in the universe. Usually expressed as 'Where are they?'

Flap Brief, usually local, frenetic period of UFO activity.

Flying triangle/black triangle Huge, usually black, triangular-shaped craft whose manoeuvres and flight characteristics seem to defy known laws of physics. Believed by some to be the latest 'state-of-the-art' Stealth technology based on AAT (see above). Others maintain that they are extraterrestrial in origin.

Foo-fighters Strange balls of light reported by combat pilots of World War II and the Korean War. Initially believed to be of German origin, and so called because of the American saying: 'Where there's Foo, there's fire.'

Gigamagnetism Term coined by researcher Alan Watts to describe the effects that very strong magnetism has on light beams. Such gigamagnetism is thought to be responsible for the bending of car headlight beams at 90 degrees during UFO encounters, causing the drivers instinctively to follow the beams and crash as a consequence.

Ground scatter Effect upon radar which sometimes occasions a false return, caused by the reflection of signals from natural and man-made sources such as the ocean, crops, rock outcrops, tall buildings, trees, etc.

Habitable zone Defined region around a star in which a planet may evolve life.

HOTOL Horizontal Take Off and Landing.

Hyperjump Observed UFO manoeuvre in which the ship apparently translocates, i.e. disappears from one point in space to reappear instantly in another.

Hyperspace Special dimension of space in which Einsteinian laws do not apply. Distances between objects having mass in this hypothetical zone are considerably shorter than in the normal space–time continuum, and thus require a lot less time to travel between them in a linear travel mode. Beloved of sci-fi fans everywhere.

Hypnogogic state State in which the subject is drowsy and internally generates images and bodily sensations which seem very real to those experiencing them.

Hysterical contagion Instances in which a number of people share a common but false belief that may none the less be subjectively real. Aka mass hysteria.

IFO Identified Flying Object. Hynek's designation for an object previously unidentified, that has subsequently been found to have a mundane or natural cause.

Implant Artificial device approximately 3–5mm (1/8–1/4in) long, said to be inserted into the witness's body during abductions, reportedly to monitor or influence their behaviour and/or serve as a location device.

Inner space hypothesis Proposal that UFO experiences are manifestations of internally generated but externally influenced stimuli.

Interdimensional Supposes that physical dimensions and consciousness can coexist at the same point in space and time, the term being applied to those beings that are allegedly able to travel or otherwise communicate between these dimensions.

LOFLITE/LOFLYTE Low Observable Flight Test Experiment. Currently the publicly acknowledged cutting edge of Stealth technology. Has been used (probably quite legitimately in some instances) as an explanation for UFO sightings.

Meteoroid Piece of space debris or ice that does not enter the Earth's atmospheric envelope.

MoD (PE) Ministry of Defence (Procurement Executive) (UK).

NASA National Aeronautics and Space Administration, based in Washington, DC. Alternatively, Never A Straight Answer!

NORAD North American Air Defense, headquartered inside Cheyenne Mountain, Colorado. Now known (since the demise of the Warsaw Pact powers) as United States Space Command. Hmmm...

NSA National Security Agency, aka Never Say Anything or No Such Agency! Said to be the United States' most secretive intelligence organization.

OST Outer Space Treaty or, more properly, Treaty on Principles Governing the Activities of States in the Exploration and Use of Outer Space, Including the Moon and Other Celestial Bodies.

Oz factor Preparatory, if intangible, 'aura', often marking imminent close encounters and abductions. Usually experienced by the witness as the onset of silence and the entering of an altered state of consciousness.

Parsec Measurement of astronomical distance equal to 3.26 light years, or 206,265AU. A parallax shift of one second of arc – a contraction of 'parallax second'.

Plasma Parcel of air containing an extremely high electrical charge, which manifests as a ball of shifting, coruscating colours. Manifestations of plasma balls have been used as explanations for UFOs.

Polarized emissions Electromagnetic radiation in which the energies are all vibrating in the same way. Such polarization is characteristic of intelligently modulated signals. Natural background radiation is not polarized.

Protected frequencies Radio frequencies not allowed to be used by transmitters because of their value and importance for radio astronomy. It has been suggested that some covert military operations have utilized these frequencies in the past, but this is unproven.

Radar-visual There are two schools of thought: first, that it refers to UFO sightings registered by a radar return only; second, that it refers to a UFO registered by radar return which is verified, confirmed or otherwise backed up by a visual sighting from an independent witness. I favour the latter.

Radio astronomy Science of observing the celestial objects and occurrences at radio wavelengths by the use of radio antennas and receivers.

RDA Radar Detected Anomaly.

Right ascension Celestial equivalent of longitude, which is measured in hours, minutes and seconds to the east from the point at which the Earth's orbit crosses the celestial equator. *See also* Declination.

RPV Remotely Piloted Vehicle. Usually utilized for military reconnaissance purposes. Generally radio controlled but with a limited range from the operator, so if witnessed as a UFO the operator is likely to be nearby.

SDI Strategic Defense Initiative, aka Star Wars – not the movie, but weapons technologies designed to be deployed and operated in or from space.

SETI Search for Extraterrestrial Intelligence.

Sky survey SETI research programme that attempts to scan as much of the sky as possible within the parameters of the search strategy.

Targeted search SETI search programme designed to examine specific stars or types of stars for evidence of extraterrestrial signals.

UAP Unidentified Aerial Phenomenon – MoD-speak for 'UFO'.

UAV Unmanned Aerial Vehicle, similar to RPV (see above) but of greater dimensions and range.

UFO If I have to tell you what this means, I suggest you find a simpler book on the subject!

USO Unidentified Submarine Object (*not* Unidentified Submerged Object, as some have claimed), which may or may not become a UFO. Usually seen at, on, or just under the ocean's surface, or in larger inland lakes.

VOA Visually Observed Anomaly. Posh term for 'UFO'.

VTOL Vertical Take Off and Landing.

Wave Similar to a UFO 'flap' (see above), but may be over an extended period of time, and cover a larger geographical area.

Window area Geographically defined area with high incidences of UFO activity over a prolonged period of time. Such areas are thought by some to be 'windows' from other dimensions, allowing immediate access to Earth's airspace from the aliens' homeworld or from similar dimensional 'windows' elsewhere.

Xenology Scientific study of extraterrestrial life-forms.

Xenophobia Literally, morbid and often irrational fear of 'foreigners'. What most sceptics and ufologists are said to exhibit, by other sceptics and ufologists!

Index